Children and
Vulnerable Witnesses in
Court Proceedings

Children and Vulnerable Witnesses in Court Proceedings

Barbara Mitchels

Wildy, Simmonds & Hill Publishing

Contains public sector information licensed under the Open Government Licence v3.0

ISBN: 9780854901913

British Library Cataloguing in Publication Data

A catalogue record for this book is available from the British Library

First published in 2016 by

Wildy, Simmonds & Hill Publishing
58 Carey Street
London WC2A 2JF
England
www.wildy.com

Typeset by Heather Jones, North Petherton, Somerset.
Printed in Great Britain by CPI Antony Rowe, Chippenham, Wiltshire.

Contents

Appendices

List of Boxes

Acknowledgements

Many thanks to Andrew Riddoch and Brian Hill of Wildy, Simmonds & Hill and to my family, all of whom have been amazingly patient and supportive.

Especial thanks to Alex Clapson and Rachel Freeth. Also grateful thanks to Anne Warren and David Kenyon of Supporting Justice, and friends and colleagues in the judiciary, lawyers, mediators, social workers, counsellors and psychotherapists, psychologists, police, probation officers and witness support workers – all actively involved in working with vulnerable adults and children in the context of police investigation and the court process – thank you all for generously contributing your ideas and sharing your expertise.

Lastly, but most importantly, I want to express the great respect and gratitude I feel towards the children and vulnerable witnesses with whom we work. Your courage and tenacity to be heard and to achieve justice is inspirational to all of us who have the privilege to work with you.

Introduction

Recently, in the aftermath of news of wide ranging investigations of sexual abuse by public figures, we have been made increasingly aware of the psychological and physical impact of all forms of abuse on its victims. Sexual abuse, violence and harassment in all its forms can leave lasting traumatic memories for its victims, irrespective of age. More recently, online sexual abuse – a criminal offence – has also been the basis of the first successful civil action in England for personal injury damages caused by the psychological impact of 'sexting' (sexual abuse by text and transmitted images in text messaging). Lawyers and other practitioners may be faced with the additional psychological distress which may be caused to vulnerable witnesses by the process of a necessary police investigation and trial, particularly when the witness has suffered any form of abuse and violence. Reporting offences and giving evidence may involve the witness having to recall in detail the experience of traumatic situations. Witnesses may then also be caught up in the major stressors of the adversarial court process, along with dealing with painful memories of traumatic events. Practitioners are only too aware that in some tragic cases, the severe psychological stress of past trauma, exacerbated by legal proceedings, has led victims and vulnerable witnesses to anxiety, depression and, for some, into despair and suicidality. This handbook was written to assist practitioners in knowing the rights of their vulnerable clients, and to pull together information which might help to identify and access available resources and support systems.

It is not only witnesses who may be adversely affected by the traumatic events which are remembered and re-experienced during the criminal process. Carers, family members, practitioners and others involved in helping witnesses and victims may be affected by the investigation and trial process. Their own personal memories of abuse may be triggered, or they may suffer vicarious trauma from hearing repeated accounts of horrific events, and they, too, may require psychological support. Social and health care professionals, the armed forces, police and the emergency services will also recognise the phenomena of 'burn-out' or 'compassion fatigue' which may result from the psychological stress and vicarious trauma of this type of work, and which should be addressed as part of the employing organisation's professional duty of care to staff. The chapters on stress and post-traumatic stress include the concepts of 'burn-out' (or 'compassion fatigue'), which may help us as busy practitioners to recognise when we are becoming stressed, or risk being overwhelmed by the pressures of the highly demanding work we undertake, and to seek appropriate rest or support for ourselves.

Child protection inevitably follows events which may have caused high levels of traumatic stress for the children concerned, and the child protection process may in itself be traumatic, especially when it involves removal of a child or another person from the family, or changes in home, school and friendships. Often, too, there is traumatic stress for the families involved. Multi-disciplinary working is as necessary in witness support as it is in child protection, and involvement in training programmes for joint investigation teams, anti-trafficking measures, and implementing the recommendations in *Achieving Best Evidence in Criminal Proceedings: Guidance on interviewing victims and witnesses, and guidance on using special measures* (MoJ, 2011a) (*Achieving Best Evidence*) all highlight the need for cohesive multi-disciplinary support for the vulnerable adults and children who are caught up in police investigations and in the judicial process.

Achieving Best Evidence (MoJ, 2011a) is still a source of useful information, and it now applies alongside other government initiatives and developments relevant to the welfare of children and other vulnerable witnesses, including: *Working Together to Safeguard Children: A Guide to Inter-Agency Working to Safeguard and Promote the Welfare of Children* (DfE, 2015a) (*Working Together*); the *Code of Practice for Victims of Crime* (MoJ, 2015) (*Victims' Code*); *The Witness Charter: Standards of Care for Witnesses in the Criminal Justice System* (MoJ, 2013c); *Working with Victims and Witnesses* (College of Policing, 2016); and *Vulnerable and Intimidated Witnesses: A Police Service Guide* (MoJ, 2011b). See also the detailed document *Guidelines on Prosecuting Cases of Child Sexual Abuse* (CPS, 2014), available at www.cps.gov.uk and the Crown Prosecution Service (CPS) 'twin' guidance documents, *Provision of Therapy for Child Witnesses Prior to a Criminal Trial: Practice Guidance*, dated 8 February 2001 (CPS, 2001a), and the subsequent *Provision of Therapy for Vulnerable or Intimidated Adult Witnesses Prior to a Criminal Trial: Practice Guidance*, issued on 24 January 2002 (CPS, 2001b) (both available at www.cps.gov.uk). These documents would benefit from updating to take into account developments in counselling and psychotherapy practice, child protection, and recent government guidance, so watch out for possible new versions of these and other relevant guidance documents.

In England and Wales, mental health law and practice has been radically reformed – the Mental Health Act 1983 has been amended by the Mental Capacity Act 2005, the Mental Health Act 2007, and the impact of the United Nations Convention on the Rights of Persons with Disabilities, which came into effect in 2008, posing far-reaching challenges to our current mental health legislation, and once again, mental health law and practice came under critical review. In March 2015, the National Health Service (NHS) set up the Mental Health Taskforce, chaired by Paul Farmer (Mind's chief executive) seeking the views of mental health service users, their families and professionals to develop a new five-year strategy for mental health, focusing on prevention, access, integration and attitudes. The Department of Health also set up a consultation 'No voice unheard, no right ignored'. Following the Law Commission review of the Deprivation of Liberty Safeguards (DoLS), in 2015 the Department of Health issued *Mental Health Act 1983: Code of Practice* (DoH, 2015). The current guidance on capacity remains *Mental Capacity Act 2005: Code of Practice* (DCA, 2007), and for consent, the *Reference Guide to Consent for Examination or Treatment*, 2nd edition (DoH, 2009).

There are also the special range of needs of the increasing population of refugees and asylum seekers in the UK. They may struggle not only with severe psychological stress from conflict and past events, plus the added traumas of their journey to the UK, but also, the likely experience of additional stress due to language differences, and the difficulties they encounter in trying to access housing, finance, education, health and social care. They may need intensive help to access appropriate support, and, of course, they too may find themselves caught up in the legal system.

Using this handbook

This is a handbook, and is not meant to be a legal authority or a formal diagnostic guide, but is intended to pull together and link a range of information and resources to be used for reference as and when needed. Inevitably, lists cannot be exhaustive, and so the handbook cannot include all the resources and information available, but provides a basis on which to start. In order to avoid unnecessary repetition, there are cross references linking topics, but sometimes specific content is repeated in places where this may be helpful.

Chapter 1 provides a glossary and definitions of terms used in the book, for example, exploring the concepts of 'vulnerability' and 'intimidation', as these terms are used in law and guidance. Chapter 2 then addresses the nature and impact of psychological stress, anxiety, panic attacks and general stress, and Chapter 3 explores ways to alleviate psychological stress in the court process, describing the law, guidance and special measures available to support children and vulnerable witnesses. Chapters 4 and 5 set out the present guidance regarding pre-trial psychological support for adult and child witnesses, respectively. Chapter 6 explores the current provisions for victim support, and Chapter 7 explores how we can, where necessary, continue to establish physical and psychological safety for our vulnerable clients, victims and witnesses after the court proceedings are over. Appendix 1 sets out the diagnostic criteria for post-traumatic stress disorder, and Appendix 2 provides charts for stress analysis, to assist in identifying and addressing the causes and triggers for stress. Appendix 3 provides references and further reading, and Appendix 4 lists some useful resources for practical advice and help.

In this book, references to court process, law, guidance and practice issues are stated as they apply in England. As these vary across jurisdictions, Appendix 4 sets out some useful resources for law and guidance relevant to practice in Northern Ireland, Scotland and Wales. The resource list is not exhaustive – there may be other local services available, and it may be helpful to consult with practitioners in local authority child protection or social care departments, local health authority lawyers, mental health practitioners, and to explore any available lists of specialist national or local resources maintained by local government or voluntary organisations.

References to 'he' or 'she' are used interchangeably in the text for variety, and all terms used in this work are meant to be generally inclusive of diversity unless specifically stated. For simplicity, when referring to counselling, psychotherapy, counselling psychology, psychiatry and other forms of psychological help, the term 'psychological therapy' is used, and the terms 'lawyer' and 'court' are also used generically unless otherwise stated.

Lastly …

I hope that the book will help practitioners to feel more confident in understanding the psychology of stress, and in knowing the rights of victims and vulnerable witnesses, and to access appropriate support and help for them. Children Panel solicitors, local authority lawyers, children's social workers and CAFCASS may help to locate or provide resources for children and young people. Social and mental health professionals, specialist lawyers, counselling services, government and voluntary organisations such as the Victim Support Service, the Citizens Advice Witness Service and the mental health charity Mind may help with the needs of adult clients.

If you are reading this book, you are likely to be concerned about the welfare of your vulnerable clients, and you may need to be assertive in protecting your clients' rights. I hope this handbook will support you in this work, and that practice will be carried forward, developing new ways to create a brighter future for vulnerable witnesses.

Barbara Mitchels

1 Glossary of Terms and Definitions

Definitions have interested philosophers since ancient times … not only have particular definitions been debated; the nature of, and demands on, definitions have also been debated. Some of these debates can be settled by making requisite distinctions, for definitions are not all of one kind: definitions serve a variety of functions, and their general character varies with function. Some other debates, however, are not so easily settled, as they involve contentious philosophical ideas such as essence, concept, and meaning.

(*Webster's Dictionary*, 2015)

There is nothing either good or bad, but thinking makes it so.

(Shakespeare, *Hamlet*: Act II, Scene II)

1.1 Colloquial use of 'vulnerable' and 'vulnerability'

Colloquially, the words 'vulnerability' and 'vulnerable' are used to include any temporary or permanent physical or mental state, special need or disability which may exist for a person at the relevant time, and which may require special attention and care for the person concerned when they are involved in the court process. However, legally, they carry specific interpretations, see para 1.2.

1.2 Meaning of 'victim' and 'vulnerable or intimidated victim'

Under the present *Victims' Code* (MoJ, 2015: Intro, para 1), services for the victims of a criminal offence will be provided if the victim is:

- a natural person who has suffered harm, including physical, mental or emotional harm or economic loss which was directly caused by a criminal offence;

- a close relative (see definition of 'Relative and nearest relative' in para 1.4) of a person whose death was directly caused by a criminal offence.

Children are by statute considered to be vulnerable by reason of their age, see section 16 of the Youth Justice and Criminal Evidence Act 1999 (YJCEA 1999) (as amended by the Coroners and Justice Act 2009). Section 16(1) of that Act makes all children under 18 years of age, appearing as defence or prosecution witnesses in criminal proceedings, eligible for special measures to assist them to give their evidence in court. Children under the age of 18 are therefore entitled to receive services under the *Victims' Code* (MoJ, 2015: Intro, para 18).

Enhanced entitlements are provided to victims of the most serious crime, persistently targeted victims and vulnerable or intimidated victims.

The *Victims' Code* (MoJ, 2015: Chapter 1, para 1.10) describes eligibility for 'vulnerable or intimidated victims' as:

> 1.10 You are eligible for enhanced entitlements under this Code as a vulnerable victim if:
>
> (a) you are under 18 years of age at the time of the offence, or
>
> (b) the quality of your evidence is likely to be affected because:
>
>> i) you suffer from mental disorder within the meaning of the Mental Health Act 1983;
>>
>> ii) you otherwise have a significant impairment of intelligence and social functioning; or
>>
>> iii) you have a physical disability or are suffering from a physical disorder.

The *Victims' Code* applies the test in section 17 of the YJCEA 1999 by which the court determines eligibility for special measures see (MoJ, 2015: Chapter 1, paras 1.13–1.15), and in particular:

> 1.11. You are eligible for enhanced entitlements under this Code as an intimidated victim if the service provider considers that the quality of your evidence will be affected because of your fear or distress about testifying in court.
>
> 1.12. When assessing whether a victim is intimidated, the service provider must take account of:
>
> • any behaviour towards the victim on the part of the accused, members of the family or associates of the accused, and any other person who is likely to be an accused or witness in a potential court case;
>
> • the nature and alleged circumstance of the offence to which a potential court case relates. Victims of a sexual offence or human trafficking will automatically be considered to be intimidated;
>
> • the victim's age and, if relevant, the victim's social and cultural background, religious beliefs or political opinions, ethnic origin, domestic and employment circumstances.

A victim's vulnerability may change during the course of an investigation due to health, intimidation or other reason. Service providers must give the victim the opportunity to be provided with an enhanced service if such a change in circumstance is brought to their attention.

1.3   Children – legal vulnerability

Children, defined here as 'children and young persons under the age of eighteen years', are by statute, considered to be vulnerable by reason of their age, see section 16 of the YJCEA 1999 (as amended by the Coroners and Justice Act 2009). Section 16(1) of that Act makes all children under 18 years of age, appearing as defence or prosecution witnesses in criminal proceedings, eligible for special measures to assist them to give their evidence in court.

However, having said this, there are anomalies. Under the UN Convention on the Rights of the Child, 17-year-olds should be treated as children by all agencies of the law including police. Practitioners working with children and young people might make carers and/or those with parental responsibility for children aware of this provision, because under the Police and Criminal Evidence Act 1984 (as amended), 17-year-olds are treated as adults while held by police, which means their parents or another 'appropriate adult' are not contacted to offer support and advice if the young person is taken into custody, unless they are deemed to be 'vulnerable'. The situation has been criticised by the Prisons Inspectorate, pointing to the fact that under all other UK law and international treaty obligations, 17-year-olds are treated as juveniles. It is hoped that this anomaly will be addressed and brought into line with other policies, but changes to the system have not yet been made.

1.4   Legal definitions relevant to mental health

Below is a glossary of basic legal terms related to mental health which are used in this book. More complex legal terms and concepts are explained in the body of the text.

The main statutory provisions in this field are the Mental Health Act 1983 (MHA 1983) as amended by further subsidiary legislation, the Mental Health Act 2007 (MHA 2007), the Mental Capacity Act 2005 (MCA, 2005), and the Care Standards legislation. For ease of reference throughout the book, the MHA 1983 as amended by the MHA 2007 is referred to throughout simply as the 'MHA'; and the Mental Capacity Act 2005 as amended by subsequent legislation is referred to as the 'MCA'.

Other statutes are relevant to specific care issues, police matters, criminal offences, and procedures, and are mentioned in the body of this book where relevant. There have been regular calls to update law and practice in the area of mental health, and with increasing scrutiny of our law under the Human Rights Act 1998 by the European Convention for the Protection of Human Rights and Fundamental Freedoms (ECHR), the increasing awareness of disability rights, the impact of the United Nations Convention on the Rights of Persons with Disabilities (UNCRPD), which came into effect in 2008, and the recurring disclosures of abuse in care systems, we might anticipate further reforms, so stay alert for changes in law and guidance which are relevant to your practice.

Appropriate admission, treatment and detention: For a guide to good practice in the process of admissions, see the *Mental Health Act 1983: Code of Practice* (DoH, 2015). This is guidance and not compulsory, but a significant help to understanding frequently used terms and definitions and also an indication of what is expected in best mental health practice.

Approved doctor: Two medical recommendations are necessary to support the application of an Approved Mental Health Professional (AMHP) or nearest relative (see definitions below) for compulsory admission to hospital. One of these must be by a 's.12 approved doctor'. The second recommendation can be given by any physician. One of the two doctors should have previous acquaintance with the patient.

This means a doctor approved for the purpose in England by the Secretary of State and in Wales by the Welsh Ministers (who have delegated the power to the Local Health Boards). The approved doctor will usually be a psychiatrist, but may also be a suitably qualified and experienced general practitioner (GP).

Approved Mental Health Professional (AMHP): AMHPs make most of the applications for admission for compulsory admission for assessment or treatment under sections 2 and 3 of the MHA.

To provide a balance (and perhaps, too, a creative tension) between medical and other social perspectives, doctors are in law specifically excluded from this particular role (section 114(2) of the MHA). AMHPs may now include: approved social workers, nurses and community health nurses, psychologists and occupational therapists, see Schedule 1 to the Mental Health (Approved Mental Health Professionals) (Approval) England Regulations 2008 (SI 2008/1206).

Detention (of a mental health patient): Detention means keeping a patient in hospital or other place where care appropriate to that person's condition is provided. Detention is subject to the 'appropriate medical treatment' test which will apply to all the longer-term powers of detention. As a result, it will not be possible for patients to be compulsorily detained or their detention continued unless medical treatment which is appropriate to the patient's mental disorder and all other circumstances of the case is available to that patient.

The changes in the MCA 2007 provide for procedures to authorise the deprivation of liberty of a person resident in a hospital or care home who lacks capacity to consent. The principles established in the MCA 2005 of supporting a person to make a decision when possible, and acting at all times in the person's best interests and in the least restrictive manner, will apply to all decision-making in operating the procedures.

Intimidated witness: 'Intimidated witnesses' are defined by section 17 of the YJCEA 1999 (as amended by the Coroners and Justice Act 2009) as:

> those whose quality of evidence is likely to be diminished by reason of fear or distress. In determining whether a witness falls into this category, the court should take account of:
>
> - the nature and alleged circumstances of the offence;
> - the age of the witness;
> - where relevant:
>   - the social and cultural background and ethnic origins of the witness,
>   - the domestic and employment circumstances of the witness,
>   - any religious beliefs or political opinions of the witness;
> - any behaviour towards the witness by:
>   - the accused,
>   - members of the accused person's family or associates,
> - any other person who is likely to be either an accused person or a witness in the proceedings.
>
> (MoJ, 2011a: para 1.10)

See also *Vulnerable and Intimidated Witnesses: A Police Service Guide* (MoJ, 2011b) which suggests that victims of and witnesses to domestic violence, racially motivated crime, crime motivated by reasons relating to religion, homophobic crime, gang-related violence and repeat victimisation, and those who are elderly and frail also fall into this category. 'Bereaved close relatives of a victim of a most serious crime are eligible for enhanced entitlements' (*Victims' Code* (MoJ, 2015: Chapter 1, para 1.8).

Learning disability (significant impairment of intelligence and social functioning): Under section 1(4) of the MHA, 'learning disability' means 'a state of arrested or incomplete development of the mind which includes significant impairment of intelligence and social functioning'. Please note, however, that under section 1(2A) of the MHA, a person with a learning disability is *not* considered to be suffering from mental disorder for many purposes of mental health law, including hospital treatment, 'unless that disability is associated with abnormally aggressive or seriously irresponsible conduct on his part'.

Achieving Best Evidence states:

> 2.67   Learning disability is not a description of one disability, but a collection of many different factors that might affect a person's ability in relation to learning and social functioning to greatly varying degrees. While some 200 causes of learning disability have been identified, most diagnoses are still 'unspecified learning disabilities'. People with high support needs may be easily identified but people with mild or moderate learning disabilities may be more difficult to identify.

> 2.68   It is impossible to give a single description of competence in relation to any particular disability, because there is such a wide range of abilities within each in terms of degree of intellectual and social impairment. However, there are some indicators that may help identify a witness with a learning disability.

> 2.69   Though generalisations cannot be made, some characteristics may exist in relation to some syndromes. For example, witnesses with autistic spectrum disorder, which includes Kanner's syndrome and Asperger's syndrome, have a huge range of abilities/disabilities, but:

> • They often have difficulty in making sense of the world and in understanding relationships;
> • They are likely to have little understanding of the emotional pain or problems of others; and
> • They may display great knowledge of certain topics and have an excellent vocabulary, but could be pedantic and literal and may have obsessional interests.

> 2.70   Some people with learning disabilities are reluctant to reveal that they have a disability, and may be quite articulate, so that it is not always immediately obvious that they do not understand the proceedings in whole or in part.

> (MoJ, 2011a: paras 2.67–2.70)

Medical treatment: This is defined in section 145(1) of the MHA as including nursing, psychological intervention and specialist mental health habilitation, rehabilitation and care, and in section 145(4):

> Any reference in this Act to medical treatment, in relation to mental disorder, shall be construed as a reference to medical treatment the purpose of which is to alleviate, or prevent a worsening of, the disorder or one or more of its symptoms or manifestations.

The explanatory note in the MHA 2007 states that:

> Practical examples of psychological interventions include cognitive therapy, behaviour therapy and counselling. 'Habilitation' and 'rehabilitation' are used in practice to describe the use of specialised services provided by professional staff, including nurses, psychologists, therapists and social workers, which are designed to improve or modify patients' physical and mental abilities and social functioning. Such services can, for example, include helping patients learn to eat by themselves or to communicate for the first time, or preparing them for a return to normal community living. The distinction between

habilitation and rehabilitation depends in practice on the extent of patients' existing abilities – 'rehabilitation' is appropriate only where the patients are relearning skills or abilities they have had before.

Mental disorder: The MHA states that it governs 'the reception, care and treatment of mentally disordered patients, the management of their property and other related matters' (section 1(1)).

'Mental disorder' is the gateway provision for the operation of many parts of mental health legislation, for example, compulsory admission to hospital, detention in hospital, confinement, and warrants to search for and remove individuals believed to be ill-treated.

There is now a unified definition of mental disorder, so that a single definition now applies throughout the MHA, and complements the changes to the criteria for detention. Under section 1(2) of the MHA, '"mental disorder" means any disorder or disability of the mind; and "mentally disordered" shall be construed accordingly'.

Under section 1(2A) of the MHA, in relation to certain specified purposes:

a person with learning disability shall not be considered by reason of that disability to be—

(a) suffering from mental disorder … or (b) requiring treatment in hospital for mental disorder … unless that disability is associated with abnormally aggressive or seriously irresponsible conduct on his part.

Under section 1(4) of the MHA, '"learning disability" means a state of arrested or incomplete development of the mind which includes significant impairment of intelligence and social functioning'.

Note that under section 1(3) of the MHA, for specified purposes set out in section 2, 'Dependence on alcohol or drugs is not considered a disorder or disability of the mind …'.

Bear in mind, though, that in some cases, a person may have comorbid conditions additional to their alcohol or drug dependence which could then fall within the definition of mental disorder under the MHA.

For further consideration of the range of this definition, see sections 2.4–2.13 of the *Mental Health Act 1983: Code of Practice* (DoH, 2015: 26–27).

Mental Health Review Tribunal (MHRT): The MHA 2007 and the Tribunals, Courts and Enforcement Act 2007 overhauled the tribunal system, and introduced a single, two-tier Tribunal for England, the one in Wales remaining in being. Each tier of the tribunal has specialist chambers headed by a President. The MHRT is part of the 'Health Education and Social Care' chamber of the First Tier Tribunal (FTT). The second tier – the Upper Tribunal (UT), acts as an appellate system to review decisions of the FTTs.

The role of the MHRT was transferred to the FTT and UT system by Article 3 of, and Schedule 1 to, the Transfer of Tribunal Functions Order 2008 (SI 2008/2833), and mental health cases are heard within the 'Health Education and Social Care' chamber of the FTT. The mental health tribunal has its own 'Mental Health Administrative Support Centre' in Leicester, and uses specialist judges and other tribunal members, and rules of procedure.

Mental illness: Mental illness was not defined as a specific term in the MHA, because there was, and still remains, a general reliance on case law and medical and psychiatric practice for a definition of mental illness on a case-by-case basis. Since the psychiatric manuals of mental disorder are constantly being updated and definitions of mental illness will change over time, this makes perfect sense, and provided that the patient's condition is defined as a category of mental illness in one of the commonly used psychiatric manuals, application of the law should follow appropriately. For examples of such a manual, see the *Diagnostic and Statistical Manual of Mental Disorders*, 5th edition (DSM-5) (APA, 2013; updated in 2015, see http://psychiatryonline.org), and *The ICD-10 Classification of Mental and Behavioural Disorders: Clinical descriptions and diagnostic guidelines* (10th revision, effective from 1 October 2015) (ICD-10) (WHO, 1992).

The concept of mental illness is in itself contested. Mental illness may be mistakenly perceived by some as a range of permanently curable illnesses, in the same way that some physical illnesses may be permanently cured – this perception may be true in some instances, but mental illness may perhaps be more clearly perceived generally as a condition, which may be severe and enduring or acute, short-term or time limited, and which may be controlled or contained with appropriate conditions of life and/or appropriate treatments. When we think of mental health legislation which might enforce treatments or conditions of living on people with certain serious mental illnesses, this means that legislation may affect a person with serious mental illness at various times in their life.

Relative and nearest relative: The terms 'relative' and 'nearest relative' are defined in section 26 of the MHA, and ranked as 'nearest' in the order of the list. They include:

(a)   husband or wife or civil partner;

(b)   son or daughter;

(c)   father or mother;

(d)   brother or sister;

(e)   grandparent;

(f)   grandchild;

(g)   uncle or aunt;

(h)   nephew or niece.

The person with whom the patient is living or had been living before admission to hospital may also be regarded as a relative or nearest relative, provided that person complies with the circumstances specified in sections 26 and 27 of the MHA. If the patient 'ordinarily resides with or is cared for by' one of the persons on the list, that person will take precedence over the others, under section 26(4) of the MHA.

The MHA 2007 gives patients the right to make an application to displace their nearest relative and enables county courts to displace a nearest relative where there are reasonable grounds for doing so.

Physical disability: *Achieving Best Evidence* recognises physical disability as potentially creating vulnerability, but sees it as:

> 2.71 less likely to be a problem, although some disabilities may be hidden, but it is important to be aware of whether or how a physical disability may affect the person's ability to give a clear statement. Most witnesses will be able to give evidence with support.

> 2.72 Some physical disabilities may require support. Hearing or speech difficulties may require the attendance of a skilled interpreter and/or intermediary.

> (MoJ, 2011a: paras 2.71–2.72)

Special measures: The YJCEA 1999 introduced a range of special measures that can be used to facilitate the gathering and giving of evidence by vulnerable and intimidated witnesses. The special measures that are available to vulnerable and intimidated witnesses with the agreement of the court are:

• the use of screens (section 23);

• the use of live TV link (section 24);

• giving evidence in private (section 25) (limited to sexual offences and those involving intimidation);

• the removal of wigs and gowns (section 26);

• the use of video-recorded interviews as evidence in chief (section 27);

• video-recorded cross-examination or re-examination (section 28).

Vulnerable witnesses are also eligible for the following special measures:

• communication through intermediaries (section 29); and

• the use of special communication aids (section 30).

The special measures listed above have now all been implemented, except section 28 which was piloted but not yet implemented (MoJ, 2011a: paras 1.14–1.17, 5.26–5.30 and Annex B).

Supervised community treatment: The MHA 2007 introduces supervised community treatment for patients following a period of detention in hospital. It is expected that this will allow a small number of patients with a mental disorder to live in the community whilst subject to certain conditions under the 1983 Act, to ensure they continue with the medical treatment that they need. Currently, some patients leave hospital and do not continue with their treatment, their health deteriorates and they require detention again – the so-called 'revolving door'.

Vulnerable witness: Vulnerable witnesses are defined by section 16 of the YJCEA 1999 (as amended by the Coroners and Justice Act 2009). Children are defined as vulnerable by reason of their age (section 16(1)). The Act makes all children less than 18 years of age, appearing as defence or prosecution witnesses in criminal proceedings, eligible for special measures to assist them to give their evidence in court (MoJ, 2011a: para 1.5).

In addition to the witness who is under the age of 18 at the time of the hearing three other types of vulnerable witness are identified by section 16(2) of the YJCEA 1999. These are:

- witnesses who have a mental disorder as defined by the Mental Health Act 1983 (as amended by the Mental Health Act 2007);

- witnesses significantly impaired in relation to intelligence and social functioning (witnesses who have a learning disability); and

- witnesses who have a physical disability.

Witnesses in this category are only eligible if the quality of evidence that is given by them is likely to be diminished by reason of the disorder or disability (section 16(1)(b) of the YJCEA 1999).

Wherever a reference is made in the legislation to the 'quality of a witness's evidence' for the purposes of defining a witness as vulnerable or intimidated, and in terms of access to special measures, it refers to the 'completeness, coherence and accuracy' of the evidence and 'coherence' refers to a witness's ability in giving evidence to give answers which address the questions put to the witness and can be understood both individually and collectively (section 16(5) of the YJCEA 1999) (MoJ, 2011a: para 1.6).

2 Psychological Stress and Stressors

> The study of trauma has become the soul of psychiatry. The development of posttraumatic stress disorder (PTSD) as a diagnosis has created an organised framework for understanding how people's biology, conceptions of the world and personalities are inextricably shaped by experience.
>
> (van der Kolk, McFarlane and Weisaeth, 1996: 4)

This chapter cannot provide detail of psychological states and conditions, and its contents are not intended to be used as a diagnostic tool. It is written to provide sufficient information for practitioners to understand some of the levels of psychological stress, to see how stress-related physiological changes might affect thinking, memory and behaviours, and to spot the need for further psychological help or formal diagnosis, especially where this might help to access appropriate treatment and/or support where necessary.

In the course of a police investigation, followed by the judicial process, witnesses may be faced with the need to recall and talk about traumatic incidents (possibly several times), providing statements or a recorded interview, and then in court proceedings, to face up to the possibility of giving live evidence, or the playing of their interview, followed by questioning about their recall of events, actions of others, and their own actions in the context of the events in issue.

Our criminal legal system is adversarial, and witnesses in criminal cases where the witness was the victim of violence, sexual offences or other personal physical and psychological violations have reported that they feel uncomfortable, or have lost their confidence. At the worst, some witnesses have felt so devastated by the experience that they become depressed and suicidal.

What few practitioners realise (except perhaps, those directly involved in this work) is that lawyers and others faced with the traumatic accounts and aftermath of others' experiences of abuse, violence and distress, may themselves become vicariously traumatised, or 'burned out'. This may result in increased workplace stress, sickness leave and even the need for potential career changes. We practitioners also need to take care of ourselves when carrying out this demanding work.

It is necessary, therefore, first to understand the nature and impact of psychological stress, its levels and its comorbid conditions – perhaps the most well-known of which are post-traumatic stress and post-traumatic stress disorder (PTSD) (see para 2.1), anxiety and panic attacks (see para 2.2) and depression (see para 2.3). There is also an increasingly recognised potential link between trauma (especially in childhood) and the later development of psychosis. Paragraph 2.3 explores the impact of traumatic stress on children and families, para 2.4 explores post-traumatic stress, and see para 2.5 and Appendix 3 for generalised stress and stressors. Chapter 3 then goes on to explore the impact of traumatic stress on those involved in the court process, and how this may be alleviated.

2.1 Post-traumatic stress and post-traumatic stress disorder

Before beginning this section, it is important to clarify that when the term 'post-traumatic stress' is used in this book, it is meant to describe a human reaction to traumatic events. It is not implied that post-traumatic stress in itself is (or will necessarily become) any form of mental disorder or formal mental illness or that post-traumatic stress will inevitably develop into PTSD. People who have lived through traumatic events may experience a high level of psychological suffering; and for a wide variety of reasons, many of those people will recover their own normal level of functioning in time, while others may develop temporary or long-term mental illness as a result of the stressors. It is difficult, if not impossible, to predict with any accuracy who will recover and who may become ill, although some research has been attempted. In the development of new categories of mental illness, there has been criticism of the medicalisation of what some see as normal life processes, for example, the inclusion of uncomplicated bereavement in the DSM-5 (APA, 2013: 716).

It may be both unhelpful and unwise for lawyers or mental health professionals to try to impose widely generalised diagnostic mental health labels on everyone who has been exposed to traumatic stressors, or who is experiencing post-traumatic stress. Cases vary widely. Many people will recover from severely stressful situations in the course of time, naturally, possibly without medication or any form of treatment, but others may need help and support towards recovery from post-traumatic stress, and will benefit greatly from mental health and/or medical support. The ways in which the severity, duration and level of disturbance of symptoms may affect a person's day-to-day life and their level of functioning may subsequently lead to diagnosis of formal mental disorder or illness (such as depression, anxiety or PTSD), and the criteria for PTSD are explored in para 2.1.2.

2.1.1 Brief history of the study of psychological stress

Hysteria

Hysteria had been regarded for centuries as a medical condition of women, named after its deemed origination in the uterus. The neurologist, Jean-Martin Charcot challenged these beliefs, and in the latter part of the nineteenth century began a systematic study of 'the Great Neurosis' in female patients from the Salpêtrière, a hospital asylum in Paris. By 1880, the cause of hysteria was proved to be psychological in that it could be artificially induced and relieved through the use of hypnosis, which Charcot used with patients in public demonstrations. Sigmund Freud, Pierre Janet and William James were among the influential physicians to hear him lecture and witness his methods of treatment. Freud, with his colleague and mentor Joseph Breuer and Janet, carried Charcot's research further by talking with hysterical patients, listening to their stories and paying attention to their emotional experiencing. Through hearing these personal histories, they concluded that the symptoms were disguised representations of psychologically traumatic events that were apparently unavailable to conscious memory. The women's affective response to these emotionally unbearable events in their lives had produced an altered state of consciousness, which Janet termed 'dissociation' and Freud termed 'double-consciousness'. Breuer and Freud accepted Charcot's theory that trauma causes hysteria, but they extended his thinking, envisaging the causal factor not as the traumatic event itself, but the individual's reaction to it. Between 1893 and 1896, Freud published his new theory of hysterical symptoms in a footnote to a translation of one of Charcot's books. The footnote includes these comments, 'I may mention here: the kernel of the hysterical attack, in whatever form this takes, is a memory, the hallucinatory living through of a scene that was significant for the outbreak of the illness' (Freud, in Jones, 1964: 241). By the mid-1890s, Breuer, Janet and Freud had discovered that relief from hysterical symptoms could be obtained by bringing the traumatic memories, along with their accompanying feelings, into the patient's conscious memory and enabling the patient to verbalise them – the 'talking cure' had evolved (Breuer and Freud, 1955: 30, in Jones, 1964: 239).

At the time Freud first published *Aetiology of Hysteria* in 1896, he attributed the origins of hysteria to memories of real experiences of childhood sexual abuse of the women concerned (Freud, 1962: 203, in Jones, 1964: 246). Freud suggested that, 'phantasies arise from an unconscious combination, in accordance with certain trends, of things experienced and heard. These trends are toward making inaccessible the memory from which the symptoms have emerged or might emerge'. However, Freud later expressed doubts concerning his original thinking about the reality of childhood sexual abuse (Jones, 1964: 247), and he then focused on the process of psychoanalysis, exploring his clients' inner world of fantasy and desires. Herman and others have suggested that Freud's patriarchal attitudes in the context of the anti-feminist political and social situation of the time may have led to his revised thinking. The implications that these 'perverted acts against children' were endemic in society reflected perceptions of a social situation which were rejected by many of Freud's professional peers and which Freud himself may have found hard to believe (Herman, 1992: 14–15). In England, there had been no specific child protection law until the nineteenth century when the Infant Life Protection Act 1872 came into force, followed by the Education Act 1880. Specific child protection legislation followed in 1889 with the Poor Law Act 1889 and the Prevention of Cruelty to, and Protection of, Children Act 1889. Until then, children had been protected in a general way rather like that for domestic and farm animals (Reder et al., 1994). Later, the NSPCC was established in 1890, and professionals and the courts were encouraged, but sometimes reluctant, to acknowledge the potentially frightening reality of extreme or widespread forms of child abuse.

The concepts of 'shell shock' and 'traumatic neurosis'

Soldiers experienced emotional reactions, symptoms of lethargy and withdrawal after the American Civil War, which at the time were attributed to 'nostalgia' due to being far from home. They also reported experiencing physiological symptoms in the chest area with unknown aetiology, which were known as 'soldier's heart' and 'irritable heart' (Bracken, 2002: 66). During the First World War, the British psychologist Charles Myers noted that some soldiers showed symptoms of screaming, weeping, inability to move, unresponsiveness and mutism, and he attributed these symptoms to organic damage to the central nervous system from the percussive effects of exploding shells, naming the syndrome 'shell shock' (Myers, 1940). Research into army history uncovered further recorded symptoms of shell shock as 'daze, fear, trembling, nightmares and an inability to function' and also symptoms of neurological dysfunction: blindness, deafness, semi-paralysis, amnesia and 'extraordinary, unnatural ways of walking' (Shepherd, 2000, in Bracken, 2002: 66). 'Conversion hysteria' is another condition described in soldiers during the First World War, with symptoms including 'paralyses, contractures, muscle rigidity, gait disorders, seizures, tremors, spasms, blindness, muteness, fugue states, and other symptoms of nervous system dysfunction'. Military doctors also noted syndromes of 'neurasthenia' and 'disordered action of the heart' (Bracken, 2002: 66).

The discrepancy in neurological symptoms would suggest that neither shell shock nor conversion hysteria are identical with the modern diagnosis of PTSD as described in the DSM-5 criteria, but they do have features in common with hysteria. It is not surprising, therefore, that following the First World War; mental health professionals considered that prolonged exposure to violent death had produced a neurotic state in men similar to hysteria. The concept of individual vulnerability or moral weakness in response to trauma as a causal factor of the neurological and emotional symptoms led some British psychiatrists, notably Lewis Yealland, to take a condemnatory moral view of this syndrome, using treatments that we would now consider most inhumane and punitive. In his *Hysterical Disorders of Warfare*, published in 1918, Yealland advocated treatment using shaming, threats and punishment and applying electric shocks to remove the hysterical symptoms of mutism, sensory loss or motor paralysis. He reported his treatment of a mute soldier with electric shocks to the throat for hours until the soldier eventually spoke, exhorting him during treatment to 'remember, you must behave as the hero I expect you to be ... "A man who has gone through so many battles must have better control of himself"' (Showalter, cited in Herman, 1992: 20).

During the First World War, other practitioners in Britain, including the physician WHR Rivers, took a different view, arguing that brave soldiers of high moral calibre could suffer from this condition. He treated shell-shocked soldiers, one of them the war poet Siegfried Sassoon, with compassion, dignity and respect, encouraging them to speak and write of their experiences. The aim of treatment was to return the men to combat. Despite his anti-war philosophy, Sassoon returned to the battle lines, expressing guilt at having survived when many fellow soldiers had perished, and also explaining that his loyalty to his comrades was the main reason for his return (Herman, 1992: 22).

In the trenches during the First World War, there was perhaps a combination of danger and pressure to be brave, with repression and denial of feelings of fear or distress. Abraham Kardiner, a psychiatrist working in America with war veterans, published a clinical and theoretical study, *The Traumatic Neuroses of War* (1941), in which he recognised the similarity between hysteria and combat neurosis. The use of the term 'hysteria' was, however, seen as pejorative, and the term 'traumatic neurosis' emerged. Kardiner's treatment of soldiers during the Second World War included psychoanalysis and also the induction of altered states of consciousness using hypnosis or 'narco-synthesis' using the drug sodium amytal, to assist cathartic re-experiencing of traumatic memories. Kardiner and the psychiatrist Herbert Spiegel recognised the importance of the relationship between the soldiers, their unit and their leaders as a factor in protection from overwhelming terror and in assisting recovery, and this was certainly Siegfried Sassoon's reason for his return to the front. During the psychological and social rehabilitation process of soldiers who had been imprisoned, on their return home after the Second World War, Adam Curle noted the importance of relationships with comrades and officers to the soldiers whilst in active service and as prisoners and the contribution of mutual comradeship to their recovery process (Curle, 2001).

During the Vietnam War in the 1970s, some anti-war veterans, with help from sympathetic psychiatrists, shunned the psychological help offered by the government through the Veterans' Association, forming self-governed 'rap groups' to relieve their psychological trauma and to raise awareness of the effects of war. The rap groups' political pressure resulted in a legal mandate for a new model of psychological treatment through self-help and peer counselling named 'Operation Outreach' within the Veterans' Administration. A five-volume report of research carried out for the Veterans Administration (Egendorf, 1981) confirmed the relationship of trauma with combat exposure, and contributed to the development of the formal diagnostic criteria for PTSD.

The different symptoms of hysteria, shell shock and combat neurosis evolved over time, and now there is the modern definition of PTSD which has also gradually developed over time (see para 2.1.2). However, the reality is that, after traumatic events, people do suffer. Those involved as the victims or witnesses of criminal actions, especially those who have experienced great fear, or any form of abuse or violation, may then suffer emotionally as a consequence. However we might choose to diagnose and label their emotional experiencing, whether we think of it as anxiety, depression, panic attacks, PTSD or anything else, it is still emotional pain and suffering, however it might be conceptualised and labelled. Our concern must be to find ways to help vulnerable clients and witnesses involved in the court system to access support that will be effective for them, taking into account their individual needs, context and diversity.

2.1.2   Post-traumatic stress and post-traumatic stress disorder

Post-traumatic stress is the general term given to the human emotional and physiological response to traumatic events. PTSD is considered to be a psychiatric illness and described in the DSM-5 (APA, 2013: 271–280), although the criteria for PTSD remained unchanged (see the website of the American Psychiatric Association (APA), www.dsm5.org). The formal diagnostic criteria of PTSD in DSM-5 are set out below. PTSD is conceptualised by the criteria of Western psychiatry, and so, although the DSM-5 now pays specific attention to diversity and cultural issues, the APA diagnoses may be less useful in non-Western cultures.

Those who experience traumatic events may experience various levels of post-traumatic stress, but will not necessarily develop PTSD (or any other psychiatric illness). Most people recover from traumatic experiences without developing PTSD. Some people are affected by traumatic events more than others. The reasons are unclear why some people have apparent greater resilience to stressors, but research suggests that there is a possibility that a number of factors might each have an influence on our reactions and resilience to stress and traumatic events (see 'The Road to Resilience', at www.apa.org).

Factors possibly influencing predisposition to, or recovery from stress:

- Personality.

- Physical health.

- Family history.

- Childhood experiences and upbringing.

- Other experiences in life.

- Pre-existing mental disorders.

- Genetic inheritance (e.g. certain traits/conditions in first-degree relatives).

- Social and community support.

- Spiritual beliefs or living within systems of meaning.

Sometimes, after a traumatic event, the stress symptoms experienced may meet the criteria of other psychiatric illnesses, for example, acute stress disorder, panic attacks or major depressive disorder. These comorbid diagnoses may exist with or without post-traumatic stress or PTSD. The symptoms of post-traumatic stress (re-experiencing, avoidance and hyperarousal) may vary over time, and may wax and wane. For many people, complete recovery from a lesser traumatic event may happen quite quickly, within months. In other cases, symptoms may last much longer, for example, over a year, and sometimes they may persist for many years. Symptoms may appear to go and then may be reactivated by triggers of the original trauma, for example, sights, sounds, smells; or by new life stressors or new traumatic events.

Typical psychological responses to traumatic events

Responses to trauma can be grouped into symptoms of *intrusion* (unwanted memories), *avoidance* (blocking out the traumatic event and feelings about it) and *hyperarousal* (agitation, over-sensitivity).

By 'intrusion' is meant that memories of the event keep coming back, in the form of thoughts, memories and dreams. Sometimes these are very real and the person feels as though the traumatic event is happening again, right now, and he is re-living it. This is uncontrollable, and the person may find it difficult, if not impossible, to shut out or stop the memories. Nightmares or intrusive waking memories may happen, making it difficult to get to sleep, or stay asleep, or the person might be afraid to go to sleep because the dreams are so bad. If the intrusions are severe, the person might experience problems if he suddenly finds himself reliving the trauma and so cannot at the same time concentrate on what he is physically doing, for example, driving, crossing a road, looking after children, or operating machinery.

The symptoms of 'avoidance' are described as a sense of 'apathy', 'tiredness', 'emotional numbing' and 'no vision of the future'. Others say that they feel 'depressed'. Some people try to avoid activities, places or people that arouse recollections of the trauma. They may try to hide their problems or feel undercurrents of tension. They might hold back feelings and memories, or become emotionally numb. Reminders of the past might act as triggers for difficult feelings, and become depressing; but some people may need to remember the past as an incentive to create a different future. This silence, or not expressing feelings, might be the result of peer pressure or a cultural or societal repression of emotions, and there might be relief in talking freely about the traumatic events. For refugees, or survivors of abuse, silence might have been a necessary survival or coping mechanism, which may be no longer necessary in a new situation of safety. Sharing feelings and problems with friends, family, the community or with professionals is seen by many people as psychologically helpful, although it may be initially difficult. For those who are witnesses, talking about events in therapy before a trial may present potential evidential problems, see Chapters 5 and 6.

The symptoms of traumatic stress described above are very similar to those of the psychiatric illnesses associated with anxiety or depression, which may exist alongside traumatic stress, increasing the sufferer's distress and dysfunction. These symptoms might include 'low energy or fatigue', 'low self-esteem', 'poor concentration or difficulty making decisions' and 'feelings of hopelessness', 'feelings of inadequacy; generalised loss of interest or pleasure; social withdrawal; feelings of guilt or brooding about the past; feelings of irritability or excessive anger; and decreased activity, effectiveness or productivity'. For anxiety disorders, see APA (2013: 189–234), as updated 2015.

Symptoms associated with mood disorders and depression include 'depressed mood', markedly diminished interest or pleasure in all or almost all activities', 'fatigue or loss of energy', 'feelings of worthlessness or excessive or inappropriate guilt' and 'diminished ability to think or concentrate or indecisiveness'. People may also have 'recurrent thoughts of death (not just fear of dying)' or thoughts of suicide. Feelings of depression or suicidality might be increased by physical illness, and by financial and social problems, insufficient money on which to live, family problems, property problems, and a lack of effective psychological help. For depressive disorders, see APA (2013: 155–189), as updated 2015.

Increased arousal and hypervigilance, evidenced by anger and irritability ('a short fuse') is also characteristic of post-traumatic stress. There may, for example, be an increase of violent outbursts, generalised verbal or physical intolerance or aggression, or there may be incidents of domestic or other forms of violence.

These groups of symptoms may have a correlation or association with physiological states. It is not yet fully understood, but it is possible that excessive stimulation of the brain and central nervous system at the time of the trauma might result in a chronic dysregulation of the body's normal evolutionary 'fight or flight' reactions to stress. See para 2.2 for discussion of the psychophysiology of post-traumatic stress.

In circumstances where there are prevailing external conditions of difficulty, for example financial hardship, physical illness, violence or aggression, or the role changes and other circumstances associated with bereavement and other forms of loss, anger and frustration may be made worse by the surrounding circumstances, and people may be less able to cope. In these circumstances, there should be greater attention given to social dimensions, and to try to help the client to access appropriate support to ameliorate their adverse circumstances where possible.

It is easy to understand how domestic violence and aggression might arise when domestic, physical or financial pressures feel intolerable. Children living with volatile family members and subjected to violence and aggression may suffer physical harm or experience developmental problems. Children subjected to or witnessing violence or other abuse at home may suffer emotional harm, a possibility that has recognition in child protection. The Children Act 1989 (CA 1989), which concerns the protection of children, was amended to include in the definition of 'significant harm', 'the impairment suffered from seeing or hearing the ill-treatment of another' (section 31 of the CA 1989). Emotional arousal and depression may lead to incidents of substance abuse, for example, alcohol, illegal drugs or the over-use of prescription drugs in an attempt to self-medicate and reduce unpleasant feelings. Sometimes feelings of anger, blame or guilt are turned inward to result in self-harm. Self-harm may sometimes be inflicted as a way of maintaining or regaining a sense of reality or self-control (van der Kolk, McFarlane and Weisaeth, 1996: 188).

Less frequently, psychotic symptoms (e.g. hallucinations) may also follow traumatic experiences.

Most people recover after the experience of trauma with social support and help from their friends, family and community, or other agencies. A few people may find that they cannot function in their day-to-day life, and continue to experience psychological suffering – these people may benefit from formal assessment and medical or psychological help, usually accessed by referral from their local doctor.

Alcohol is often used as a self-medication to relieve the symptoms of post-traumatic stress, and 'may well be an effective short term medication for sleep disturbances, nightmares and other intrusive PTSD symptoms' (van der Kolk, McFarlane and Weisaeth, 1996: 191). But the use of alcohol as self-medication can lead to undesirable consequences, not the least of which might be alcohol dependence or addiction, and physical damage to the body. Cessation of drinking may cause a psychological rebound effect, in which the unwanted memories return in full force. Van der Kolk comments that the self-help group Alcoholics Anonymous has intuitively grasped this idea, and includes effective post-traumatic treatment strategies in the Twelve Steps programme.

Some people are tempted into other forms of self-medication and the use of psychotropic drugs without a doctor's advice and prescription. This might temporarily affect the psychological effects of trauma, 'Heroin has powerful effects on muting feelings of rage and aggression, whereas cocaine has significant antidepressant action' (van der Kolk, McFarlane and Weisaeth, 1996: 191); but substance misuse, or dependence – particularly on cocaine or alcohol – can exacerbate conditions, and may lead to addictions or mental illnesses.

For the impact of post-traumatic stress on family dynamics, see para 2.4.

Formal diagnostic criteria for post-traumatic stress disorder

The DSM-5 is a manual used by psychiatrists and psychologists as a normative reference for the diagnosis and treatment of psychiatric disorders (APA, 2013). The diagnostic features and criteria for PTSD as presently defined are set out on pp 271–280, and summarised in Appendix 1, from which it can be seen that the criteria can be considered as comprising five distinct groups.

The first group, A, describes exposure in one of several ways to a traumatic event that involved actual or threatened death or serious injury, or sexual violence in a number of ways.

The second group, B, describes the presence of persistent 'intrusion' symptoms of the traumatic event, including recurrent and intrusive distressing memories of the traumatic event, distressing dreams, 'flashbacks' where it feels as though the event is recurring, and intense or prolonged reactions to internal or external cues (triggers) which remind the person of the traumatic event. These might be expressed by children aged over 6 in re-enactment or repetitive play involving themes or aspects of the trauma, or children may have frightening dreams in which the content is not necessarily recognisable.

The third group, C, describes the persistent avoidance of stimuli associated with the trauma. This avoidance might include efforts to avoid thoughts, feelings or conversations associated with the trauma, or to avoid activities, places or people that arouse memories of the trauma.

Group D is negative alterations in thinking (cognition) or mood associated with the traumatic event, often described as 'emotional numbing'. This is a restriction of the range and depth of memories and feelings related to the event. The person may be unable to remember important aspects of the trauma, or have a negative set of beliefs about herself, others or the world (e.g. guilt, blame, it's all my/his/their fault ... if only .../No one can be trusted ... etc.). The person may lose interest or pleasure in activities that she used to enjoy, and may see little or no future for herself or others. Other symptoms are feelings of being detached or estranged from others, and a possible loss of positive and loving feelings. All these can have a significant impact on family relationships – see para 2.5.

The final group of symptoms, E, describes alterations in psychological arousal and reactivity which begin or worsen after the trauma, as evidenced by a list of symptoms (of which at least two must be present for the diagnosis). These include irritability or outbursts of anger or aggression, reckless or destructive behaviour, hypervigilance and an exaggerated startle response, difficulty concentrating, or difficulty falling or staying asleep.

If these clusters of symptoms cause clinically significant distress or impairment in social, occupational or other important areas of functioning and they persist for more than one month, then PTSD may be diagnosed. PTSD is specified as 'delayed expression' if it starts more than six months after the originating traumatic event.

2.2 The psychophysiology of traumatic stress, anxiety and panic attacks

2.2.1 The hormonal changes of post-traumatic stress and post-traumatic stress disorder

This section is written with the caveat that the explanations that follow are based on the current state of neuroscientific understanding available, but medical science is moving forward very fast, and these theories are likely to be explored with further research in medicine and neuroscience. The functioning of the brain is becoming clearer through research and new developments in psychiatry, psychopharmacology and the use of electronic imaging processes which generate the ability to map and track brain activity. As an example, neuroscience research, using functional magnetic resonance imaging (fMRI), created the ability to 'map' and see on a screen the brain's activity and monitor its reactions, and in 2006, this discovery enabled scientists Owen, Laureys and Schiff to make a breakthrough and communicate with a patient who is in a persistent vegetative state (PVS, sometimes referred to as 'locked in syndrome'). This patient had been unable to speak, or communicate in any other way, following severe brain injury. They found that some PVS patients could be enabled to respond to questions, without requiring them to speak or make any physical movement, by simply asking the patient to imagine a specific activity, such as playing a game of tennis, or walking around their home. These imagined activities stimulate two different areas of the brain, which then can be clearly seen with the imaging equipment. The researchers postulated that these responses could then be used to represent 'yes' or 'no' replies to specific questions, and so enable these patients to establish effective communication, see (Owen et al., 2006). For more recent research using electroencephalograph (EEG) imaging, see (Chennu et al., 2014).

To return to post-traumatic stress, in para 2.1 we saw in the criteria for diagnosis of PTSD a mix of symptoms which appear to be opposites, for example at times a person may experience emotional numbing and negative or low mood, and at other times, that person may experience hyperarousal showing as hypervigilance, irritability, anger or aggression. Often sufferers refer to this pattern of numbing and hyperarousal as 'mood swings' which may be repeated frequently over time. Anxiety and panic attacks share some of these same hyperarousal symptoms. The somatic symptoms of hyperarousal arise as a result of endocrinal activity in the body, and this pattern can, in normal circumstances, be understood as part of the human body's instant automatic physical preparation for 'fight or flight' when experiencing a perceived threat. In PTSD, the swings of the 'fight or flight' pattern followed by the emotional numbing may be both exacerbated and prolonged. These 'mood swings' from the 'highs' of the hypervigilance, i.e. hypersensitivity, irritability, anger, aggression, down to the 'lows', i.e. emotional numbness, negativity, apathy, depression, are the result of hormonal action and PTSD is a severe and prolonged exacerbation of the normal human reaction pattern to stressors. The normal response to stressful events will be less severe and of shorter duration.

A number of neurotransmitters (the body's chemical messengers) may be released and play a central role in post-traumatic stress, generally referred to as the 'fight or flight' hormones. These hormones may affect the body's physical and mental functioning, including cognition, memory, and emotions.

Symptoms of post-traumatic stress and associated disorders may include insomnia, palpitations, tremors, sweating, feeling cold, diarrhoea, confusion, blushing, tension headaches, choking sensations or giddiness, decreased libido and gastrointestinal disturbances. Muscular aches in the head or back, restlessness, heaviness or fatigue in the legs, and pains in the abdomen, head, shoulders, back or pelvic area are also common.

In generalised anxiety disorder, people may experience cold, clammy hands, dry mouth, nausea, urinary frequency, trouble swallowing (described as 'a lump in the throat') and an exaggerated startle response.

If traumatic stress is prolonged, the longer-term effect of hyperarousal can potentially lead to circulatory problems, hypertension, ulcers and gastrointestinal problems, and dysfunction of the thyroid glands. Following traumatic stress, the body's immune system may be depleted, and the body becomes more susceptible to infections and to other immunological ailments.

Psychotropic medication for PTSD is difficult, because it needs to address the very different symptoms arising in the mood swings caused by hormonal changes in the body. The problem is that the swings can vary widely in frequency, duration and severity, making appropriate medication difficult. This book cannot address the complexities of the psychopharmacology for this group of disorders, but there are many excellent general works on prescribing for reference – see, for example, *The Maudsley Prescribing Guidelines in Psychiatry* (Taylor, Paton and Kapur, 2015); *Oxford Handbook of Prescribing for Nurses and Allied Health Professionals* (Beckwith and Franklin, 2011); and the *American Psychiatric Publishing Textbook of Psychopharmacology* (Schatzberg and Nemeroff, 2009). There are also specific textbooks on psychopharmacology for the treatment of PTSD.

2.2.2   Impact of hormonal changes on day-to-day living in post-traumatic stress disorder

Appropriate and inappropriate reactions and responses

Van der Kolk (1994: 255) records that Kolb (1987) was the first to propose that excessive stimulation of the central nervous system at the time of trauma might result in temporary or permanent neuronal changes that may have a negative effect on learning, memory, habituation and stimulus discrimination. Given the hormonal changes described, we can understand on a physical level the reasons why a person may also have difficulty in remembering accurately parts of traumatic events, or may experience difficulty in controlling his emotions or reacting appropriately to a situation (see the PTSD criteria in para 2.1).

Emotional hyperarousal may cause abnormal reactions on two different levels; firstly, reactions in response to specific reminders of the trauma; and, secondly, responses to intense but neutral stimuli, such as loud noises, sudden movements, etc. It may therefore be difficult to react appropriately to certain situations.

2.2.3   Traumatic stress, the role of the amygdala and memory

One of the distinctive features of post-traumatic stress and PTSD is the persistent re-experiencing of the traumatic event. To understand why this re-experiencing occurs in PTSD, we need to consider the body's biological systems for memory storage and retrieval. Research in the last two decades has led to greater understanding of the biological systems of the laying down and triggering of memories.

Van der Kolk describes the cycle of hyperarousal and re-experiencing of trauma:

> traumatised patients seemed to react to reminders of the trauma with emergency responses that had been relevant to the original threat but had no bearing on current experience. They were unable to put the trauma behind them, victims had trouble learning from experience; their energy was funnelled toward keeping their emotions under control, at the expense of paying attention to current exigencies. They became fixated on the past, in some cases being obsessed with the trauma, but more often by behaving and feeling as if they were traumatised over and over again without being able to locate the origins of these feelings.

> (van der Kolk, 1994: 253)

Van der Kolk suggests there could be a physiological explanation for this constant, repeated re-experiencing of the past and post-traumatic stress may be seen as a cyclical process:

> Physiological arousal in general can trigger trauma-related memories; conversely, trauma-related memories precipitate generalised physiological arousal. The frequent reliving of the event in flashbacks or nightmares probably causes a re-release of stress hormones that further kindles the strength of the memory trace. Such a positive feedback loop could cause sub clinical PTSD to escalate into clinical PTSD in which the strength of the memories appears to be so deeply engraved that Pitman and Orr (Pitman 1990) have called it 'the black hole' in the mental life of the PTSD patient: it attracts all associations to it and saps current life of its significance.

> (van der Kolk, 1994: 260)

Post-traumatic stress is inextricably linked with the process of laying down and retrieval of memory, on cognitive and physiological levels. The process by which events are perceived and stored in memory usually occurs below the level of conscious awareness:

> The limbic system maintains and guides the emotions and behaviour necessary for self-preservation and survival of the species, and is critically involved in the storage and retrieval of memory. During waking and sleeping states, signals from the sensory organs travel to the thalamus, from which they are distributed to the cortex (setting up a 'stream of thought'), the basal ganglia (setting up a 'stream of movement') and the limbic system (setting up a 'stream of emotions' that determines the emotional significance of the sensory output). Most processing of sensory input occurs outside of conscious awareness, with only novel, significant, or threatening information being selectively passed to the neocortex for further attention.
>
> (van der Kolk, 1994: 260)

The amygdala, an organ in the brain's limbic system, is thought to have a 'gateway' function in the formation and storage of memory traces. Some theorists argue that:

> When a deeply traumatic event occurs ... the emotional reaction is so strong that communication between the amygdala and the hippocampus is barred, preventing the sensory memories from passing from one to the other and keeping them trapped in wordless form in the amygdala.
>
> (Griffin and Tyrrell, 2001: 10)

The psychobiological basis for this activity of the amygdala is not yet fully understood.

The amygdala's functions appear to include the attribution of emotional meaning of incoming stimuli and assignation of free-floating feelings of significance to sensory input, which the neocortex then further elaborates and imbues with personal meaning. It integrates internal representations of the external world in the form of memory images with emotional experiences associated with those memories.

Whilst low and intermediate levels of arousal can improve learning, high stress levels may adversely affect memory:

> As arousal and stress levels dramatically increase, memory deteriorates and fewer details are recalled, including events, which occurred immediately prior to or following each high stress episode, such that an inverted U shaped learning curve is produced. Under excessive and prolonged conditions of stress, excitation and arousal, learning and memory may be completely eclipsed, inducing a profound amnesia, and abnormal reactivity and injury to the hippocampus. As is well known, the hippocampus assists in storing words, places, conversations, written material, contextual details and spatial relationships in long-term memory.
>
> (Joseph, 1998: 169–170)

Hippocampal injury disrupts the ability to convert short-term memory into long-term memory. This means that traumas which are prolonged or repeatedly suffered are often more difficult to remember than a single episode of severe turmoil.

Joseph here is also describing the adverse effect of traumatic stress on memory, which is partly due to the role of norepinephrine (noradrenalin). Both very low and very high levels of norepinephrine activity in the central nervous system interfere with memory storage. The release of excessive norepinephrine, as well as other neurohormones such as endogenous opioids, oxytocin and vasopressin at the time of the trauma probably plays a role in creating the hypermnesias and amnesias that are a quintessential part of PTSD. The amnesia may extend backwards in time for minutes, days or even weeks. Sometimes some or all memory may be recovered.

Traumatic stress may cause long-term damage to the hippocampus, causing lesions. The high levels of corticosteroids released during trauma inhibit the hippocampus, producing memory deficits. In research, administration of 80 mg of prednisone to humans was found to disrupt memory, learning and stimulus discrimination. High levels of corticosteroids can induce hippocampal atrophy, as can be seen in Cushing's syndrome, where overproduction of corticosteroids leads to hippocampal atrophy and memory loss. Distractibility and hyper responsiveness also occurs with hippocampal lesions. 'Incoming messages cannot be acted on, learning cannot take place, injured or damaged cells cannot be repaired due to RNA/DNA interference, and in consequence memory dysfunction and hippocampal atrophy results' (Joseph, 1998: 177). Overwhelming fear might cause this type of arousal. When the hippocampus is desynchronised by high arousal, the subject may be unable to react as they would normally to adverse environmental stimuli, and act to avoid or escape threat.

Paradoxically, whilst conscious memory may be impaired, van der Kolk suggests that some sub-cortical emotional responses may be indelible, because physical damage in the form of cortical lesions may prevent their extinction. 'Emotional memory may be forever' (van der Kolk, 1994: 261). However, although the memories may remain, medication and psychotherapy may enable a person to recall past traumatic events with less negative emotional impact. A range of psychological therapies have now been developed which may be helpful to relieve the distressing symptoms of anxiety, panic attacks, post-traumatic stress and PTSD, harnessing the information learned from research. For further discussion of these, and their place in the forensic process, see Chapters 5 and 6.

Perhaps, too, we can consider the possibilities for positive change in neurogenesis and neuroplasticity – the repairing function of the brain, which may allow us to regain certain lost or impaired brain functions following physical damage. This is an area of neuroscience still developing rapidly; see *The Plastic Mind* (Begley, 2009). For a fascinating and well-researched book on the functions of the two hemispheres of our unequally divided human brain, see *The Master and His Emissary* (McGilchrist, 2010).

2.3   Effects of traumatic stress on children and families

In para 2.1, we explored the formal diagnostic criteria and the psychophysiology of PTSD. We saw that it may be triggered by a situation in which a person experiences, witnesses or is confronted with an event or events which involve actual or threatened death, serious injury or sexual violence to the self or others. These events are referred to as traumatic events. The person's response to the traumatic event might involve fear, helplessness or horror. Traumatic events may vary from a brief, single event (e.g. accident, violence, sexual assault), to prolonged or repeated episodes, and include illness, violence, sexual assaults, torture, abuse, the events of war, and all forms of adult or childhood abuse. These lists are simply examples – and are not exhaustive – many events can be traumatic. After any traumatic event, many people will experience some form of psychological and physical effects. This is a natural part of the human response to stress. Some people have described this as a 'normal reaction to an abnormal event'. When these post-traumatic stress reactions continue for a long time, or if the symptoms are very severe, and if they significantly disrupt the person's day-to-day life, pharmacological or psychological help may be required.

We have seen that other factors can also cause post-traumatic reactions:

(1)   Directly experiencing the traumatic event(s).

(2)   Witnessing, in person, the event(s) as it occurred to others.

(3)   Learning that the traumatic event(s) occurred to a close family member or close friend. In cases of actual or threatened death of a family member or friend, the event(s) must have been violent or accidental.

(4)   Experiencing repeated or extreme exposure to aversive details of the traumatic event(s) (e.g. first responders collecting human remains; police officers repeatedly exposed to details of child abuse).

The age of the child will influence the effect of traumatic stress on the child's development and the way in which he responds to the trauma.

In relation to PTSD criteria, DSM-5 distinguishes between children aged 6 years and over, and those under the age of 6 (APA, 2013). The

DSM-5 criteria in part B 3.1 refer to adults and children over 6 years of age. For similar criteria for children under the age of 6, see APA (2013: 272–274).

Children and families who have been through illness, bereavement, accident, violence or abuse, or refugees from the events of war, may have directly experienced, witnessed or heard about traumatic events within their community or family. The family as a whole, or individuals in it, may have also experienced the loss of their loved ones, homes, security or work. They may have experienced radical changes in their roles within their family and community, which may go along with the potential additional loss of family support, friendships and other community services and support systems.

Professionals who are involved in child protection work following events such as domestic violence, child abuse or neglect will be working with children and families who have experienced traumatic events. The legal and social work processes in child protection, which may involve interviews and court proceedings, are often accompanied by changes in the pre-existing family systems, family structure or roles, and perhaps also the relocation or the removal of a child (or adults) from the family home. All this may in itself be a highly traumatic process for the child and the family. If we are aware of the possible physical and psychological responses to trauma for the members of the family, we can understand why the children and their families affected by such traumatic events may behave differently from their usual patterns, or present challenging behaviours, and perhaps we can respond more appropriately and help them more effectively. An understanding of the psychological, physical and emotional impact of disrupted attachments will also contribute to helping families through crises, and responding appropriately to their needs. For resources on attachment theory, there are many useful publications – see for example the detailed six-volume reference work, *Attachment Theory* (Slade and Holmes, 2014); also Prior and Glaser (2006); Seedall (2011); Brisch and Kronenberg (2002). Help and/or information in family attachment issues may be obtained through local government or independent social workers and children's guardians – for contact details for NAGALRO and CAFCASS, see the resources in Appendix 6.

In children, stress-induced corticosterone production may decrease their hippocampal activity, including hippocampal mediated memory storage and categorisation, but some mental representation may be laid down by means of the system that stores affective memory without symbolic, spatial or temporal processing. Children therefore perhaps might not remember traumatic events clearly, or they may recall some parts of events, or have memories which are not fully processed, making it difficult for them to give a full, clear, detailed account of what has happened.

These psychobiological effects of the post-traumatic stress syndrome may affect the child's reactions to stimuli, and also the child's general behaviour and attitudes. The hyperarousal, intrusive symptoms and depression of PTSD may impact on the child's ability to concentrate on daily tasks and schoolwork and to assimilate and remember new information. Behaviours at school and achievement at school tasks and exams may be affected.

In children, distressing dreams can occur after the traumatic event. They may be of the event; general nightmares of monsters; of rescuing others; or of things that are threatening or scary to the child or others. In some cases, it may be difficult or even impossible to relate the frightening content of the dream to the traumatic event.

When intrusive memories occur, young children may not have the clear sense that they are reliving the past, but the reliving of the trauma may occur through repetitive and/or re-enactment in their play (e.g. a child who was involved in a traffic accident may repeatedly re-enact car crashes with toy cars), and the child may not necessarily exhibit distress when playing in this way. The events may be represented in different ways in the child's drawings or other forms of expression.

In other circumstances, children may feel that they are reliving the past, and during dissociative reactions (flashbacks) they may lose their connection with the present.

Children may present with intense or prolonged psychological distress at exposure to internal or external cues that symbolise or resemble an aspect of the traumatic event (sights, smells, sounds, certain types of touch, etc.). They may show marked physiological reactions to reminders of traumatic events. Children may wish to avoid activities, places or people associated with the traumatic events, or conversations or interpersonal situations that remind them of it.

Arousal may show itself in hypervigilance, sleep disturbance, lack of concentration, temper tantrums, irritable behaviour and angry outbursts (with little or no provocation), which may be expressed as verbal or physical aggression towards others (including extreme temper tantrums).

Another feature of PTSD is negative alterations in cognition and this may show in children through negative emotional states (fear, sadness, shame, confusion, guilt, etc.) or marked lack of interest in fun activities or in play. They may become withdrawn and/or show little expression of positive emotions. Because it may be difficult for children to report diminished interest in significant activities and restriction of affect (feelings), these symptoms should be carefully evaluated alongside reports from parents, teachers and other observers.

In older (e.g. adolescent) children, the sense of a foreshortened future may be evidenced by the belief that life will even be too short to include thinking about becoming an adult. This could lead to reckless or self-destructive behaviour. There may also be 'omen formation', that is a belief in an ability to foresee the future, especially untoward or unhappy events. If this is linked with the 'magical thinking' of childhood (a sense of responsibility for causing events), then in relation to the remembered traumatic events, there may also be feelings of inappropriate responsibility.

Children may also experience various physical symptoms as a result of stressors, such as feeling sick, stomach aches and headaches. If children live in circumstances in which they do not get much adult attention when they try to express their negative feelings (which can happen especially when the adults around them are themselves stressed), and if the adults do not take much notice of a tentative expression by a child of negative feelings such as sadness, but seem to pay more heed to the child when he describes a physical symptom (such as responding when a child says he feels ill, has a headache, tummy ache or feels sick), those children may become more likely to express or exhibit emotional discomfort as an experience of physical pain or illness.

Atle Dyregrov, a specialist in trauma work with both adults and children, wrote in 1995 that we do not yet know enough about trauma processing in relation to the different development tasks of childhood (Dyregrov, 1995: 46). He continued exploring in research and his more recent book *Supporting Traumatised Children and Teenagers* (Dyregrov, 2010) which draws on research and the author's extensive experience, providing practical and accessible information about ways of helping children and young people through trauma. See also his more recent co-authored book, *Effective Grief and Bereavement Support* (Dyregrov and Dyregrov, 2008).

Children, like adults, may suffer from anxiety, hyperarousal and behavioural disturbances – see the preceding section on DSM-5 criteria relating to children. The effects of long-term child abuse may reach into a child's adult life. The severity of the effects may be proportional to the duration of the trauma and the age of the child when it began. The effects of disrupted attachment resulting from parental behaviours and/or separation from attachment figures in childhood has long been recognised in Western psychiatry (Bowlby, 1969; Winnicott, 1957). Attachment disorders and separations may arise from bereavement, illness, and marital or family break-up, internal displacement in wartime, refugee status, or for child protection or other societal reasons. Children who have suffered early separations or disrupted attachments may be less resilient to stressors. Separation linked with a traumatic experience may worsen the effects of post-traumatic stress, and the syndrome of post-traumatic stress may manifest in a wide variety of ways as child survivors grow and develop.

2.3.1   Children under 7 years of age

Pre-school children are learning to trust others, developing basic
security and attachments, and developing control over their body and
impulses. They are developing identity and autonomy, and seeking to
understand their outer world. If they face death or crisis at this, their
most passive and vulnerable age, they may have a limited capacity for
understanding what is happening, or the long-term implications of the
events. They may have heightened anxiety about separations and
rejections, and are more vulnerable to the death of a caregiver. Their
lack of understanding may be to some extent a protective factor, as is
their openness and ability to be concrete and direct. Their reactions to
death may include anxiety about strangers, crying, clinging, and the
need for much reassurance. They may show regressive behaviour such
as bedwetting, soiling and sleep disturbances. The depressive symptoms
may be apparent in loss of interest in play and temper tantrums
(Dyregrov, 1995: 43–44).

In children under 7, predominant problems relate to separation, sleeping,
feeding, changed behaviour and various forms of physical disturbances for
which paediatricians cannot find an organic cause.

2.3.2   Children over 7 years of age

School-age children are 'decreasing their dependence on their parents,
and increasing contact with the world outside the family'. They have a
'greater repertoire of coping strategies to meet and handle death and crisis
situations' and in fantasies, 'through changing, undoing, reversing, or
taking revenge, they can counteract feelings of helplessness' (Dyregrov,
1995: 44). Schoolwork may suffer from the child's inability to concentrate
or apathy. Depressive symptoms are common after bereavement, and
anxiety or guilty feelings may emerge, but the child may be unable or
unwilling to share his feelings with adults or his peer group. Dyregrov
suggests that denial or suppression of feelings seems to increase with age
(Dyregrov, 1995: 45).

If feelings are suppressed for any reason, or if there is a family or societal
culture where negative or painful feelings are not freely expressed,
reactions to post-traumatic stress may emerge in physical symptoms,
subconsciously giving a tangible reason for complaint. Children and
young people may tend to react the same way as they move towards
adulthood. The problems most frequently found in schoolchildren are
related to a changed attitude towards everyday duties, school and
authorities, but also to other problems, such as psychosomatic reactions
and diseases, depression and even suicide attempts.

2.3.3   Adolescents, and young people of 16–18 years of age

Dyregrov (1995: 44–45) describes the developmental tasks of adolescents as directed towards mastery of biological, psychological and social changes, developing adult sexuality and the adult sexual role. Concerns centre on dependence and independence, fear of rejection and ambivalence towards parents. The 'magical thinking' of childhood may be reactivated and inappropriate feelings of responsibility for events, guilt and self-reproach may arise. Adolescents may, however, think about the long-term consequences of death and loss.

Dyregrov suggests that the intensity of adolescents' feelings or the avoidance of confrontation may cause their reactions to be expressed more through challenging behaviour and conflicts with their environment. 'Violent human-caused deaths may activate adolescents' own destructive fantasies and aggression' (Dyregrov, 1995: 45). They may endeavour to gain a control over death, and engage in risk-taking activities. In a peaceful situation this may be sublimated by adolescents into sport, but this may pose different challenges in refugee populations or in other post-conflict situations where the trauma is severe and/or recent, and the political, cultural or social climate may tend to encourage or exacerbate risk-taking behaviour. When we are working with vulnerable refugee families, or those who may have been caught up in violent conflict, we need to bear this in mind.

Children and young people of any age who have suffered loss and bereavement might also have to cope with changing roles within the family, carrying out additional or new household tasks or wage-earning work to replace the role of lost adults. Competition may arise between attendance at school and other tasks. Children and young people may find themselves with competing social and family pressures or needs. Through physical or psychological causes, adults may become dependent on their children. Refugee children may have additional stress and responsibility of role reversal, where significant family members are missing and the family is struggling to survive both physically and emotionally (Harris Hendricks, Black and Kaplan, 1993: 12).

There may be a significant difference between the parents' and children's perception and evaluation of the children's problems; sometimes children may report more problems than their parents or carers have noticed. Possibly, some parents may simply not have noticed, or have discounted their children's problems. This can happen for many reasons, one of which may be perhaps because they are too caught up in their own difficulties. Other parents may have a tendency to deny (or magnify) their children's problems, possibly indicating a disturbed parent–child relationship, and/or possibly also an emotional condition of the parent.

The intensity of mental disturbances for children and families is likely to be influenced by the general family system, including the attitudes, beliefs and behaviours prevailing in the family. It is therefore an advantage if families can be regarded as a system, and assessment and treatment may need to apply to the family as a whole (rather than simply seeing a child as 'the problem'). Systemic family therapy may be the treatment of choice by psychologists for family dysfunction.

As we have seen, the psychophysiological responses traumatic events may cause impairment of memory. It is suggested that children suffering from post-traumatic stress are more at risk for traumatic memory loss than older individuals (Joseph, 1998: 171). In infants, the memory system that encodes affective quality of experience matures before the central nervous system. The central nervous system links the representations of events with symbolic and linguistic organisation of mental experience. With maturation, there is an increasing ability to link experience with existing mental schema, but this process is also vulnerable to disruption.

In normal child development, the hippocampus matures slowly until the third or fourth year, and the myelination cycle is not complete until well after the first decade. There may be prolonged immaturity of the corpus callosum, which is limited in its ability to transfer information between right and left hemispheres until well after the age of 5. As the right hemisphere and right temporal lobe are dominant for storage of personal and emotionally laden experiences, callosal immaturity prevents the language-dominant left hemisphere from gaining access to this data. Joseph explains that this may be why most individuals might have difficulty recalling events that occurred prior to the age of three and a half, because these memories are stored, but cannot be easily retrieved and expressed (Joseph, 1998: 171).

When a child is asked to give an account of past events, the age-related laying down of memory and the impact that post-traumatic stress has on memory storage and retrieval needs to be considered, and psychological advice can be helpful in understanding why a child witness may give an account of events in a certain way.

2.4   Why do some people suffer from post-traumatic stress disorder and others not?

There have been hypotheses put forward about why some people seem to be more vulnerable to post-traumatic stress than others, and why some people seem to make more rapid recoveries than others. Pitman, Shin and Rauch (cited below) put forward interesting alternative hypotheses about possible causation, but some practitioners may feel that these reflect linear, mechanistic thinking, in that for example, they take little account of the influences of social and the other factors relevant to the individual and their community such as those listed earlier in para 2.1.2 – 'Factors possibly influencing predisposition to, or recovery from stress'. Also, Pitman, Shin and Rauch refer to 'abnormality' which is a concept which some practitioners may find difficult to define, because they would understand post-traumatic stress more as a human reaction, involving suffering and distress, but they would not necessarily conceptualise it in terms of pathology.

Research relating to PTSD has discovered much of the psychophysiology, i.e. the physiological symptoms and effects of post-traumatic stress in relation to the psychological effects, but we are still left with many unresolved questions as to causation. Post-traumatic stress and PTSD appear to be either the result of, caused by or accompanied by abnormal physiological states. The unresolved questions of causation were very well summarised in the hypotheses suggested by Pitman, Shin and Rauch, set out below, but only further research will get us closer to the answers.

1. That there is a pre-existing brain abnormality which increases the risk of exposure to PTSD causing events – [i.e.] less ability to avoid risks, or to learn from past events

2. A pre-existing abnormality increases vulnerability to PTSD after exposure to traumatic events

3. The traumatic exposure causes the brain abnormality, and the abnormality produces PTSD

4. The traumatic exposure produces PTSD, and that leads to the abnormality

5. Traumatic exposure produces PTSD, and sequelae, which then lead to complications (e.g. alcoholism), which then leads to the abnormality

(Pitman, Shin and Rauch, 2001: 54)

2.5   Post-traumatic growth

Some people who have experienced post-traumatic stress have, despite their suffering, also discovered or developed within themselves levels of self-compassion, insight, strength and fortitude of which they had formerly been unaware, and are able to carry this knowledge forward into the future. They may develop new skills, knowledge and survival strategies, and they may find new directions and meaning in life. Professor Stephen Joseph's book, *What Doesn't Kill Us* (Joseph, 2012) in which he describes his theory of post-traumatic growth is well worth reading.

See also *Post-Traumatic Stress* (Regel and Joseph, 2010).

2.6 What is stress? Assessment and identifying stressors

When we are working with vulnerable witnesses or clients, awareness of their levels of stress and helping clients to identify the particular stressors in that individual client's life can be helpful in finding effective ways to support them. It may also help us as practitioners to know our own personal stressors, and perhaps help us to reduce problems which impact on our work or home life.

Stress is an ordinary part of day-to-day life, and can have a useful function as a driver towards creating energy and achievement (e.g. in working for examinations or preparing for interviews). However, when stress levels become too high, the effect may be to create anxiety that may reduce our energy, ability to give attention to detail and efficiency, and so here, high stress levels are counterproductive.

We also need to be aware as practitioners of 'vicarious traumatisation' – in other words the traumatic stress in us created by hearing repeated accounts from clients or others of traumatic events (see the DSM-5 criteria and description in para 2.1). However, many stressors in our day-to-day lives are not necessarily related to traumatic events or vicarious trauma, but we may simply become stressed or feel overwhelmed or overburdened by the pressures of ordinary life.

Appendix 2 comprises a map of the possible sources of stress in daily life. A diagram sets out potential stressors, followed by a questionnaire, which can be self-administered or used with a counsellor, psychologist or other mental health practitioner to identify the possible causes of our stress (our stressors), and from there we can consider ways to address the stressors and reduce their impact.

3 Alleviating Stress in Court Proceedings: Law, Special Measures and Guidance on the Treatment of Vulnerable Witnesses

He had an accident that damaged his ability to speak. He wants to give evidence. Can he do so? What help is there for him in court?

She suffers from mental illness – and I'd like to support her in court. Is she a vulnerable witness? If she is, does this entitle her to my support?

He is afraid to come face to face again with the mugger who knifed him, or of meeting the man's friends outside the court. What can we do to help?

All witnesses are likely to feel some measure of anxiety when thinking about their attendance at court and the possibility of giving evidence. Their concerns may come from a wide variety of factors. These may include a general lack of self-confidence; fears specifically related to the court proceedings; concerns about the evidence they may have to give, or anxieties related to potential exposure to public attention. This list is by no means exhaustive. Witnesses may wish to seek help or support, and this may be available to them through the Witness Service (available in all criminal courts in England and Wales), or through private or publicly funded psychological or psychosocial support, but all too often, witnesses are not made aware of their rights and of the resources which they might wish to access. Professionals might wish to create and maintain a list of the local resources available in their area, and some useful national organisations are listed in Appendix 6. If the witness is a child, or a vulnerable adult, his concerns may be addressed with additional support through special measures, described in paras 3.2–3.7.

Professionals can help witnesses at the outset of proceedings by exploring the extent of the witness's concerns, needs and available support which may include:

- concerns that the witness may have:
  - about his self-confidence,
  - about the evidence he may have to give,
  - about the general nature of the legal process and court proceedings,
  - about getting to court, or giving evidence,
  - about other issues relevant to the case;
- medical or mental health conditions or concerns the witness may have;
- medical and psychological support available to the witness;
- family and community support networks available to the witness.

Once these issues are identified, professionals can then see where the areas of need lie, and begin to help the witness bring into action his existing support networks, and to plan any additional support which may be necessary for his wellbeing.

This chapter explores the relevant law guidance and the possible support that is currently available for witnesses.

3.1   Legal rights of vulnerable or intimidated witnesses

Article 6(1) of the ECHR establishes the right to a fair trial. This concept includes openness in judicial proceedings and underpins the requirement for a prosecution witness to be identifiable not only to the defendant, but also to the open court. It supports the ability of the defendant to present his case and to test the prosecution case by cross-examination of prosecution witnesses. In some cases, it may also encourage other witnesses to come forward.

The CPS states that:

> the principle of open justice can sometimes act as a bar to successful prosecutions, particularly in homicides, organised crime and gun crime. Witnesses may fear that if their identity is revealed to the defendant, his associates or the public generally then they or their friends and family will be at risk of serious harm.

The CPS goes on to say that:

> [the] police in most cases will establish whether a witness is in fear and should inform the prosecutor. Ideally, a discussion about the type of 'protection' that should be applied for will take place between the police and the prosecutor at the pre charge stage. Occasionally information about a witness being in fear may come from another source (for example the Witness Care Unit or the Witness Service).

> When informed that a witness is fearful of giving evidence, prosecutors must liaise closely with the police to consider the range of options available to them both at common law and by virtue of statute. Prosecutors should seek to ensure that, wherever possible, the witness's fear is allayed and that they are given the requisite protection. Prosecutors must also ensure that the witness's rights under the ECHR are acknowledged and protected.

(www.cps.gov.uk)

We have seen that Article 6(1) of the ECHR establishes the right to a fair trial. This concept includes some protection for witnesses in that Article 6 also states that:

> Judgment shall be pronounced publicly but the press and public may be excluded from all or part of the trial in the interests of morals, public order or national security in a democratic society, where the interests of juveniles or the protection of the private life of the parties so require, or to the extent strictly necessary in the opinion of the court in special circumstances where publicity would prejudice the interests of justice.

(ECHR: Article 6, p 9)

The provisions for the protection of witnesses are also in line with Article 8(1) of the ECHR, the right to respect for private and family life (ECHR: Article 8, p 10). Section 17 of the YJCEA 1999 makes provision for 'special measures' to protect child witnesses, and intimidated adult witnesses – for details of how special measures should operate in the guidance *Achieving Best Evidence* (MOJ, 2011a) and relevant codes of practice, see paras 3.2–3.7.

The *Code of Practice for Victims of Crime* (MoJ, 2015) was issued in October 2015, see www.gov.uk. It revises an earlier version of the *Victims Code* (MoJ, 2013b) which had replaced an older version (MoJ, 2006). The changes have been criticised for reducing the level and availability of support for the victims of crime; see the response produced by Victim Support to the consultation document *Improving the Code of Practice for the Victims of Crime* and the *Draft Code of Practice for the Victims of Crime* at www.victimsupport.org.uk.

Although the Witness Charter does not have the force of law, the *Victims' Code* places a statutory obligation on criminal justice agencies, being issued under section 33 of the Domestic Violence, Crime and Victims Act 2004. It implements relevant provisions of the EU Directive establishing minimum standards on the rights, support and protection of victims of crime (2012/29/EU); Directive 2011/92/EU combating the sexual abuse and sexual exploitation of children; and Directive 2011/36/EU preventing and combating the trafficking of human beings. The *Victims' Code* sets out the services to be provided to victims of criminal conduct by criminal justice organisations in England and Wales. Each organisation should produce operational guidance about how to fulfil their relevant duties, and 'service providers' are encouraged to discuss with victims the level of service they require to meet their needs. The 'service providers' are the organisations listed in the *Victims' Code* and who have obligations imposed by the *Victims' Code*, and they include the police, the CPS, witness care units and the courts – for the complete list, see *Victims' Code* (MoJ, 2015: 2). Other organisations, including voluntary sector organisations, which are not listed, may also provide services for victims but they are not covered by the *Victims' Code*.

The Victims' Commissioner has a responsibility to keep the *Victims' Code* under regular review, to listen to victims' points of view and to try to improve the services and support available. The *Victims' Code* contains details of complaints procedures. Failure to comply with the *Victims' Code* will not lead to legal proceedings against that organisation, but it may be considered by a court in reaching its decision. The Parliamentary and Health Service Ombudsman may consider complaints, referred by MPs, from those who complain that a body has not met its obligations under its provisions.

Achieving Best Evidence (MoJ 2011a) provides general guidance on approaches to interviewing and working with vulnerable and intimidated witnesses (see para 3.3.1). In addition, it sets out guidance on the use of a specific range of special measures which are each discussed separately in paras 3.3–3.10. Here, just to set the scene, it may be helpful to briefly explain that the YJCEA 1999 (sections 23–30) embodied in legislation the concept of using special measures to facilitate the gathering and giving of evidence by vulnerable and intimidated witnesses, with the agreement of the court. These are:

- the use of screens (section 23);

- the use of live TV link (section 24);

- giving evidence in private (section 25) (limited to sexual offences and those involving intimidation);

- the removal of wigs and gowns (section 26);

- the use of video-recorded interviews as evidence in chief (section 27).

Vulnerable witnesses are also eligible for the following special measures:

- communication through intermediaries (section 29); and

- the use of special communication aids (section 30).

Achieving Best Evidence comments that 'The Special Measures listed above have now all been implemented. Section 28 video-recorded cross-examination has not been implemented' (MoJ, 2011a: paras 1.14–1.17). However, it has been piloted, and the outcome of the pilot trials may be made available in the future.

The main concern of sections 23–30 of the YJCEA 1999 as explained in *Achieving Best Evidence* is not necessarily the welfare of the witness, but, as the title might imply, to achieve the best evidence for the court. Therefore the use of special measures is not primarily intended to alleviate distress or inconvenience for vulnerable witnesses but might go some way towards helping a witness survive the court process. Access to special measures is a matter for the court, and contingent on:

- 'whether the witness is 'vulnerable' or 'intimidated' as defined by sections 16 and 17 respectively;

- whether any of the special measures or any combination of them are likely to improve the quality of the witness's evidence;

- which of the available special measures are most likely to maximise the quality of the witness's evidence' (MoJ, 2011a: para 1.19).

The YJCEA 1999 provides other protective measures which may have the effect of helping the witness psychologically to have more confidence and less anxiety in giving evidence.

- Vulnerable and intimidated victims in certain classes of sexual offences are exempted from cross-examination by the accused in person, if the defendant is unrepresented (sections 34–35).

- At the discretion of the court, an unrepresented defendant may be prohibited from cross-examining a vulnerable and intimidated victim in person (section 36).

- In the case of rape and other sexual offences, the court may restrict the evidence and questions about the victim's (complainant's) sexual behaviour (section 41).

- There may be restrictions imposed on media reporting information which is likely to identify adult witnesses (section 46).

In section 39 of the Children and Young Persons Act 1933 there is power to prohibit publication of certain matters such as name, address, school, or other identifying material in newspapers, and pictures of the child or young person, and in section 49 there are restrictions on reports in which children or young persons are concerned that may be applied in relation to child witnesses.

Please refer to para 3.3, and note that although a competent witness can be legally required to attend court and give evidence, or to give his evidence under a court direction for special measures, he should not be compelled to give an initial interview:

> the fact that a witness is compellable does not mean they can be legally required to give any kind of preliminary statement to the police – even the sort of statement that is made under this guidance.

(MoJ, 2011a: para 2.10)

Achieving Best Evidence confirms (in relation to reluctant witnesses) that investigators should listen to the witness's concerns, and inform the witness of the outline of the alleged offence, and that it is suspected that he may have witnessed all or part of the events connected with it. Investigators may also inform the witness of his right to protection and the resources available, but:

> No pressure should be brought to bear on these witnesses to talk to police or to give evidence; the function of the investigator in these circumstances is simply one of providing enough information to allow the potential witness to make an informed choice. …

> Records should be kept of these sessions either in the form of notes or by way of a visual or audio-recording, as appropriate in the circumstances.

(MoJ, 2011a: paras 2.141–2.142)

3.2   Who is a vulnerable or intimidated witness, and entitled to special measures?

Achieving Best Evidence is available at www.cps.gov.uk and was issued by the CPS, Department of Education, and Department of Health, along with the Welsh Assembly Government. It takes into account the changes to special measures provisions in the Coroners and Justice Act 2009, and the *Advice on the Structure of Visually Recorded Interviews with Witnesses* (ACPO, 2010; 2nd edn, 2013) and it aims to improve the quality of video-recorded statements. It is not legally enforceable, but 'significant departures from its practice may have to be justified in the courts' (MoJ, 2011a: para 1.1). Those witnesses who do not receive sufficient support, and their families and loved ones, might wish to have stronger enforcement and redress.

Achieving Best Evidence is wide ranging, and:

> covers the interviewing of witnesses both for the purposes of making a video-recorded statement and also for taking a written statement, their preparation for court and the subsequent court appearance. It applies to both prosecution and defence witnesses and is intended for all persons involved in relevant

investigations, including the Police, adults and children's social workers, and members of the legal profession.

(MoJ, 2011a: para 1.3)

3.2.1   Vulnerable witness

Achieving Best Evidence defines those who are vulnerable and intimidated witnesses eligible for special measures, and sets out the special measures available for them.

> Vulnerable witnesses are defined by Section 16 of the Youth Justice and Criminal Evidence Act 1999 (as amended by the Coroners and Justice Act 2009). Children are defined as vulnerable by reason of their age (Section 16(1)). The Act makes all children less than 18 years of age, appearing as defence or prosecution witnesses in criminal proceedings, eligible for Special Measures to assist them to give their evidence in court.

(MoJ, 2011a: para 1.5)

In addition to the witness who is under the age of 18 at the time of the hearing, three other types of vulnerable witness are identified by section 16(2) of the YJCEA 1999. These are:

• witnesses who have a mental disorder as defined by the Mental Health Act 1983 (as amended by the Mental Health Act 2007);

• witnesses significantly impaired in relation to intelligence and social functioning (witnesses who have a learning disability); and

• witnesses who have a physical disability. Witnesses in this category are only eligible if the quality of evidence that is given by them is likely to be diminished by reason of the disorder or disability (section 16(1)(b)).

> Wherever a reference is made in the legislation to the 'quality of a witness's evidence' for the purposes of defining a witness as vulnerable or intimidated, and in terms of access to Special Measures, it refers to the 'completeness, coherence and accuracy' of the evidence and 'coherence' refers to a witness's ability in giving evidence to give answers which address the questions put to the witness and can be understood both individually and collectively (section 16(5)).

(MoJ, 2011a: para 1.6)

Although *Achieving Best Evidence* recognises mental disorder, it also reflects the understanding that this may be the most difficult category to identify for support through special measures because of the fluctuating nature of many mental disorders. A person with mental disorder may need special assistance only at times of crisis. Note that a brief interview may not reveal mental disorder, but if clear evidence and/or a clear diagnosis becomes available which suggests the need for special measures, then these should take account of any emotional difficulties, to enable the witness to give evidence with the least possible distress. Currently, there appears to be no accepted and consistent approach to the assessment of witness competence. It is likely that varying criteria may be used by experts called to make assessments. In addition, mental instability might be aggravated by factors such as alcohol, or use of (or withdrawal from) drugs or other substances. These effects may be temporary and the time necessary to elapse before a witness is able to give clear evidence may vary according to the type and severity of the intoxication from a few hours to a few days, or longer.

3.2.2   Intimidated witnesses

'Intimidated witnesses' are defined by section 17 of the YJCEA 1999 (as amended by the Coroners and Justice Act 2009) as:

> those whose quality of evidence is likely to be diminished by reason of fear or distress. In determining whether a witness falls into this category, the court should take account of:
>
> - The nature and alleged circumstances of the offence;
> - The age of the witness;
> - Where relevant
>   - The social and cultural background and ethnic origins of the witness
>   - The domestic and employment circumstances of the witness
>   - Any religious beliefs or political opinions of the witness;
> - Any behaviour towards the witness by:
>   - The accused
>   - Members of the accused person's family or associates
>   - Any other person who is likely to be either an accused person or a witness in the proceedings.
>
> (MoJ, 2011a: para 1.10)

Witnesses are regarded as intimidated in cases of complainants in cases of sexual assault (section 17(4) of the Act). Witnesses to specified gun and knife offences are defined as falling into this category by section 17(5) of the Act (as inserted by the Coroners and Justice Act 2009) (MoJ, 2011a: para 1.11).

Vulnerable and Intimidated Witnesses: A Police Service Guide (MoJ, 2011b) suggests that victims of and witnesses to domestic violence, racially motivated crime, crime motivated by reasons relating to religion, homophobic crime, gang-related violence and repeat victimisation, and those who are elderly and frail, also fall into this category. The families of homicide victims also fall into this category (see MoJ, 2011a: para 1.11).

Achieving Best Evidence recognises some of the learning from research, i.e. that witnesses may be intimidated not only by the nature of the offence such as sexual offences and assaults, but also cases where the witness knows the alleged offender, and offences of victimisation which are of a repeated nature, such as stalking and racial harassment (MoJ, 2011a: para 1.12). *Achieving Best Evidence* also recognises that the categories 'vulnerable' or 'intimidated' are not mutually exclusive, so that while some witnesses may belong to just one category (e.g. a child who witnesses a robbery in the street may be vulnerable, but not subject to intimidation), other witnesses may be considered both vulnerable and intimidated – for example 'an elderly victim of vandalism who has dementia on an inner-city estate' and 'others may not be vulnerable but may be subject to possible intimidation (e.g. a young woman who fears violence from her current or former partner or someone who has been the subject of a racial attack)' (MoJ, 2011a: para 1.12).

Intimidated witnesses are very likely to feel unsafe, and they may wish for support. They should be told about the protection that might be available for them, including witness protection schemes where available, see (MoJ, 2011a: paras 2.125–2.133). Discussions need to take place quickly, see *Early Special Measures Discussions between the Police and the Crown Prosecution Service* (MoJ, 2009).

Box 3.1 Information about intimidated witnesses

Achieving Best Evidence recommends obtaining as much information as is possible about the witness, including:

- gender;
- sexuality (where the alleged offence might contain a trans/homophobic element);
- preferred name/mode of address;
- domestic circumstances (including whether the witness is currently in a 'safe' environment);
- relationship of the witness to the alleged perpetrator;
- any medication being taken and its potential impact on the interview;
- current emotional state (including trauma, distress, shock, depression, fears of intimidation/recrimination, and recent significant stressful events experienced);
- likely impact of recalling of traumatic events on the behaviour of the witness;
- current or previous contact with public services (including previous contact with police, the local children's or adult services authority or health professionals); and
- any other relevant information or intelligence known.

(MoJ, 2011a: para 2.133)

3.2.3   Significant impairment of intelligence and social functioning (learning disability)

Achieving Best Evidence defines:

> Learning disability is not a description of one disability, but a collection of many different factors that might affect a person's ability in relation to learning and social functioning to greatly varying degrees. While some 200 causes of learning disability have been identified, most diagnoses are still 'unspecified learning disabilities'. People with high support needs may be easily identified but people with mild or moderate learning disabilities may be more difficult to identify.
>
> (MoJ, 2011a: para 2.67)

> It is impossible to give a single description of competence in relation to any particular disability, because there is such a wide range of abilities within each in terms of degree of intellectual and social impairment. However, there are some indicators that may help identify a witness with a learning disability.
>
> (MoJ, 2011a: para 2.68)

> Though generalisations cannot be made, some characteristics may exist in relation to some syndromes. For example, witnesses with autistic spectrum disorder, which includes Kanner's syndrome and Asperger's syndrome, have a huge range of abilities/disabilities, but:
>
> - They often have difficulty in making sense of the world and in understanding relationships;
> - They are likely to have little understanding of the emotional pain or problems of others; and
> - They may display great knowledge of certain topics and have an excellent vocabulary, but could be pedantic and literal and may have obsessional interests.
>
> (MoJ, 2011a: para 2.69)

> Some people with learning disabilities are reluctant to reveal that they have a disability, and may be quite articulate, so that it is not always immediately obvious that they do not understand the court proceedings in whole or in part.
>
> (MoJ, 2011a: para 2.70)

3.2.4   Physical disability

Physical disability is not specifically defined in *Achieving Best Evidence*, but witnesses with physical disabilities are recognised as potentially requiring support to give their evidence – see the following extracts:

> Recognition of this type of disability is less likely to be a problem, although some disabilities may be hidden, but it is important to be aware of whether or how a physical disability may affect the person's ability to give a clear statement. Most witnesses will be able to give evidence with support.
>
> (MoJ, 2011a: para 2.71)

Some physical disabilities may require support. Hearing or speech difficulties may require the attendance of a skilled interpreter and/or intermediary.

(MoJ, 2011a: para 2.72)

3.3   Competence and compellability of vulnerable or intimidated witnesses

Under section 53(1) of the YJCEA 1999, in principle, 'all persons are (whatever their age) competent to give evidence' provided that in accordance with section 53(2), that person can: (a) understand questions put to him as a witness; and (b) give answers to them which can be understood.

If the competence of a witness is questioned, the YJCEA 1999 requires the court to determine, on a balance of probabilities, whether or not the witness is competent; and it is the job of the party calling the witness to satisfy the court as to the witness's competence. See section 54(1) and (2) of the YJCEA 1999.

In determining the question of competence, the court shall treat the witness as having the benefit of any directions made under section 19 of the YJCEA 1999 which the court has given or proposes to give regarding special measures, section 54(4).

Note that under section 54(6) of the YJCEA 1999, 'any questioning of the witness (where the court considers that necessary) shall be conducted by the court in the presence of the parties'. This means that if the witness is likely to be vulnerable or intimidated, those supporting the witness need to raise with the court the issue of any special measures to which the witness might be entitled under section 19 at the outset of the case, for the protection of the witness during any questioning regarding competence.

Expert evidence may be received to assist the court in making a decision as to competence, section 54(5) of the YJCEA 1999.

Competence is not dependant on the age of a child. See *R v B* [2011] Crim LR 233, where the Court of Appeal held that:

> although the chronological age of the child will inevitably help to inform the judicial decision about competency, in the end the decision is a decision about the individual child and his or her competence to give evidence in the particular trial.

A competent witness is also compellable, i.e. the witness can be legally required to attend court and give evidence, or to give his evidence in another way under a court direction for the use of special measures. However, as *Achieving Best Evidence* points out:

the fact that a witness is compellable does not mean that they can be legally required to give any kind of preliminary statement to the police – even the sort of statement that is made under this guidance.

(MoJ, 2011a: para 2.10)

Achieving Best Evidence confirms (in relation to reluctant witnesses) that investigators should listen to the witness's concerns, and inform the witness of the outline of the alleged offence. They should tell the witness of their right to protection and the resources available, but 'No pressure should be brought to bear on these witnesses to talk to police or to give evidence; the function of the investigator in these circumstances is simply one of providing enough information to allow the potential witness to make an informed choice.' Records should be kept of such a session by way of notes or an audio-recording, as appropriate.

(MoJ, 2011a: paras 2.141–2.143)

3.4   Interviews with vulnerable or intimidated witnesses

3.4.1   Initial brief interviews

We have saw in the last paragraph of para 3.3 that, although a competent witness can be legally required to attend court and give evidence, or to give his evidence under a court direction for special measures, *Achieving Best Evidence* recognises that the witness cannot be compelled to give an initial interview to the police (MoJ, 2011a: para 2.10). In cases where the CPS believes the evidence of a particular witness is essential, the *Code for Crown Prosecutors*, 7th edition (MoJ, 2013a), leaves it open to the CPS to drop the case if it thinks that it would be particularly damaging to the witness to proceed (see also the revised Code (CPS, 2015)).

Interviews should be planned in advance, taking account of the witness's expressed preferences and discussed where appropriate with carers.

> In some cases, it might be advisable for there to be a discussion with the Crown Prosecution Service (CPS) in accordance with the guidance set out in *Early Special Measures Discussions between the Police and the Crown Prosecution Service* (Office for Criminal Justice Reform, 2009). Where such a discussion takes place, there should be a decision about the form in which the statement is to be taken (video-recorded or written). Such decisions must take account of the witness's expressed preferences and, if appropriate, those of their carers.

(MoJ, 2011a: para 2.2)

Decisions about whether to make a video-recorded interview cannot always be taken at the outset. Initial questioning may have to take place as a matter of urgency, but should be brief – intended to elicit a brief account of the events, to inform the investigation plan and arrange any necessary medical attention or support for the witness. There is guidance for the way in which an initial interview should be conducted.

> In these circumstances, any early discussions with the witness should, as far as possible, adhere to the following basic principles:
>
> a) Listen to the witness.
>
> b) Do not stop a witness who is freely recalling significant events.
>
> c) Where it is necessary to ask questions, they should, as far as possible in the circumstances, be open-ended or specific-closed rather than forced-choice, leading or multiple.
>
> d) Ask no more questions than are necessary in the circumstances to take immediate action.
>
> e) Make a comprehensive note of the discussion, taking care to record the timing, setting and people present as well as what was said by the witness and anybody else present (particularly the actual questions asked of the witness).
>
> f) Make a note of the demeanour of the witness and anything else that might be relevant to any subsequent formal interview or the wider investigation.
>
> g) Fully record any comments made by the witness or events that might be relevant to the legal process up to the time of the interview.
>
> (MoJ, 2011a: 2.5–2.6)

3.4.2   Preparation for interviews with vulnerable adult witnesses

Briefly, vulnerable adult witnesses are those who have a mental disorder, learning disability or physical disorder that is likely to have an impact on the quality of their evidence. For more detailed definitions of 'vulnerable adult', 'victim' and 'vulnerable or intimidated victim', see Chapter 1, paras 1.1 and 1.2, and *Achieving Best Evidence* (MoJ, 2011a: paras 1.2 and 1.6). For video-recorded interviews, see para 3.5.

It might also be useful to refer to *Vulnerable and Intimidated Witnesses: A Police Service Guide* (MoJ, 2011b), which contains prompts to assist the police in recognising vulnerable adult witnesses. *Achieving Best Evidence* offers guidance (MoJ, 2011a: paras 2.61–2.94). Below is a summary based on the guidance. Specialist mental health and social care workers may feel that some of the information in the guidance is too generalised, or they may disagree with its application to specific people, but it is helpful to be aware of the advice which is given to police and interviewers, and the parameters within which they are asked to carry out their work.

A brief interview may not be sufficient to identify a witness as vulnerable, as, for example, mental disorders may fluctuate. If a clear diagnosis becomes available which suggests the need for special measures, the interviewer should take account of any potential emotional difficulties and try to cause the witness the least possible distress. The use of prescribed medication and abuse of drink, drugs or other substances may cause temporary impairment and recovery possible over time to enable an interview to take place. Some people with a learning disability may be reluctant to reveal that they have a disability, and if they are articulate, it might not be immediately obvious that they may not understand the proceedings in whole or in part.

Achieving Best Evidence (MoJ, 2011a: paras 2.67–2.70) accepts that the recognition of significant impairment of intelligence and social functioning (learning disability) is not easy for those working with witnesses, as disability may take so many forms, and there is such a wide range of abilities within each, but it suggests that:

> Though generalisations cannot be made, some characteristics may exist in relation to some syndromes. For example, witnesses with autistic spectrum disorder, which includes Kanner's syndrome and Asperger's syndrome, have a huge range of abilities/disabilities, but:
>
> - They often have difficulty in making sense of the world and in understanding relationships;
> - They are likely to have little understanding of the emotional pain or problems of others; and
> - They may display great knowledge of certain topics and have an excellent vocabulary, but could be pedantic and literal and may have obsessional interests.
>
> (MoJ, 2011a: para 2.69)

Physical disability is seen as 'less likely to be a problem' but may affect the witness's ability to 'give a clear statement'. 'Most witnesses will be able to give evidence with support'. 'Hearing or speech difficulties may require the attendance of a skilled interpreter and/or intermediary' (MoJ, 2011a: paras 2.71–2.72).

Preparation and establishing rapport are important to put the witness at ease and to facilitate communication. Communication should be facilitated by use of appropriate assistance, for example the use of sign systems such as British Sign Language (BSL), Sign Supported English (SSE), Sign-a-long and Makaton, alphabet boards, Rebus, and Bliss symbol boards, etc. The witness's own idiosyncratic use of signs and symbols should be understood, for example, signs for 'yes', 'no' and 'don't understand'. Wherever possible, witnesses should point to, or otherwise indicate, the required symbols themselves. There should be opportunities for rest and refreshment, with short interviews where necessary (MoJ, 2011a: paras 2.90–2.94).

Mental disorders are not seen as precluding the giving of reliable evidence. *Achieving Best Evidence* recognises that 'the recall of traumatic events can cause significant distress, and recognition of the mental state of the witness and its effect on their behaviour is crucial' (MoJ, 2011a: para 2.73):

> Witnesses with a mental disorder, such as schizophrenia or other delusional disorders, may give unreliable evidence through delusional memories or by reporting hallucinatory experiences, which are accurate as far as the witness is concerned but bear no relationship to reality (e.g. they might describe a non-existent crime). Challenges to these abnormal ideas may cause extreme reactions and/or distress. Interviewers should probe these accounts carefully, sensitively and in a non-judgemental way with a view to identifying which elements of the account may be delusional and which elements might have a firmer foundation in reality.
>
> (MoJ, 2011a: para 2.74)

Practitioners may wonder whether interviewers should be expected to have the necessary qualifications and skills to identify delusions and hallucinatory experiences, and/or to distinguish these from a truthful account of certain types of serious criminal offences. Expert help such as a psychiatrist or psychologist may be necessary to clarify such evidence:

> Witnesses may suffer from various forms of anxiety through fear of authority, exposure or retribution. Extreme fear may result in phobias, panic attacks or unjustified fears of persecution. Anxious witnesses may wish to please, they may tell the interviewer what they believe they wish to hear or fabricate imaginary experiences to compensate for loss of memory. The evidence given by depressed witnesses may be influenced by feelings of guilt, helplessness or hopelessness. Witnesses with antisocial or borderline traits may present with a range of behaviours such as deliberately giving false evidence. These disorders cause the most difficulties and contention in diagnosis, and require very careful assessment.
>
> (MoJ, 2011a: para 2.75)

> Witnesses, particularly some older witnesses, may also have dementia, which can cause cognitive impairment. A psychiatrist or clinical psychologist with experience of working with older people should be asked to assess their ability to give reliable evidence and the effect such a procedure might have on their health and mental welfare.
>
> (MoJ, 2011a: para 2.76)

> Witnesses with a mental disorder may show some of the behaviour seen in witnesses with a learning disability, such as confusion, memory loss and impaired reasoning. For this reason, many of the interview practices that are likely to help witnesses with a learning disability may also benefit witnesses with

a mental disorder. Properly preparing the witness for the interview may help to identify and reduce confusion, emotional distress and anxiety. Cognition may not be an immediate difficulty, but attention to the way a statement is given and how questions are posed must always be considered.

(MoJ, 2011a: para 2.77)

The witness may wish to please the person in authority. They may be suspicious of the person, aggressive, or wish to impress the interviewer. Interviewing teams should be aware of such possibilities. Consultation with people who know the witness well should give some indication of their likely behaviour and some suggestions as to how interviewers can best interact with the witness.

(MoJ, 2011a: para 2.78)

Interviewers are advised to spend some time in preparation for an interview establishing rapport with the witness, and allowing the witness to develop some sense of familiarity with the personnel involved in the interview.

Learning disability may lead to some difficulties in a witness interview. It may take many forms, and the level at which learning disability may interfere with giving evidence will therefore vary widely. Suggestibility and compliance, or 'learned helplessness' in a witness may lead to problems in being decisive or in giving cogent evidence:

Some witnesses with a learning disability may wish to please people in authority. Some may be suspicious of people, or aggressive, or may wish to impress the interviewer. Interviewing teams should be aware of such possibilities. Consultation with people who know the witness well should give some indication of their likely behaviour and some suggestions as to how interviewers can best interact with the witness.

(MoJ, 2011a: para 2.81)

Some witnesses with a learning disability may show confusion, memory loss and impaired reasoning. Properly preparing the witness for the interview may help to identify and reduce confusion, emotional distress and anxiety.

(MoJ, 2011a: para 2.82)

In some instances of mild and moderate learning disability, a difficulty with cognition may not be immediately apparent. The experience that many people with learning disabilities have of discrimination towards them in society is likely to act as an incentive to conceal or minimise their disability whenever possible. Where there are concerns that a witness has a learning disability, even if the extent of the disability is considered to be relatively mild, it is essential that a great deal of care is taken in framing questions and evaluating the witness's response to them.

(MoJ, 2011a: para 2.83)

Some witnesses with a learning disability communicate using a mixture of words and gestures (e.g. Makaton signs/symbols when used as an augmentative communication system). While an intermediary should be considered in every case where a witness has a learning disability, the services of an intermediary are essential in circumstances where a witness communicates using a mixture of words and gestures.

(MoJ, 2011a: para 2.84)

Some witnesses with a learning disability do not use speech but communicate using alternative methods of communication. Such alternative methods include sign and symbol systems. Examples of sign systems include Makaton signing and Sign-a-long (these systems may be used either as an augmentative system with speech or as an alternative system without it). Examples of symbol systems include Rebus, Bliss and Makaton. The symbols may be printed on boards or cards, or contained in booklets. They vary from being iconic and concrete to being more abstract in their composition. They may be personalised and can be composed of words, pictures and symbols. While an intermediary should be considered in every case where a witness has a learning disability, the services of an intermediary are essential in circumstances where a witness uses an alternative method of communication instead of speech.

(MoJ, 2011a: para 2.85)

Achieving Best Evidence suggests that a series of short interviews preferably, but not necessarily, held on the same day, may be more helpful than one long interview (MoJ, 2011a: para 2.86).

Achieving Best Evidence recognises that 'race, gender, culture, ethnicity and first language should be given due consideration by the interviewing team'. The team's knowledge of 'the witness's religion, customs, culture and beliefs may have a bearing on their understanding of any account given by the witness, including the language and allusions the witness might make, for example to reward or punishment' (MoJ, 2011a: para 2.106, p 37). It is interesting that *Achieving Best Evidence* acknowledges the potential impact of racism, discrimination and oppression, for example where witnesses are refugees or asylum seekers, or of dual heritage, but it makes no mention here of taking into account a witness's gender identity or sexual preferences if known, knowledge of which may also have a bearing on the witness's account of events and the team's perceptions of the account given.

3.4.3   Vulnerable adult witnesses: psychological impact of events

Where the witness may have experienced abuse, neglect, domestic violence and/or discrimination based on race or disability, the interviewers must consider its potential impact on the interview. There is no single 'diagnostic' symptom of abuse or discrimination, but some of

Box 3.2   Checklist – information about vulnerable adult witnesses

While circumstances will sometimes limit what can be found out about the witness prior to the interview taking place (e.g. as a result of time constraints where the alleged perpetrator is in custody), as much of the following information should be obtained about the witness as is possible:

- age;
- gender;
- sexuality (where the alleged offence might contain a trans/homophobic element);
- preferred name/form of address;
- the nature of the witness's disability or mental disorder and the implications of this for the interview process;
- any medication being taken and its potential impact on the interview (including its timing);
- domestic circumstances (including whether the witness is currently in a 'safe' environment);
- the relationship of the witness to the alleged perpetrator;
- current emotional state (including trauma, distress, shock, depression;
- fears of intimidation/recrimination and recent significant or stressful events experienced);
- the likely impact of recalling traumatic events on the behaviour of the witness;
- current or previous contact with public services (including previous contact with the police, the local authority adult services or health professionals); and
- any relevant information or intelligence known.

(MoJ, 2011a: para 2.105)

the possible effects on vulnerable adult witnesses are set out in *Achieving Best Evidence* (MoJ, 2011a: Boxes 2.10–2.13). The guidance comments that 'When considering the possibility of abuse or discrimination, it must be understood that vulnerable adult witnesses who have experienced it will not necessarily exhibit all, or indeed any, of the behaviours set out in these boxes'. The guidance strongly warns interviewers against assumptions based on stereotypes and encourages a non-judgemental approach. These lists in the guidance are of necessity very basic, and cannot take in all the effects of trauma which witnesses may have encountered. Please refer to Chapter 2 of this book for more detailed consideration of the impact of post-traumatic stress on individuals, children and families.

Box 3.3　Checklist – considerations for vulnerable adult witnesses

Some possible relevant considerations include the following, although this list is in no way intended to be exhaustive:

- customs or beliefs that could hinder the witness from participating in an interview on certain days (e.g. holy days) or may otherwise affect the witness's participation (e.g. when fasting);
- the relationship to authority figures within different minority ethnic groups; for example, witnesses from some cultures may be expected to show respect to authority figures by not referring to them by their first names, and by not correcting or contradicting them;
- the manner in which love and affection are demonstrated;
- the degree to which extended family members are involved in caring for the witness;
- the degree of emphasis placed on learning skills in independence and self-care; and
- issues of shame; for example, carers in some cultures may inhibit the witness from talking about a sexual assault for fear of shaming the family.

(MoJ, 2011a: para 2.109)

Box 3.4　Some possible effects of abuse and neglect

These include:

- Poor self-esteem;
- Post-traumatic stress disorder;
- Self-injury and suicidal behaviour;
- Increased emotional problems, e.g. anxiety and depression;
- Decreased cognitive functioning;
- Sexualised behaviour; and
- Negative social behaviour, e.g. increased aggression, non-compliance and criminal activity.

(MoJ, 2011a: Box 2.10)

Box 3.5 Some possible effects of racism

These include:

- Fear;
- Poor self-esteem;
- Fear of betrayal of community;
- Mistrust of people from outside own community;
- Difficulty in establishing positive (racial) identity; and
- Increased vulnerability to racist abuse.

(MoJ, 2011a: Box 2.11)

Box 3.6 Some possible effects of discrimination based on disability

These include:

- Decreased autonomy;
- Increased dependency:
- Difficulty in establishing positive self-identity;
- Experience of being isolated (geographical, physical, social);
- Experience of being patronised by people who do not have a disability;
- Experience of being treated as a 'voiceless object';
- Feelings of being perceived as 'asexual'; and
- Increased vulnerability to abuse.

(MoJ, 2011a: Box 2.12)

Box 3.7 Some possible effects of domestic violence

These include:

- Fear for safety of self and others in family;
- Sadness/depression possibly reflected in self-harm or suicidal tendencies;
- Anger, which may be demonstrated in aggressive behaviour;
- Negative impact on health (e.g. asthma, eczema or eating disorders); and
- Negative impact on behaviour (e.g. aggression).

(MoJ, 2011a: Box 2.13)

3.5   Capacity and consent issues in interviewing vulnerable witnesses

Mental capacity is a legal concept, according to which a person's ability to make rational, informed decisions is assessed. It is presumed in law that adults and children over the age of 16 have the legal power to give or withhold consent in medical and health care matters, provided that they have mental capacity. This presumption is rebuttable, for example in the case of mental illness. For adults, law relating to mental capacity is now governed by the Mental Capacity Act 2005, the Mental Health Act 2007 and the Mental Capacity Act 2005 (Appropriate Body) (England) Regulations 2006 (SI 2006/2810). Collectively, these are referred to here as the 'MCA'. Relevant publications and websites are listed in Appendix 5 and Appendix 6. The MCA empowers individuals to make their own decisions where possible, and protects the rights of those who lack capacity. Where an individual lacks capacity to make a specific decision at a particular time, the MCA provides a legal framework for others to act and make that decision on their behalf, in their best interests, including situations in which the decision is about their care and/or treatment (DoH, 2015: 96).

Note that neither mental disorder nor any form of disability should be linked with an assumed lack of mental capacity. The 2015 guidance clearly provides that:

> It is important for professionals to be aware that those with a mental disorder, including those liable to be detained under the Act, do not necessarily lack capacity. The assumption should always be that a patient subject to the Act has capacity, unless it is established otherwise in accordance with the MCA.

> (DoH, 2015: 99, para 13.15)

Under Article 12(2) of the UNCRPD, there is a requirement that 'persons with disabilities enjoy legal capacity on an equal basis with others in all respects of life'. This seems to mean that people with mental disabilities are generally expected to exercise choice in their ordinary day-to-day decision making. Article 12(3) requires states to provide people with disabilities all reasonable support in their decision making. Article 12(4) requires that the support systems 'respect the rights, will and preferences of the person'.

Under the MCA 2005, mental capacity is a legal concept, according to which a person's ability to make rational, informed decisions is assessed. There is no single, definitive test for mental capacity to consent; however, section 2(1) of the MCA 2005 sets out the criteria for deciding when a person does not have capacity in relation to the MCA 2005:

For the purposes of this Act, a person lacks capacity in relation to a matter if at the material time he is unable to make a decision for himself in relation to the matter because of 'an impairment of, or a disturbance in the functioning of, the mind or brain'.

This means that there is a two-tier test of capacity:

• Does the person have an impairment of, or a disturbance in the functioning of, the mind or brain?

• Does the impairment or disturbance mean that the person is unable to make the specific decision at the time that it needs to be made?

This test for capacity takes a 'function specific' approach, which means that it looks to assess a person's understanding in relation to each decision that has to be made and recognises that, while a person may have capacity to make some decisions, the person may not have capacity to make other decisions. It is not a question of whether a person has capacity to make particular types of decisions generally.

The assessment of mental capacity is also based on a set of principles in which it is situation-specific and depends upon criteria set out in section 3(1) of the MCA 2005:

A person is unable to make a decision for himself if he is unable:

    a) To understand the information relevant to the decision

    b) To retain that information

    c) To use or weight that information as part of the process of making the decision; or

    d) To communicate his decision (whether by talking, using sign language or any other means).

The quality of the decision-making process is therefore dependent on the quality of the information given to the person, and the manner in which relevant information is provided. The person only needs to retain the information long enough to make the decision, so short-term memory will suffice. Ability to evaluate the potential consequences of making the decision (or not) is important. However, if a person fulfils the criteria for capacity, that person may not then be assumed to lack capacity just because he wishes to make a decision that is regarded by others as unwise.

Note that *Achieving Best Evidence* (MoJ, 2011a) was issued before other relevant recent guidance, the content of which may impact on consent and capacity issues and decisions affecting the health and welfare of the witness – for example, *Working Together* (DfE, 2015a); *Victims' Code* (MoJ, 2015); *The Witness Charter: Standards of Care for Witnesses in the Criminal Justice System* (MoJ, 2013c); *Working with Victims and Witnesses* (College of Policing, 2016); and the *Mental Health Act 1983: Code of Practice* (DoH, 2015).

Box 3.8 Five statutory principles of the Mental Capacity Act 2005

- *Principle one*
  A person must be assumed to have capacity unless it is established that they lack capacity.

- *Principle two*
  A person is not to be treated as unable to make a decision unless all practicable steps to help them to do so have been taken without success.

- *Principle three*
  A person is not to be treated as unable to make a decision merely because they make an unwise decision.

- *Principle four*
  An act done, or decision made, on behalf of a person who lacks capacity, must be done, or made, in their best interests.

- *Principle five*
  Before the act is done, or the decision is made, regard must be had to whether the purpose of the act or the decision can be as effectively achieved in a way that is less restrictive of the person's rights and freedom of action.

(DoH, 2015 : 98–99, para 13.14)

In assessing capacity and consent for some groups of vulnerable witnesses, regard should be had to the principles set out in the MCA 2005 and the *Mental Capacity Act 2005: Code of Practice* (DCA, 2007) described above, and mental health and medical practitioners might also wish to refer to the *Reference Guide to Consent for Examination or Treatment*, 2nd edition (DoH, 2009) where this is relevant to the witness, for example in planning preliminary or subsequent interviews for a victim or witness who also requires examination and/or treatment.

A person may be mentally incapacitated on a temporary basis (e.g. unconscious in hospital after an accident), or on a longer-term or permanent basis (e.g. those who suffer from severe long-term mental illness or other impairments of mental functioning), and in those circumstances, the capacity to make medical decisions is likely to be assessed by a medical doctor or psychiatrist. The assessment of a person's mental capacity for other tasks may be made by other professionals; for example, the decision on a person's capacity to make a will may be made by a lawyer; or the decision on whether a person can engage in therapy may be made by a therapist. In decisions about giving interviews to the police, the witness may make the decision in consultation with the police and with carers where appropriate, but if there is any doubt about the capacity of the witness to consent to an interview and to give evidence, advice should be sought from an appropriate registered medical practitioner, psychiatrist or psychologist.

Note: under the Criminal Procedure and Investigations Act 1996, any report obtained in order to assess capacity or consent issues may have to be disclosed to the defence prior to a trial as unused prosecution material.

Box 3.9 Matters to take into account when capacity is an issue

If, following assessment, capacity is an issue, matters to be taken into account when considering the best interests of a witness (as specified in section 1(6) of the Mental Capacity Act 2005) include:

- The person's past and present wishes and feelings;
- The beliefs and values that would be likely to influence the person's decision if they had capacity; and
- The other factors that the person would be likely to consider if they were able to do so.

Views to be considered

As specified in sections 4(4) and 4(7) of the Mental Capacity Act 2005, the following should be considered:

- Such views as the witness is able to express (with such assistance as is necessary); and
- Where it is practicable and appropriate to consult them, the views of
    - anyone named by the person as someone to be consulted on the matter
    - in question or on matters of that kind;
    - anyone engaged in caring for the person or interested in their welfare;
    - any person with lasting power of attorney granted by the person; and
    - any deputy appointed for the person by a court.

                                          (MoJ, 2011a: paras 2.99–2.100)

Notes

If a person involved in the care of a witness is also suspected of abusing them, this should be taken into account when considering the person's best interests.

A record should be made of the scope of the consultation, the person(s) consulted, and all decisions taken.

Any considerations and/or decisions made at this time about the necessity and potential evidential impact of pre-trial therapy should also be carefully recorded.

All witnesses should freely consent to an interview, and if the interview is to be video-recorded, the witness should be fully aware of this and agree to it. For video-recorded interviews, see para 3.4. The consent does not necessarily have to be in writing, but should be recorded or noted in some form for evidential purposes. As set out in para 3.3, there is no legal requirement for a witness to give a preliminary interview to the police, but a competent witness may be compelled to come to court to give evidence (MoJ, 2011a: para 2.10).

Informed consent for an interview requires that the witness has a clear understanding of the nature and purpose of the interview, and the use to which it will be put. Interviewers should explain in a way appropriate to the witness:

- The benefits/disadvantages of having or not having the interview video-recorded;
- Who may see the video-recorded interview (including the alleged offender both before the trial and at court); and
- The different purposes to which a video-recorded interview may be put (e.g. if it appears the video may be useful in disciplinary proceedings against a member of staff who is suspected of abusing a vulnerable adult in their care).

(MoJ, 2011a: para 2.95)

3.6   Making Special Measures Directions under the Youth Justice and Criminal Evidence Act 1999 (as amended by the Coroners and Justice Act 2009)

The needs of the witness should have been assessed and resolved as far as possible before the plea and case management hearing (PCMH). At the PCMH, either directions will be made for special measures or a date fixed for a hearing to consider what is necessary and appropriate to meet the witness's needs. A similar system exists in the magistrates' and youth courts, called a pre-trial review hearing (PTR). Legal representatives should have all the necessary information to assist this decision, including information available about the mental and medical condition of the witness and witness attendance times.

A joint plea and case management questionnaire is then agreed between the advocates and handed to the court to assist the court at the PCMH. The plea and case management questionnaire contains specific questions about measures to assist witnesses giving evidence, including reporting restrictions (part 19); third party material (part 20); video evidence (part 22); electronic equipment such as live links (part 25);

cross-examination on previous sexual history (part 26); concurrent family proceedings (part 33); and other special arrangements such as interpreter, intermediary communication assistance, the need for breaks, etc. (part 34). If the court has not considered the needs of the witnesses, the judge may be expected to ensure that this is raised (MoJ, 2011a: para 5.2).

If a video recording is made, the legal representatives need to have seen it before the PCMH, so that the court can make decisions at the PCMH about admissibility, editing, etc.

If new information comes in about the witness after the PCMH and before the trial hearing, the court has a responsibility to consider any changes in the needs of the witness and to make appropriate directions.

Note: If a young witness is aged under 18 when a video recording of his evidence is made, but over 18 at the time of a court hearing for trial, he is entitled to special measures as if he were still a child (sections 21(9) and 22 of the YJCEA 1999), and the same presumptions apply.

If a young witness who had a Special Measures Direction made in relation to him becomes over 18 at the time of a trial, then the special measures no longer apply. However, there is the possibility of protection for the witness as a vulnerable adult witness if he fulfils the criteria; or, if he is a defendant on trial, some level of protection may be possible at the discretion of the court, see para 3.13.

Applications for Special Measures Directions can be made at the pre-trial hearing, under Part 29 of the Criminal Procedure Rules 2014 and Part 18 of the Criminal Procedure Rules 2015, before the beginning of the trial. An application can also be made before a 'Newton' hearing to which witnesses are called to settle the facts of the case before sentence is passed, or on an appeal. New directions will be needed for a retrial or an appeal. Special measures include:

- Screening a witness from the accused (section 23).

- Evidence given by live link (section 24).

- Evidence given in private (section 25) (limited to sexual offences and those involving intimidation).

- Removal of wigs and gowns (section 26).

- Video-recorded evidence in chief (section 27).

- Video-recorded cross-examination or re-examination (section 28).

- Examination of witness through an intermediary (section 29).

- Communication aids (section 30).

3.6.1   Screening a witness from the accused (section 23)

Making the choice between using screens and live link

When courts are making the decision between use of a live link (see para 3.6.2) and a screen, they might consider that the live link has the advantage that the witness does not physically have to come to the court, which may have both psychological and physical advantages, especially for witnesses who might have difficulty in travelling. The screen will allow the witness to be present in person before the jury or magistrates, and it has been suggested that this might be helpful for the court in forming decisions of fact, as they may have a better physical sense of the witness.

However, if the witness does *not* want the defendant to see him, and to be totally shielded while he gives evidence, the courtroom screen may present a better choice. Witnesses should at pre-trial stage be made aware that the alternative of the live link would then show their image to the whole court during the evidence (sometimes on a large plasma screen/monitor) which will be visible to the defendant, too. However, note it is possible in some cases (e.g. where a child witness wants to use live link but would be distressed by being seen by the defendant) to use *both* the live link and obscured monitor/screen, see *Achieving Best Evidence* (MoJ, 2011a: Appendix B, B.9.9–9.10).

Exceptions: Where the witness is a child witness, or a witness over 18 to whom section 21 or section 22 of the YJCEA 1999 applies, the live link is usually taken to be the more appropriate measure, but the witness can express a wish to opt out from the measure and give evidence in court. In such a case, if the witness is a child, there will be a presumption that screens will then be used in court. Section 21(4)(A), as amended by section 100 of the Coroners and Justice Act 2009 (MoJ, 2011a: Appendix B, B.9.11).

Screens

Screens may be authorised to shield a witness from seeing the defendant. The screen is normally erected around the witness rather than the defendant. It must not prevent the judge, magistrates or jury and at least one legal representative of each party to the case (i.e. the prosecution and each defence representative) from seeing the witness, or the witness from seeing them. If an intermediary or an interpreter is appointed to assist the witness, that person too must be able to see the witness and be seen by the witness. The YJCEA 1999 does not specifically provide for the witness's need to see the Witness Service Volunteer (if there is one), but the court should ensure that this need is met where a screen is erected.

The court is also authorised to provide for an 'arrangement' which is not a screen, but which has the same effect of preventing a witness from seeing the defendant. An arrangement used in some older cases required the defendant to move from the dock to a position in court where he could not be seen by the witness. Such an arrangement might have the undesirable effect of making it more difficult for the defendant to communicate with his legal representatives, which could become a factor in determining whether he was accorded a fair trial within the meaning of Article 6 of the ECHR. Screens, if erected around the defendant, could also have this unintended effect. If such an arrangement or screens are adopted, therefore, careful consideration must be given to ensuring that the rights of the defendant are properly preserved, for example by ensuring that a break in the witness's evidence is taken in order to afford the defendant an opportunity to consult with his legal representative about any further questions which should be put in the light of what the witness has said.

Where the trial involves a jury, the judge may warn them not to be prejudiced against the defendant as a consequence. This is done as part of the judge's duty to protect the accused from the unfairness that would ensue if, for instance, the jury were to assume that the defendant must have done something wrong to merit the erection of a screen (MoJ, 2011a: Appendix B, B.9.1–9.3).

3.6.2   Evidence given by live link (section 24)

When courts are making the decision between use of a screen (see para 3.6.1) and a live link, they might consider that the use of a remote live link has the advantage that the witness does not physically have to come to the court, which may have both psychological and physical advantages, especially for witnesses who might have difficulty in travelling. However, if the live link is from another room at the court premises, then this potential advantage would be lost.

The live link picture is usually shown on a screen to the court (and this may be a large plasma screen), and so the defendant will also see the screen picture of the witness giving live link evidence. The witness needs to be aware of this at the pre-trial stage.

Exception: Note it is possible in some cases (e.g. where a child witness wants to use live link but would be distressed by being seen by the defendant) to use *both* the live link and an obscured monitor/screen (see MoJ, 2011a: Appendix B, B.9.9–9.10).

'Live link' usually means a closed circuit television link, but also applies to any technology with the same effect. The essential element of a live link is that it enables the witness to be absent from the courtroom where the proceedings are being held, but at the same time to see and hear, and be seen and heard by, the judge, the magistrates or jury, at least one legal representative of each party to the case, and any intermediary or an interpreter appointed to assist the witness. The judge, magistrates, court clerk or justices' clerk control the equipment, and should be comfortable with it and familiar with any likely difficulties, such as the distorted image which may appear on the witness's monitor if those in court lean too close to the camera. Judges and magistrates must also ensure that the witness understands what is happening. This is most obviously of importance for a child witness or a witness who has learning disabilities, but it should not be assumed that any witness is conversant with the equipment. It may be useful for the judge or magistrate to inquire as to whether the witness has paid a pre-trial visit to the court at which the facility has been explained and/or demonstrated (see MoJ 2011a, para 4.20).

There is a presumption that a witness who gives evidence by live link for a part of the proceedings will continue to give evidence by this means throughout. Where a party to the proceedings argues that the method of receiving the witness's evidence should change, the court can make a direction to this effect if the interests of justice so require.

If there are no live link facilities at the magistrates' court where the proceedings would normally be held, the proceedings may be transferred to another court where a live link is available. Alternatively, if the witness is an adult and screening them is considered to be equally likely to enable the witness to give his best evidence, then the court may choose to screen the witness instead. Particular care will need to be given to making a decision in such circumstances where the witness is a child.

The YJCEA 1999 makes the live link available to vulnerable and intimidated witnesses, whether or not their evidence in chief is presented in the form of a video-recording, and there may be some witnesses for whom the live link is the only special measure required to enable them to give their best evidence. Even in the case of a child witness who is subject to a presumption that a recording will be used as evidence in chief, it may be necessary to resort to the use of the live link alone if no recording is available or an available recording has been ruled inadmissible.

Consideration should be given to whether use of a live link away from the court house where the trial is taking place could be used for a witness. This could be at another court or a separate 'remote' facility which has live link capability (MoJ, 2011a: Appendix B, B.9.4–9.7).

3.6.3   Court hearings held in camera: evidence given in private (section 25)

Evidence is usually given in open court, with the protections described here. However, exceptions may be justified where the evidence to be given is of a very intimate nature, and the presence of the defendant's supporters or members of the public may make the giving of the evidence exceptionally difficult, or where the court believes that someone may take advantage of their entitlement to be in court to intimidate the witness. In these circumstances, section 25 of the YJCEA 1999 permits the courtroom to be cleared of everyone apart from the accused, legal representatives and anyone appointed to assist the witness.

The Special Measures Direction will describe individuals or groups of people who are excluded. The court has to allow at least one member of the press to remain, if one has been nominated by the press. The freedom of any member of the press excluded from the courtroom under this section to report the case will be unaffected, unless a reporting restriction is imposed separately.

The court also has the power under section 37 of the Children and Young Persons Act 1933 to clear the public gallery when a person under 18 gives evidence in proceedings relating to conduct that is indecent or immoral (MoJ, 2011a: Appendix B, B.9.12–9.15).

3.6.4   Removal of wigs and gowns (section 26)

> The Crown Courts have traditionally exercised their discretion to dispense with the wearing of wigs and gowns by the judge and by legal representatives in cases where child witnesses are concerned. The inclusion of this power as a Special Measure in the 1999 Act makes it clear that the same dispensation can be made in the case of vulnerable and intimidated adult witnesses.
>
> (MoJ, 2011a: Appendix B, B.9.16)

This special measure is optional. Perhaps some witnesses might wish the court to keep to its traditional way of dressing, and the court will respect their wishes.

3.6.5   Video-recorded evidence in chief (section 27)

This topic is covered in *Achieving Best Evidence* (MoJ, 2011a: Appendix B, B.9.17–9.28). Discussions about special measures should happen between the police and the CPS early in the investigation to see whether an application for video-recorded evidence should be made. See *Early Special Measures Discussions between the Police and the Crown Prosecution Service* (MoJ, 2009).

Police and other interviewers should be aware that video-recorded interviews may present emotional or other problems for some witnesses, either in the process of making of the video-recording or, for example, because the recording equipment or procedures may trigger past traumatic memories for the witness. For example, the presence of cameras and other equipment may be terrifying if the witness has suffered forms of sexual and/or physical abuse which was filmed or video-recorded at the time.

We saw in para 3.4 that informed consent requires that the witness has a clear understanding of the nature and purpose of the decision to be made (in this case the making of a video-recorded interview), and the use to which that video-recording will be put (MoJ, 2011a: para 2.95). The witness may need clarification about where the video-recording will be kept, and how and when it will be shared with others. Interviewers should explain all this to the witness in a way appropriate to his understanding. The potential consequences of making a video-recorded interview may be considerable, for example the recorded video evidence may be seen in its entirety by the court, the parties to the case, including the alleged offender, and possibly others including police, experts, etc. The video may also be regarded as useful evidence in other situations, for example in disciplinary proceedings, or complaints. The witness may be concerned that the alleged offender might see the video before the trial and discuss its content with others, or that copies of the video-recording may fall into the hands of the alleged offender and be misused in some way. These concerns should be heard, considered carefully and addressed before consent is given.

Following completion of the witness questionnaire, which is then considered by the legal representatives, a joint plea and case management questionnaire is agreed between the advocates and handed to the court to assist the court at the PCMH. A similar system exists in the magistrates' and youth courts, called a PTR. The PCMH contains specific questions about measures to assist witnesses giving evidence, including video evidence (part 22). If a video recording is made, the legal representatives need to have seen it before the PCMH, so that the court can make decisions at the PCMH about admissibility, editing, etc.

The witness will need to be aware of his rights in terms of the powers of the court in protecting his evidence, and the special measures available to him, which may include the making of directions by the court restricting access to the video-recorded evidence, and/or protecting the witness in other ways (see paras 3.7–3.13). However, information can only be withheld from the defence if the court accepts an application on the basis of public interest immunity. This is likely to apply only where either the defendant does not know the identity of the witness and there are reasonable grounds to believe that the witness could be at risk of serious intimidation, or the witness reveals something in interview that could undermine undercover police operations or reveal private addresses not known to the defendant. If an application for public interest immunity is to be made, the police and the CPS will need to discuss any editing requirements at an early stage (MoJ, 2011a: para 5.6).

Note, also, that:

> A video-recorded interview is usually only admissible as evidence-in-chief at trial where the witness is 'available for cross-examination'. The exceptions to this general rule are set out in the hearsay provisions in section 116 of the Criminal Justice Act 2003 that give the judge discretion to allow the court to hear the pre-trial statements of witnesses who are unable to give evidence for various specified reasons. These include the fact that the witness is dead, or 'by reason of his bodily or mental condition unfit to attend as a witness', or does not give evidence at trial through fear or because he or she is kept out of the way'. This might include a witness who is abroad and it is not reasonably practicable to ensure their attendance, or where the witness cannot be found. It must be remembered, however, that the judge has the final word on whether or not the statement will be admitted.
>
> (MoJ, 2011a: para 2.12 and Appendix C)

Editing or excluding video-recordings of evidence

Video-recordings may be edited, or even excluded, in the interests of justice. The court has to 'weigh the prejudice against the accused of admitting that part, against the desirability of showing the whole video' (MoJ, 2011a: Appendix B, B.9.17). The guidance clearly has in mind that one the reasons for omitting part of a video might be for failure of the interviewer to comply with the rules (B.9.18–9.19).

Videos may be edited, or excluded in the interests of justice because the witness has changed his mind about perceptions expressed in the video.

A video may also be excluded if the witness is not available for cross-examination, unless the parties have not agreed that this is unnecessary.

When the video is shown as the evidence in chief, with the court's permission the witness may be asked questions that range beyond the evidence given in the video.

Where a witness gives evidence in court which is different from (i.e. is inconsistent with) a previously recorded video, they may be examined on the content of the video by way of cross-examination.

3.6.6   Video-recorded cross-examination or re-examination (section 28)

This measure has not yet been implemented.

3.6.7   Examination of witness through an intermediary (section 29)

This topic is covered in *Achieving Best Evidence* (MoJ, 2011a: Appendix B, B.9.29–9.37).

An intermediary will not be appointed by the court if a witness is entitled to special measures for reasons of fear and distress alone. Deaf witnesses can choose an intermediary, or to rely on an interpreter or a communication aid (see para 3.6.8).

It may be that a defendant will gain the power to request assistance by an intermediary when he gives evidence if section 104 of the Coroners Act 2009 comes into force.

Intermediaries need to be approved by the court, and specialists in assessing communication needs and facilitating communication. They have a responsibility to avoid making false or misleading statements which is similar to the responsibility of an interpreter.

Certain vulnerable witnesses may give evidence through an intermediary: during an investigative interview; during evidence in chief and cross-examination in court or via the live link; and during any pre-trial familiarisation visit. Detailed procedural guidance can be found in *Working with Victims and Witnesses* (College of Policing, 2016), available on the College of Policing website, www.app.college.police.uk.

The intermediary is expected to provide a written report to the court explaining any difficulties that the witness may have with certain types of questioning, and to assist the court and others in asking questions of the witness. The intermediary may communicate to the witness the questions asked, and then communicate the answers the witness gives in reply. The intermediary is allowed to explain questions and answers, if that is necessary to enable the witness and the court to communicate.

The intermediary does not decide what questions to put. This is the responsibility of the judge or magistrates, or of the legal representative, who should ensure that the questions put to a witness are proper and appropriate to the witness's level of understanding.

3.6.8   Communication aids (section 30)

Sign and symbol boards, etc. can be used to overcome difficulties in understanding or answering questions. These can be used in conjunction with an intermediary (MoJ, 2011a: Appendix B, B.9.38).

3.7   Other witness protections

In addition to the special measures provisions for vulnerable and intimidated witnesses, the YJCEA 1999 affords:

- protection of witnesses in certain cases from cross-examination by the accused in person (sections 34–38);

- restriction on evidence and questions about the complainant's sexual behaviour (section 41); and

- restrictions on the reporting by the media of information likely to lead to the identification of certain adult witnesses in criminal proceedings (section 46).

Reporting restrictions on the identification of children under 18 are provided by sections 39 and 49 of the Children and Young Persons Act 1933 (see para 3.7.3).

3.7.1   Protection of witnesses in certain cases from cross-examination by the accused in person (sections 34–38 of the Youth Justice and Criminal Evidence Act 1999)

Facing a person asking questions in court can be daunting, and when the witness is a victim and/or vulnerable in any way, and if the person accused (the defendant) has no lawyer to ask questions on his behalf, the witness can be protected from a direct cross-examination by the defendant. It is a general rule in criminal trials that a defendant may choose to conduct his own defence, and may cross-examine the witnesses for the prosecution. The court can make an exception preventing an unrepresented defendant (i.e. the accused in person) from cross-examining a prosecution witness. If the defendant fails to appoint a legal representative, then the court is empowered to appoint a representative to act for the defendant, so that the witness's evidence can be heard and tested in cross-examination, (section 38 of the YJCEA 1999):

> Section 34 of the 1999 Act prevents defendants charged with rape or other sexual offences from personally cross-examining the complainant of the offence. The ban is absolute in order to provide a measure of reassurance to complainants that in no circumstances will they be required to undergo cross-examination by the alleged offender. It extends to any other offences with which the defendant is charged in the proceedings. It was brought about by cases in which defendants sought to abuse their position as cross-examiner by, for example, dressing in the clothes which were worn at the time of the rape to intimidate the witness.

(MoJ, 2011a: para 5.37)

Under Section 35 of the 1999 Act, unrepresented defendants are prohibited from cross-examining in person any child who is a complainant of, or a witness to sexual offences, offences of violence, cruelty, kidnapping, false imprisonment or abduction.

(MoJ, 2011a: para 5.38)

The prohibition on cross-examining child witnesses extends to witnesses who were children when they gave their evidence-in-chief, even if they have passed that age by the time of cross-examination. For the purposes of this provision, witnesses count as children if under 18 in the case of sexual offences, and if under 14 in the case of the other offences to which the provision applies.

(MoJ, 2011a: para 5.39)

3.7.2   Restriction on evidence and questions about the complainant's sexual behaviour (section 41 of the Youth Justice and Criminal Evidence Act 1999)

For guidance see *Achieving Best Evidence*, Chapter 5 (MoJ, 2011a: paras 5.42–5.51).

Section 41 of the YJCEA 1999 restricts the circumstances in which the defence can bring evidence about the sexual behaviour of a complainant in cases of rape and other sexual offences.

The restrictions in section 41 of the YJCEA 1999 apply to all complainants in cases involving sexual offences, whether male or female, adult or child. The defence may not normally ask any questions or bring any evidence about the complainant's sexual behaviour on occasions other than those that are the subject of the charges at trial, and this includes questions and evidence about the complainant's previous relationships with the defendant:

> The House of Lords (now called the Supreme Court) gave a judgment (in *R v A* [2001] UKHL 25; [2002] 1 AC 45; [2001] 2 Cr App R 21) that has subsequently qualified these restrictions. Restricting the use of such evidence protects the complainant from humiliation and the unnecessary invasion of their privacy, and it prevents the jury from being prejudiced by information that might divert them from the real issues they have to consider. Their Lordships accepted the need for such restrictions but acknowledged that in some cases the evidence of a complainant's sexual behaviour might be so relevant that to exclude it would endanger the fairness of the defendant's trial. This may be particularly so where the previous sexual behaviour was with the defendant. In such a case it would be the duty of the court to interpret Section 41 so as to admit the evidence. The courts have to find a balance between protecting the interests of the complainant and ensuring that the trial is fair.

(MoJ, 2011a: para 5.42)

Section 41 does not restrict the provision of relevant information by the prosecution about a complainant: for example, where it is the prosecution's case that the defendant raped his own wife, and his defence is consent, there would be no difficulty about informing the jury of the previous relationship between the defendant and the complainant as it would be relevant to the background of the case.

(MoJ, 2011a: para 5.43)

If the defence wishes to introduce evidence or ask questions about the complainant's sexual behaviour, they will have to make an application to the court. The court may grant leave in a case where:

- The evidence/question relates to a specific instance of alleged sexual behaviour by the complainant; and
- To refuse it might have the result of rendering unsafe a conclusion on a relevant issue (such as a conviction by a jury arrived at in ignorance of the complainant's sexual behaviour); and
- One of the following four conditions is also satisfied:
  - The evidence/question is relevant to an issue in the case that is not an issue of consent (such as whether intercourse took place).
  - The defendant's honest but mistaken belief in consent, which is currently a defence to a crime such as rape where lack of consent is an element of the offence, falls into this category, as it is not an issue of consent as such
  - The issue is whether the complainant consented and the evidence/question relates to sexual behaviour that took place at or about the same time as the event which has given rise to the charge. This might cover cases where a couple were seen in an intimate embrace shortly before or after one is alleged to have sexually assaulted the other. 'At or about the same time' is unlikely to cover behaviour occurring more than a day before the incident which is the subject of the charges.
  - The issue is whether the complainant consented and the evidence/question relates to behaviour which is so similar to the defendant's version of events at or about the time of the alleged offence that it cannot reasonably be dismissed as coincidence. The House of Lords in *R v A* decided that this exception would have to be given a broad interpretation to cover any case where the evidence is so relevant to the issue of consent that to exclude it would endanger the fairness of the defendant's trial. It was accepted that this might involve stretching the language of the Act. The particular concern of the House in *R v A* was whether the defence should be able to allude to a previous sexual relationship between the complainant and the defendant where consensual intercourse had taken place some time before the alleged rape. It was thought that there were cases where this would be necessary to ensure a fair trial even though it could not strictly be said that the previous behaviour was so similar that it could not be dismissed as coincidence. It does not follow that in every case where the defendant and the complainant have had such a relationship that it will fall within this exception, but the House of Lords accepted that

it is more likely that the court will need to be told about a previous relationship between the complainant and the defendant than between the complainant and a different person
- The evidence/question is intended to rebut or explain evidence advanced by the prosecution about the complainant's sexual behaviour. This might include a case where the prosecution adduce evidence to show that the complainant was a virgin before the defendant allegedly raped her, and the evidence the defence wishes to bring shows that she was not.

(MoJ, 2011a: para 5.44)

An application to ask questions/bring evidence about the complainant's sexual behaviour is made in private, and the complainant is not allowed to be present, although the defendant may attend. The court must give reasons in open court for allowing or refusing an application and specify the extent to which they are allowing any evidence to be brought in or questions to be put. This makes it clear to the complainant, as well as to the legal representatives, how far the questioning can go, and in relation to which issues.

(MoJ, 2011a: para 5.45)

Please note: witnesses need to be carefully warned and prepared – one cannot promise that their sexual history and past experiences will not be questioned.

The guidance states:

Because the issue of whether evidence or questions relating to sexual behaviour can only be resolved by a court and at a stage of proceedings where the defence case is fairly clearly defined, it is highly unlikely that any assurances can be given to a complainant that their sexual history will not be subject to cross-examination at trial. In the light of the decision in *R v A* it is advisable that a complainant should be warned to expect that any claims by the defendant that they have had a sexual relationship with the complainant are likely to be scrutinised by the court.

(MoJ, 2011a: para 5.46)

3.7.3   Restrictions on the reporting by the media of information likely to lead to the identification of certain adult witnesses in criminal proceedings (section 46 of the Youth Justice and Criminal Evidence Act 1999)

The general rule is that justice must 'be seen to be done', i.e. trials must take place in public, but there can be two exceptions. The public (including the media) may be excluded from the court with proceedings taking place *in camera* (in private). Secondly, the public and media may be allowed to remain in court subject to permanent or temporary restrictions on their ability to report the proceedings, including bans on reporting information likely to lead to the identification of the witness.

Also reporting restrictions can be made on the identification of adults in criminal proceedings, under section 46 of the YJCEA 1999.

Reporting restrictions on the identification of children can be made under sections 39 and 49 of the Children and Young Persons Act 1933, which imposes restrictions on identifying defendants, victims and witnesses in youth court proceedings if they are a child or young person under the age of 18.

There is an automatic ban on reporting the identity of complainants in sex offence cases, under section 1 of the Sexual Offences (Amendment) Act 1992.

3.7.4   Pre-trial supporters in investigative interviews and witness memory refreshment

For details of the relevant provisions for witness support, see *Achieving Best Evidence* (MoJ, 2011a: Chapter 4, pp 99–130, and Appendix L). In relation to children, additional guidance is provided in the *National Standards for Child Witness Preparation* (see MoJ, 2011a: Appendix K).

It is vital that the supporter does not coach the witness in any way at any stage of the process.

Supporters (e.g. friends or relatives of children or vulnerable witnesses) may be helpful during the investigative interviews. However, these supporters cannot be a party to proceedings, and they may not be involved in pre-trial support or be a supporter for the witness at the trial hearing.

To avoid any concerns about the evidence, therefore, one supporter may be present during the investigative interview and the 'witness memory refreshment', i.e. when the witness views his video-recorded statement to refresh his memory before the trial.

3.7.5   Professional pre-trial and trial hearing supporter

Another (different) supporter would then support the witness pre-trial and at the hearing. A pre-trial supporter should be a trained person with knowledge of the court process, but does not have to be an usher or court official:

> Assistance and support is available from Witness Care Units, Victim Support and the Witness Service as well as a range of other organisations. In the case of child witnesses, various local arrangements exist which may involve local authorities or organisations such as the NSPCC and Barnardo's. Agreement

should be reached on a local basis as to who is responsible for pre-trial preparation and also for ensuring that the necessary preparation has been or is being undertaken. Regardless of which profession is identified as best placed to co-ordinate pre-trial preparation and support, it is vitally important that it begins as soon as the witness's vulnerability is identified and the police and/or the CPS become aware that they may need to attend court.

(MoJ, 2011a: para 4.26)

At the trial, the witness supporter may accompany the witness into the live link room, and there are rules governing this:

Support during the court process itself, in the live link room or when giving remote live link evidence, is to be provided when it is necessary. There are evidential constraints that apply to the person providing support (see Appendix L). The identity of a supporter in the live link room or at the remote location must be the subject of an application to the court as part of a live link application (Sections 24 (1A), (1B) and 27(9A) of the Youth Justice and Criminal Evidence Act 1999). The procedures are set out in Part 29 of the Criminal Procedure Rules (see rule 29.10(f)). A practice direction issued by the Lord Chief Justice outlines who can act as a supporter in the live link room. Reference is made to 'an increased degree of flexibility' being appropriate, and as long as the supporter is completely independent of the witness and is not involved in the case (for example, as a witness), they do not need to be the usher or another court official (Consolidated Criminal Practice Direction, Part III. 29, Support for Witnesses Giving Evidence by Live Television Link, is available at www.justice.gov.uk).

(MoJ, 2011a: para 4.21)

Supporters may not discuss the evidence with the witness, nor express an opinion about it. If the witness begins to talk about the evidence, the supporter must make a note – in the witness's words – of what was said, notify the police, and ask the witness to speak to the person who conducted the investigative interview. The written record is disclosable. For full details of the rules and requirements relating to supporters, see *Achieving Best Evidence* (MoJ, 2011a: Appendix L).

3.8   Applications to hold a Crown Court hearing in camera

The general rule is that justice must 'be seen to be done', i.e. trials must take place in public, but there can be two exceptions. First, the public (including the media) may be excluded from the court with all or part of the legal proceedings taking place *in camera* (in private). This application might be made where the presence of people in the public gallery or elsewhere in the court might unduly influence or intimidate a witness, or in any other way adversely affect the justice of the trial.

Secondly, the public and media may be allowed to remain in court subject to permanent or temporary restrictions on their ability to report the proceedings, including bans on reporting information likely to lead to the identification of the witness. For reporting restrictions, see para 3.7.3.

3.9   Concealing the name of a witness or providing full witness anonymity

While witnesses should be assured that their details will be kept confidential during the investigation, investigators must be honest in letting them know that the suspected offender is likely to find out their name (not their address) when their statement is served on the defence after charge. Where a witness expresses concern about the prospect of a suspected offender discovering their identity consideration should be given to:

- The various options for action described in *Working with Intimidated Witnesses: A Manual for Police and Practitioners Responsible for Supporting Intimidated Witnesses* (Office for Criminal Justice Reform 2006);
- Explaining the appropriate special measures to the witness;
- In certain exceptional cases, applying for an investigation anonymity order and/or a witness anonymity order (see Sections 74–95 Coroners and Justice Act 2009).

(MoJ, 2011a: paras 3.136–3.144)

Witnesses should not be asked to give their address aloud in court unless for a specific reason. Witnesses who are nervous about the possibility of retaliation should be advised of this rule. If the witness's address is necessary for evidential purposes, it should be possible for it to be written down rather than read out in open court.

(MoJ, 2011a: para 5.13)

Note also that reporting restrictions on the identification of children under 18 are provided by sections 39 and 49 of the Children and Young Persons Act 1933 (see para 3.8).

3.10   Witness protection

In some very serious cases the risk to a witness is so great that they may need to relocate to another part of the UK and even change their identity. Witness protection is the means of providing protection measures for people involved in the criminal justice process who find themselves at risk of serious personal harm as a result of that involvement.

Witness protection, as defined within the Serious Organised Crime and Police Act 2005, is generally directed to those persons who have provided crucial evidence and against whom there is a substantial threat. This definition does not preclude police forces and law enforcement agencies from offering protection measures to witnesses and others at risk.

The CPS website states that 'ramifications for individual witnesses who have to participate in witness protection are immense and it should only be used sparingly' (see www.cps.gov.uk).

3.11   Interpreters

Sign language:

> When a witness gives evidence assisted by a sign language interpreter, all persons present in the courtroom (including the defence representative) should be able to see the witness and the interpreter. If it is decided that such a witness should not give evidence in open court, either the TV link should be used, ensuring the picture includes a view of the witness's hands, or screens should be used in combination with a video camera giving the defence representative a view of the witness. Allowance should be made for proceedings to take longer than usual.
>
> Sign language interpretation is very tiring. Depending on the length of testimony and the number of witnesses using the interpreter, it will be necessary to take frequent breaks or to have more than one interpreter available.

(MoJ, 2011a: paras 5.52–5.53)

3.12   Protection of defendants (the accused) who give evidence

The special measures created by sections 23–30, 39 and 49 of the YJCEA 1999, discussed earlier in this handbook, do not apply to a person who is on trial.

However, a defendant is entitled to a fair trial under the ECHR (Article 6), and so section 19(6) of the YJCEA 1999 allows the court a discretion to offer a defendant the measures that existed before the YJCEA 1999 came into force.

The measures that might be available to a defendant include the following.

3.12.1   For defendants under 18 years of age

Where the defendant's ability to participate effectively in the proceedings as a witness giving oral evidence in court is compromised by his level of intellectual ability or social functioning:

- *Evidence by live link* (under section 33C of the YJCEA 1999 which were inserted by section 47 of the Police and Justice Act 2006).

- *Assistance by an intermediary to give evidence*, if this is necessary to ensure a fair trial (by use of an order made under the court's inherent powers until provisions made under section 104 of the Coroners and Justice Act 2009, inserting sections 33BA and 33BB into the YJCEA 1999 are brought into force).

3.12.2   For defendants over 18 years of age

If the defendant is unable to participate effectively in the proceedings as a witness because he suffers from a mental disorder or has a significant impairment of intelligence and social functioning:

- *Evidence by live link* (under section 33C of the YJCEA 1999 which were inserted by section 47 of the Police and Justice Act 2006).

- *Assistance by an intermediary to give evidence*, if this is necessary to ensure a fair trial (order can be made by use of court's inherent powers until provisions made under section 104 of the Coroners and Justice Act 2009, inserting sections 33BA and 33BB into the YJCEA 1999 are brought into force).

3.13   Special considerations in prosecuting cases of child sexual abuse

The CPS has issued *Guidelines on Prosecuting Cases of Child Sexual Abuse* (CPS, 2014) (CPS Guidelines), available at www.cps.gov.uk.

The CPS Guidelines clearly set out the way in which it is expected that the police and CPS will approach these cases, and how they should be handled by prosecutors. They are intended to be inclusive and should be applied to cases where a sexual offence has been committed against a child or young person, unless there are good reasons why not in a particular case and these reasons are noted clearly by the prosecutor. The Guidelines also include cases of adult victims of sexual abuse in childhood.

Embodied in this part of the CPS website are other guidance documents all of which are relevant.

The CPS Guidelines should be read in conjunction with other relevant guidance, including the CPS Rape and Sexual Offences (RASO) Legal Guidance (available at www.cps.gov.uk) which sets out the approach to be taken in cases involving allegations of rape and sexual assault. Of particular relevance are the following:

- Chapter 2, which sets out the principal offences of the Sexual Offences Act 2003;

- Chapter 3, which deals with the issue of consent;

- Chapter 21, which discusses some of the myths and stereotypes around rape and sexual violence;

- CPS Youth Offenders Legal Guidance, section entitled 'Sexual Offences and Child Abuse by Young Offenders' (available at www.cps.gov.uk); and

- Human Trafficking and Smuggling Legal Guidance (available at www.cps.gov.uk), which sets out detailed advice on trafficking related issues.

The CPS Guidelines require early consultation between the police and the CPS, making the local RASO Unit the central point of expertise in the area. Paragraphs 9–16 describe the different contexts in which abuse can take place and the forms of pressure that might be placed on a victim to keep silent and not report offences.

The CPS Guidelines envisage that support (apart from counselling) will be offered to victims to help them in the process of investigation and in court (paras 20–22), including the appointment of an Independent Sexual Violence Adviser (paras 23–25). It refers to the *Victims' Code* (MoJ, 2015) and the twin guidance documents *Provision of Therapy for Child Witnesses Prior to a Criminal Trial: Practice Guidance* (CPS, 2001a) and *Provision of Therapy for Vulnerable or Intimidated Adult Witnesses Prior to a Criminal Trial: Practice Guidance* (CPS, 2001b).

The point is made that:

> Providers of counselling or therapy should ensure that records are kept and that the child or young person (and if relevant, parents or guardian) is advised at the start of the process that there may be a requirement to disclose the fact that counselling has taken place, particularly if detail of the alleged offending is raised. Experience over a number of years has shown that properly conducted and recorded counselling or therapy has not caused problems with the criminal trial process. Where the therapist or counsellor is known to the investigation, they should be briefed at an early stage to inform them about the court process and their disclosure obligations.
>
> Prosecutors have a duty to disclose the fact that a victim has undergone therapy or counselling and to disclose any other matter which is determined by the usual tests as to whether it is relevant to an issue in the case. This is part of the continuing duty on the CPS to disclose.

(CPS, 2014: paras 33–34)

Reference is also made to *Achieving Best Evidence* (MoJ, 2011a) as guidance on interviewing the witness, and his right to make a Victim Personal Statement (VPS).

In paras 48–56, the CPS Guidelines describe the possible reactions and behaviours of a victim following abuse, and explain behaviours and attitudes which could be misinterpreted, or used to attack the credibility of the witness. Helpers might find it illuminating to pay attention to this part of the Guidelines.

Helpers might also wish to look at the investigations that may be made to assess the credibility of the young person's allegations – listed in the CPS Guidelines at paras 65–67. In particular, prosecutors' attention is drawn to a number of common myths and stereotypes surrounding this type of offending, listed in Annex C.

In relation to identifying children who may be at risk of exploitation, the Office of the Children's Commissioner for England (OCCE) issued an interim report '*I thought I was the only one. The only one in the world*' (OCCE, 2012), followed by a series of booklets written for children and young people:

- *Protecting children from harm – Looking into child sexual abuse in the family network* (version for young people) (OCCE, 2015a).

- '*If only someone had listened*' – *Office of the Children's Commissioner's Enquiry into Child Sexual Exploitation in Gangs and Groups* (children and young people's version) (OCCE, 2015b).

- '*Sex without consent, I suppose that is rape*' – *How young people understand consent to sex* (children and young people's version) (OCCE, 2015c).

- '*It's a lonely journey …*' – *A Rapid Evidence Assessment on child sexual abuse within the family environment* (children and young people's version) (OCCE, 2015d).

- '*Basically … porn is everywhere*' – *A Rapid Evidence Assessment of the Effect that Access and Exposure to Pornography has on Children and Young People* (children and young people's version) (OCCE, 2015e).

The OCCE listed the following in the interim report (OCCE, 2012: 51–52):

Typical vulnerabilities in children prior to abuse

- living in a chaotic or dysfunctional household (including parental substance use, domestic violence, parental mental health issues, parental criminality);
- history of abuse (including familial child sexual abuse, risk of forced marriage, risk of 'honour' based violence, physical and emotional abuse and neglect);
- recent bereavement or loss;

- gang association either through relatives, peers or intimate relationships (in cases of gang associated child sexual exploitation only);
- attending school with young people who are sexually exploited;
- learning disabilities;
- unsure about their sexual orientation or unable to disclose sexual orientation to their families;
- friends with young people who are sexually exploited;
- homeless;
- lacking friends from the same age group;
- living in a gang neighbourhood;
- living in residential care;
- living in hostel, bed and breakfast accommodation or a foyer;
- low self-esteem or self-confidence;
- young carer.

The following signs and behaviour are generally seen in children who are already being sexually exploited:

- missing from home or care;
- physical injuries;
- drug or alcohol misuse;
- involvement in offending;
- repeat sexually-transmitted infections, pregnancy and terminations;
- absent from school;
- change in physical appearance;
- evidence of sexual bullying and/or vulnerability through the internet and/or social networking sites;
- estranged from their family;
- receipt of gifts from unknown sources;
- recruiting others into exploitative situations;
- poor mental health;
- self-harm;
- thoughts of or attempts at suicide.

(CPS, 2014: para 57)

The CPS Guidelines (CPS, 2014) also refer to any previous convictions of the child or young witness, and suggest that:

Full details of a victim's previous convictions will be required from the police including:

- type of offence;
- location of offence;
- who they were with, e.g. other young people or adults significantly older than them;
- what explanation they gave to the police at the time of arrest or in interview; and
- any other relevant circumstances.

(CPS, 2014: para 62)

Witnesses should be aware that the defence also has to disclose a list of their defence witnesses, and so this could present an opportunity for the witness to know who might be at court, which may be relevant to the provision of special measures.

The CPS has its own legal guidance on special measures at www.cps.gov.uk.

The CPS Guidelines (CPS, 2014: paras 96–98) refer to the psychological impact on adults of remembering childhood abuse later in their life, as an adult, and the potentially severe mental health problems that may arise for some of them. For consideration of the availability of psychological support for vulnerable adult witnesses in the legal process, see Chapter 4.

4 Psychological Support for Vulnerable Adult Witnesses

He has depression, and thinks he is not strong enough to give any evidence, but has not made a final decision. He says that he needs some support from his GP and a counsellor. How can we help him without compromising the case?

She remembers the mugging and it still upsets her, especially at night. If she has therapeutic help for the post-traumatic stress, can she still give evidence?

How can I help my client find a suitable therapist before the trial? Are there rules or procedures that we have to follow?

She was standing on the pavement when the accident happened, and now the police would like to interview her. She is not sure about it. She is only just out of hospital, she does not really remember that day clearly, and she feels confused about what will happen next.

This chapter addresses psychological support for adult witnesses. For protection and support for child witnesses, see Chapter 5.

Many witnesses experience some level of emotional distress at some point during the process of criminal proceedings. For those who have experienced traumatic circumstances, their psychological distress may be severe.

The CPS Guidelines (CPS, 2014) refer to the psychological impact on adults who were victims of sexual abuse in childhood, of a subsequent investigation and possibly giving evidence:

> 96. Some victims of sexual abuse may not feel confident or strong enough to report until many years after the abuse has taken place, and often not until they are adults. This delay in reporting can be for a wide range of reasons, but many of the same considerations for child victims will also apply to adults who were victims of sexual abuse in their childhood, particularly around assessing the credibility of the overall allegation and the need for effective and proactive case-building.

97. Prosecutors should be mindful of the potential for severe re-traumatisation faced by some victims. The process of giving an account of the abuse may cause flashbacks where an adult finds themself in the same emotional state as when the sexual abuse took place and with the resilience and understanding of a child of that age. Consistent and effective support should be provided including keeping under constant review whether there is a need for counselling and special measures.

98. It is recognised that some adult victims of childhood sexual abuse may suffer severe mental health problems as a result of their experience and may never be able to give evidence in court. However, it should not be overlooked that they may have important information which might be of assistance in supporting the account given by other victim(s) against the same offender(s).

(CPS, 2014: paras 96–98)

Pre-trial, witnesses may experience strong emotional reactions to the circumstances giving rise to the case, perhaps also fearing police interviews and legal questioning, even if special measures can assist. The trial process itself often presents fears, which may include the possibility of seeing or otherwise coming into contact with the defendant (the accused) or others associated with the defendant, perhaps for the first time since the incident. There is also some trauma for victims and witnesses by seeing themselves again on video or photographs, especially if they have waited a long time for the trial. For example, following the disclosure of sexual abuse or any other violent physical assault, victims may experience physical and/or psychological changes and seeing themselves as they were at the time of a past video recording or photograph can be traumatic. There may also be fear of having to engage with the facts of the traumatic circumstances again, and perhaps the fear of the witness's personality or behaviour being judged, or perhaps their evidence being disbelieved, by the court or by others present in the court.

Waiting to give evidence may be stressful for very many different reasons, and the presentation of evidence in court can in itself be a stressful process. After the trial, there may be, for some witnesses, a sense of relief that it is all over, but not all will feel this way, and witnesses may also face further stressors in the aftermath of the trial. The stress assessment diagram and charts in Appendix 2 may be of use to helpers in assisting witnesses to identify any causes of stress and assess stress levels, to understand whether help might be appropriate, and looking at the areas of the witness's life where support might be useful.

Some types of criminal case, for example rape, domestic violence, sexual assaults, harassment, gun or knife crimes, or any other forms of violence or threat, will result from traumatic experiences, which the witness is likely to be expected to recall in detail and answer questions in the course of his evidence and cross-examination. Feelings of fear, anger, shame or guilt about the events may be strongly attached to the traumatic experiences which are then re-lived in the re-telling of the story in court, or in the cross-examination.

Cases continue to be reported in the press where witnesses involved in the judicial process have been severely affected or re-traumatised by the police investigation and the court process. Some witnesses have been so affected by the judicial process that they have become ill, made attempts on their own life or, in some cases, have committed suicide following their provision of evidence in court. This has led to renewal of concerns about the welfare of vulnerable witnesses and a re-examination of the way in which they are treated and the support they receive during a police investigation and throughout the judicial process. Trauma and post-traumatic stress does not necessarily stop after a trial. In fact, once the adrenalin rush and sustained effort of the trial has ended, the witness may feel further psychological reactions in the aftermath. See Chapter 2 for discussions of the physical and psychological patterns of post-traumatic stress, anxiety and depression. The existence of post-traumatic stress provides cogent evidence to support the argument that, where necessary, psychological and social support should continue after the court case has finished.

4.1 Pre-trial counselling and psychotherapy with vulnerable adults

The CPS recognised that therapy may be required for a witness before a trial, and therefore issued guidance on pre-trial therapy, *Provision of Therapy for Vulnerable or Intimidated Adult Witnesses Prior to a Criminal Trial: Practice Guidance* which, although dated 2001, was issued on 24 January 2002 (CPS, 2001b). There is a parallel version of this guidance issued earlier in relation to pre-trial therapy for children and young people, *Provision of Therapy for Child Witnesses Prior to a Criminal Trial: Practice Guidance* issued on 8 February 2001 (CPS, 2001a) (see www.cps.gov.uk). These two documents currently remain in force as guidance to police, CPS and therapists, until revised or withdrawn. The guidance in relation to pre-trial therapy for children is worded similarly to that for vulnerable adults, but attention is given to the additional issues of consent and child protection. For further discussion, see Chapter 6. There is an argument for revision of these two guidance documents to take in subsequent law and government guidance documents (including e.g. *Achieving Best Evidence* (MoJ, 2011a); the *Victims' Code* (MoJ, 2015); mental health law and the *Mental Health Act 1983: Code of Practice* (DoH, 2015); child protection law and *Working Together* (DfE, 2015a), etc.), and to bring them into line with developments in psychological therapy modalities and practice. In the

CPS guidance, the specific terms 'psychotherapy' and 'counselling' are defined, but the definitions might not now fit the various modalities of counselling and psychotherapy in modern practice. Many therapists, for instance, carry both titles. In this chapter, therefore, the terms 'counsellor', 'psychotherapist' and 'psychologist' are all included in the generic terms 'therapist', and 'psychological therapy' unless a specific meaning is otherwise indicated.

4.2   Key issues for pre-trial therapy

The CPS guidance has to find a way to balance any competing needs of the witness and the interests of justice. The two documents are aimed at those who arrange or commission psychological therapy, and the therapists and lawyers who are involved in making decisions in cases where pre-trial therapy is a consideration.

A key issue in a criminal trial is that pre-trial discussions of any kind might have a potential effect on the reliability, actual or perceived, of the evidence of the witness and the weight which will be given to that evidence in court. Pre-trial discussions may lead, for example, to allegations of coaching and, ultimately, the failure of the criminal case on the basis that the evidence is unreliable. So a vulnerable witness, his therapists and the police need to weigh up, as soon as possible, the need for that witness to receive therapeutic help, balancing that need against the interests of justice and any perceived risk to the case.

The CPS guidance (2001b) states three issues relevant to pre-trial therapy:

- many victims express the wish to see the alleged offender convicted and punished;

- there is a wider public interest in ensuring that offenders are brought to justice to prevent further offences;

- all accused persons are entitled to a fair trial.

(CPS, 2001b: para 1.1)

It should also be borne in mind that the therapists concerned may themselves be called to court as witnesses in relation to any psychological therapy undertaken by the witness with them prior to the criminal trial. However, the good news is that the overarching concept in this guidance is the primary importance of the welfare of the witness, even at the cost of the trial if necessary, and the guidance is crystal clear on this (see CPS, 2001b: paras 4.3–4.6).

4.3   Definitions

Therapy: In the guidance, the term 'therapy' covers a range of psychological treatment approaches, but does not include physical therapy.

Psychotherapy – purpose:

> Psychotherapy includes interventions designed to decrease distress, psychological symptoms and maladaptive behaviour, or to improve adaptive and personal functioning through the use of interpersonal interaction, counselling or activities following a specific treatment plan. Treatment focuses on some facet of how clients feel (affect), think (cognition) and act (behaviour).

(Kazdin, 1990: 21–5, in CPS, 2001b: para 2.2)

Psychotherapy – modalities:

> Psychotherapies and counselling can be grouped in a number of ways; for example, psychodynamic, cognitive-behavioural, systemic, experiential. They are underpinned by different models of understanding and techniques, and vary in the context in which they are given (individual, family, group, etc.) and frequency of session.

(CPS, 2001b: para 2.3)

Psychotherapy may address a number of issues, including:

- treatment of emotional and behavioural disturbance, for example post-traumatic stress disorder;
- treatment of an adult who has been highly traumatised and shows symptoms which give rise to concern for his/her mental health.

(CPS, 2001b: para 2.4.2)

Counselling: This will address a number of issues, including;

- the impact of the incident on the adult;
- improving the self-esteem and confidence of the adult;
- providing the vulnerable or intimidated adult with information with regard to dealing with and avoiding abusive situations. The purpose of this is to help the adult to protect him/herself and to access appropriate help.

(CPS, 2001b: para 2.4.1)

Both counselling and psychotherapy may require long term involvement with the vulnerable or intimidated adult.

(CPS, 2001b: para 2.4.2)

It will be seen from these definitions that counselling is seen generally as working on the impact of the event, developing self-esteem and confidence, information-giving with regard to dealing with and avoiding abusive situations, and helping the adult to access appropriate support and protection. Psychotherapy is seen as more in-depth work with the witness on emotional, cognitive and behavioural issues.

The CPS guidance (in para 6.1) makes a distinction between 'formal preparation of a witness for giving evidence in court' and the provision of psychotherapy and counselling by qualified practitioners.

The preparation for court may be to:

- provide information about the legal process, for example the respective roles of judge, advocates, jury;
- address any particular concerns or fears which the adult may have in relation to giving evidence;
- reduce anxiety.

(CPS, 2001b: para 2.5.2)

Information should be available in a variety of forms to enable accessibility, for example, braille, British Sign Language, etc. The CPS guidance refers to an earlier version, but *Achieving Best Evidence* (MoJ, 2011a) has information about preparation for court, and assistance may be requested from the Witness Service, which provides support for court, see Chapter 3.

4.4   Risks of pre-trial therapy

Discussions with a witness before a trial which in any way touch on the proceedings or his evidence might potentially affect the quality and the reliability of the evidence of the witness concerned. Discussions may include de-briefings, informal contact with friends and family, training and therapy. Witnesses of fact are not allowed to sit in court and hear the evidence of others, in order not to taint their evidence. Expert witnesses are exempt from this rule, being trusted to be able to assess all that they hear and evaluate it, giving their evidence in a professional manner. In particular, concerns arise about the possibility of a witness of fact giving an inconsistent account of what happened, perhaps contradicting his earlier statement to police or the content of an earlier video-recorded interview.

Another concern is that through discussions, a witness could begin to imagine events differently and perhaps come to recall them differently, so – intentionally or inadvertently – to fabricate evidence. This could happen to fill in gaps in information, or rationalisations to explain inconsistencies in the accounts of the witness and others. Fortified by discussions about the events, a witness may become more convinced of his account, but nevertheless remain mistaken.

In therapy, therefore, it is vital that the work is undertaken with these risks in mind, to ensure that, as far as possible 'justice is seen to be done' and the actual or perceived risks are eliminated.

For this to happen, good record keeping in therapy is essential.

4.5 Records, confidentiality and disclosures in pre-trial therapy

In pre-trial therapy, practitioners must pay particular attention to issues of confidentiality and record keeping, particularly with regard to information sharing. In relation to vulnerable adults, capacity and consent may be issues for undertaking psychological therapy and perhaps, too, in relation to the witness's competence to give evidence, assessment for special measures and arrangements for the trial hearing. Therapists will need to be aware of current law and their own professional body's guidance, in addition to the government guidance, and match all this as seamlessly as possible with their own policies and procedures. In the NHS, local authority and government-regulated practice, policies are set and will contractually bind therapists as part of their employment or contract for services to compliance with government guidance.

Clients must know what to expect from their psychological therapy and where the boundaries of confidentiality lie. They need to be told, for example, that records of the therapy will be kept, and that disclosure of information concerning their pre-trial therapy is likely to be required by the court.

Therapy records should be accurate and up to date, and all material that may be relevant to the issues in the case must be preserved (CPS, 2001b: para 3.7). Disclosure should not be viewed as a tool to enable the prosecution or defence to satisfy their curiosity. It is a principle designed to ensure that information that is of genuine relevance to a criminal case is available to the parties and the court (CPS, 2001b: para 3.9).

Requests for information to be obtained from third parties may be made at various stages in a criminal case by:

- the police;
- the prosecutor;
- the defence;
- the court.

(CPS, 2001b: para 3.11)

The requests should explain the issues in the case, so far as they are known, and be reasonably precise. Speculative inquiries are discouraged. The purpose should be to elicit a genuine and focused search for relevant documents or information. Careful maintenance of records of therapy will facilitate this focused approach. Where a therapist receives a request for information or documents, legal advice should be obtained before complying with the request. If, for example, the therapist is employed by a Social Services Department or NHS Hospital, the legal department of such a Department or Hospital will provide advice.

(CPS, 2001b: para 3.12)

Therapists should not withhold information. However, given the therapist's duty of confidentiality to clients as part of their duty of care, the CPS guidance recognises that it will usually only be appropriate to breach confidentiality in compliance with a court order. It emphasises that:

Those aspects of the therapy that have no material relevance to criminal proceedings should not have to be disclosed. However, the issue of relevance may need to be reviewed at different stages of the criminal case, as more becomes known about the prosecution and defence cases.

(CPS, 2001b: para 3.14)

In addition to informal requests for information, if there are real grounds to believe that material which could affect the outcome of the prosecution is being withheld, an application may be made to the court for a witness summons to obtain the material. If, as will usually be the case, a therapist, having taken appropriate legal advice, believes that the material should not be disclosed, he or she may oppose the witness summons application. In that case the court may hold a hearing at which the therapist's employer may be legally represented. The court, having heard representations from the advocate representing the applicant for the witness summons and the advocate for the therapist's employer, will decide whether or not to issue a summons requiring the disclosure of the material.

(CPS, 2001b: para 3.13)

Note: This wording could benefit from clarification. It is assumed that a self-employed therapist may attend court in his own right.

The CPS guidance makes it very clear, in bold type, '**Confidentiality cannot, therefore, be guaranteed in advance**'. (This means, in effect, that a therapist cannot promise a vulnerable witness client absolute confidentiality. In fact, given other statutory duties of disclosure, for example, in cases of terrorism, etc. which will apply to all therapy, no therapist can safely make this promise, see *Confidentiality and Record Keeping in Counselling and Psychotherapy* (Bond and Mitchels, 2014).) The guidance then goes on to state:

Bearing this in mind, it is important that an understanding is reached with the vulnerable or intimidated adult witness (and where appropriate, any other emotionally significant person) at the outset of any therapy undertaken of the circumstances under which material obtained during treatment may be required to be disclosed.

(CPS, 2001b: para 3.15)

4.6   Making decisions about pre-trial therapy

The Crown Prosecution Service (CPS) is responsible for reviewing and conducting the majority of criminal cases involving adult vulnerable or intimidated witnesses. Once a crown prosecutor considers that there is a realistic prospect of conviction, the public interest must be considered.

(CPS, 2001b: para 4.1)

This means that, in a criminal case, the CPS must decide in the public interest whether (or not) to bring a case against the accused. If the CPS decides to proceed, then additional considerations will follow:

The prosecution in these criminal cases must do what it can to:

- identify cases in which the provision of therapy before the criminal trial might be thought to have some material impact on the evidence;
- assess the likely consequences for the criminal trial in these cases;
- ensure that these cases are dealt with as quickly as possible;
- safeguard the confidentiality of therapy sessions wherever possible whilst ensuring that the defence and the court are aware of the existence of information which might undermine the prosecution case or assist the defence.

(CPS, 2001b: para 4.2)

These questions are not unique to therapy which takes place before the criminal trial, but the ethical, medical, welfare and legal issues are of particular importance in these cases.

Note that the guidance is clear that the decision about therapy is not a matter for the police or CPS to decide:

Whether a vulnerable or intimidated witness should receive therapy before the criminal trial is not a decision for the police or the Crown Prosecution Service. Such decisions can only be taken by the vulnerable or intimidated witness, in conjunction with the professionals from the agencies providing service to the witness.

(CPS, 2001b: para 4.3)

It should be understood that those involved in the prosecution of an alleged offender have no authority to prevent an adult vulnerable or intimidated witness from receiving therapy.

(CPS, 2001b: para 11.1)

The best interests of the vulnerable or intimidated witness are the paramount consideration in decisions about the provision of therapy before the criminal trial. In determining what is in the best interests of the vulnerable or intimidated witness, it will be essential to consider the wishes and feelings of the witness and, where appropriate, of those who are emotionally significant to the witness. The witness will need to be given information on the nature of the therapy proposed in a form which is accessible. Account should be taken of issues associated with gender, race, culture, religion, language, disability and any communication difficulties both in initial discussions about the proposed therapy and in the provision of the therapy itself.

(CPS, 2001b: para 4.4)

The provision of certain types of pre-trial psychological therapy, for example traumatic incident reduction, or other types of imaginal re-exposure therapies which might be used to alleviate the symptoms of PTSD, or any therapeutic modality requiring discussion of issues relevant to the case, might cause the evidence to become unreliable or unsafe, and the impact of therapy may go so far as to cause the police and the CPS to abandon the prosecution. As we saw earlier, the interests of justice have to be weighed against the needs of the witness, and sometimes there will be a compromise that will satisfy both needs. The CPS will advise on the impact of the therapy on the evidence, but the overriding principle that will apply in this situation, as stated in (CPS, 2001b: paras 4.4 and 4.6) is the best interests and the wellbeing of the witness:

If there is a demonstrable need for the provision of therapy and it is possible that the therapy will prejudice the criminal proceedings, consideration may need to be given to abandoning those proceedings in the interests of the wellbeing of the vulnerable or intimidated witness. In order that such consideration can be given, it is essential that information regarding therapy is communicated to the prosecutor.

(CPS, 2001b: para 4.6)

4.7 Guidelines on assessment for pre-trial therapy

Assessment of the need for therapy during the pre-trial period (when the vulnerable or intimidated witness may become a witness in the subsequent trial) should only be undertaken following consultation with the witness, where appropriate, those who are emotionally significant to the witness and the relevant professionals. The police and the Crown Prosecution Service should be informed about any planned or ongoing therapy at the assessment stage.

(CPS, 2001b: para 8.1)

Practitioners have commented that, in their experience, the identification of the needs for therapy may be very poor and many professionals that are responsible for the first stage of needs assessment with victims and witnesses, police officers and witness care officers are still anxious about offering pre-trial therapy. This can create a barrier for victims and witnesses getting the help they need.

The CPS guidance goes on in para 8.2 to provide for a meeting of 'all relevant professionals' to discuss an assessment and treatment strategy, at which the views of the witness and those emotionally significant to him would be made known and considered as part of the decision-making process if the witness is not present at the meeting. This may include decisions about support from other agencies, including therapy. Issues to be considered would include the funding of therapy, who will undertake transport to appointments, who would undertake any family work, and inter-agency professional communication (CPS, 2001b: paras 8.2–8.3). This, of course, all has a bearing on confidentiality and sharing information in the context of pre-trial therapy, which would need appropriate consent. For mental capacity and consent for adults, see Chapter 3, paras 3.3 and 3.5.

The point that priority must be given to the best interests of the vulnerable or intimidated witness is again emphasised (CPS, 2001b: para 8.5). The task of assessment may, according to the CPS guidance, be carried out by a variety of professionals. Some professionals listed in the guidance at para 8.7 may not be qualified to assess emotional needs, while others may not be able to assess levels of disability requiring special measures. The assessment is expected to recommend the type of therapy or intervention required by the witness (CPS, 2001b: para 8.9). More than one professional may therefore be needed to carry out an assessment, and therapy may be carried out by a different person with appropriate qualifications and experience:

> It is important that anyone involved in an assessment, or in subsequent therapy, should be a trained professional person with a recognised competence, such as a social worker, psychiatrist, psychologist, psychotherapist, nurse or other relevant qualified person. On occasions, an assessment may be carried out by a different professional from the one who will undertake the therapy. It is for the agency funding or commissioning assessment and therapy to satisfy itself of the relevant competence of those undertaking either assessment or therapy.

(CPS, 2001b: para 8.7)

A witness may have special needs, which may include physical or learning difficulties, hearing or speech difficulties, or the need for an interpreter, where the native language of the witness is not English. Specialist communication may be necessary, for example sign language or Braille, and if an interpreter is used, he must abide by a code of conduct which ensures accuracy and integrity in his work.

The CPS guidance gives brief advice on assessment questioning:

> There is some evidence that some people who have been intimidated or physically beaten and some severely emotionally disturbed people are more likely to produce erroneous or ambiguous responses to leading questions from interviewers, than are less vulnerable people. Particular care, therefore, should be taken to ensure that any assessment:
>
> • uses short, plain words;
> • does not ask convoluted, hypothetical or leading questions;
> • uses open-ended questions wherever possible;
> • checks that the witness has understood the questions.
>
> (CPS, 2001b: para 9.5)

There are occasions when it may seem advisable from the point of view of the evidence to delay therapy until after the case:

> Some victims or witnesses may be so seriously traumatised that their needs can only be met by a placement within a containing environment, based on therapeutic principles as well as the provision of any necessary specific treatment. If the assessment identified this to be the case and it is considered that a less intense short-term provision of outpatient treatment will not be adequate, or may be unsatisfactory, it may be better, after considering the views of the witness and professionals involved, to delay therapy until after the criminal proceedings have been completed. However, such a witness can be offered general support as well as information and support about the court process. In such cases, prosecutors will wish to do all that they can to expedite the proceedings.
>
> (CPS, 2001b: para 9.6)

Practitioners have commented that in their experience, proceedings are not always expedited as recommended in the guidance. The timing of the trial is entirely dependent on when the case is ready to be presented, court time and custody time limits. Victims and witnesses' needs may be secondary to those factors.

However, this rationale should *not* be used to prevent a vulnerable or intimidated witness from receiving appropriate therapy if the witness and professionals agree that the witness's wellbeing and best interests require it, and the decision about whether or not a witness should have therapy, or whether to delay therapy, is not one for the CPS or police to make (see CPS, 2001b: para 4.4).

4.8   Guidelines on the use of pre-trial therapy

The CPS guidance makes a distinction in para 6.1 between 'formal preparation of a witness for giving evidence in court' and the provision of psychotherapy and counselling by qualified practitioners.

Therapists and those providing formal preparation for giving evidence in court need to be aware of the possible impact of their work on subsequent evidence. Some relevant training or experience would be necessary to create this awareness. The CPS guidance states that:

> some types of therapeutic work are more likely to be seen as prejudicial and therefore undermine the perception of the credibility and reliability of the witness, or to influence the memory of the witness in the account they give.

> (CPS, 2001b: para 6.2)

When exploring the modalities that may be appropriate, the guidance then becomes less clear in its wording. 'Preparation for court and carefully planned preventive work which does not focus on past abuse presents less of a problem than interpretive psychodynamic psychotherapy' (CPS, 2001b: para 6.3).

There are many therapeutic modalities, of which psychodynamic psychotherapy is just one, but to widen out the point being made, it would seem that the main two aspects causing concern for the CPS here are the use of interpretation, and also the possible discussion of past events relevant to the trial in the therapy. The CPS guidance later on specifies additional modalities which are seen as clearly problematic:

> There are therapeutic approaches that would very definitely present problems as far as evidential reliability is concerned. These would include hypnotherapy, psychodrama, regression techniques and unstructured groups.

> (CPS, 2001b: para 10.4)

There are grey areas in the guidance in establishing which specific kinds of pre-trial therapy (apart from cognitive-behavioural therapy which is specifically mentioned) might be considered appropriate for witnesses, i.e. which modalities are less likely to prejudice the evidence.

If a witness needs any form of therapy that will necessitate talking in detail about the events material to the case, for example specific trauma therapy involving intensive discussion or imaginal re-exposure to the traumatic events, then this is likely to be perceived as potentially damaging to the cogency of the witness's evidence, as the therapist may be thought to be going over the evidence and so 'rehearsing the witness' or 'coaching the witness' or in other ways affecting the witness's recall of the event. This may happen quite unintentionally on the part of the therapist, simply as a result of the recounting of events in the course of therapy:

> Witnesses may derive therapeutic benefits from talking about their experiences, but any detailed recounting or re-enactment of the offending behaviour may be perceived as coaching. Therapists should recognise that the criminal case is almost certain to fail as a consequence of this type of therapeutic work. This should be differentiated from the accepted practice of

allowing witnesses, prior to giving evidence, to refresh their memory by reading the statement or viewing the video-recorded interview.

(CPS, 2001b: para 11.11)

However, as we have seen (CPS, 2001b: para 4.4), if intensive trauma therapy were considered absolutely necessary in the interests of the witness's mental health and welfare, then the trial may have to be abandoned if the therapy would adversely affect evidence which is vital to the case.

A clearly stated preferred modality is cognitive-behavioural therapy, to improve self-esteem and confidence, and/or including:

- the reduction of distress about the impending legal proceedings;
- the treatment of associated emotional and behavioural disturbance that does not require the rehearsal of abusive events.

(CPS, 2001b: para 6.4)

The CPS guidance warns:

Professionals should avoid the use of jargon and take care to use language that will not be perceived, if repeated by a witness, as evidence of the witness being instructed. The language content of the therapy and counselling sessions is guided by the witness but equally it must be recognised that witnesses do use different forms of language in differing situations and contexts.

(CPS, 2001b: para 11.12)

During therapy, witnesses should never be encouraged to extend their account of the offending behaviour which they have suffered. However, it is acceptable to offer general reassurance and support to a witness during this difficult process.

(CPS, 2001b: para 11.13)

Any disclosures of materially new allegations by the witness undergoing therapy, including possible disclosures of their own abusive behaviour, or any material departure from or inconsistency with the original allegations should be reported to the Social Services Department (in line with procedures set down in the guidance 'No Secrets – Guidance on developing and implementing multi-agency policies and procedures to protect vulnerable adults from abuse' Department of Health March 2000) and to the Police and other relevant statutory agencies.

(CPS, 2001b: para 11.14)

Note: The *No Secrets* guidance (DoH, 2000) is now outdated. Practitioners comment that the guidance here seems to assume that a therapist would know what allegations are 'materially new' or which are 'a material departure or inconsistency with original allegations'. In order to know this, the therapist would need to be informed about the details of the case. The

CPS may be wary of disclosing the full details of the case to a therapist, for evidential reasons.

The CPS guidance states 'both therapist and vulnerable or intimidated adult witness should be aware of the related criminal case, which may or may not have commenced', and 'Careful recording is essential' (CPS, 2001b: para 6.5). The guidance here is unclear about whose responsibility it is to make the witness and the therapist aware of a new or impending case – and how this should be done. If the police are carrying out an investigation, and are aware that a witness is likely to be vulnerable or intimidated, they need to ascertain whether that witness is having or has had any therapy, and whether the therapy discussions have in any way touched on issues relevant to the case.

The situation of a witness who is neither vulnerable nor intimidated is left open. This CPS guidance does not apply to such witnesses, but we should be aware that any witness in a criminal case may have had or still be in therapy, either for issues entirely unrelated to the prosecution, or for issues relevant to the case.

An assessment of the impact of therapy on the evidence of a vulnerable or intimidated witness should be carried out before the decision is made to bring a case. However, if therapy had already started some time before an arrest is made or before the case is brought against a defendant, this raises some areas of difficulty for the CPS, in that the witness may need his therapy to continue for his own wellbeing, which may in turn pose evidential problems. The CPS will advise on this, or perhaps, if the criminal case is at an advanced stage, a judge in chambers may be consulted as to the best course of action (CPS, 2001b: para 8.6).

4.9 Which therapist is appropriate to undertake pre-trial work?

Therapy may be provided through the NHS, voluntary sectors, or privately. 'Therapists may specialise in work with particular groups, for example people with learning disability, or with victims of particular offences, for example rape' (CPS, 2001b: para 7.1). There is no register of therapists appropriately qualified to work with vulnerable and intimidated witnesses, perhaps partly because the needs of such witnesses vary so much, and partly because there are so many therapeutic modalities and training organisations. Some of the professional organisations for counsellors and psychotherapists have specialist interest groups. This means, as the CPS guidance recognises, that 'Treatment responses will need to draw on both general therapeutic skills and specialised knowledge of the particular cause of vulnerability. Skills in communication with the particular witness will always be important' (CPS, 2001b: para 7.2).

Those who provide therapy for vulnerable and intimidated witnesses should have appropriate training and supervision, and membership of an appropriate professional body or other recognised competence would be expected. The therapist should also have a good understanding of how the rules in criminal proceedings require the modification of techniques (see CPS, 2001b: para 7.3).

Pre-trial therapy has to be undertaken by therapists who are confident in their ability to meet their client's needs in the context of preparing for court proceedings and at the same time to comply with the requirements of the judicial process. Specific training may be helpful for therapists who undertake pre-trial work. Section 7 of the CPS guidance (2001b) addresses the qualities expected of the therapists undertaking this work. Revisions of this guidance may re consider both the therapeutic modalities considered appropriate and the recommended therapist qualities and training, recognising that these may vary according to the client needs and the nature of the case.

4.10   Recovered memories

The CPS guidance (CPS, 2001b: paras 10.1–10.5) deals with problem areas. The guidance explains that there have been concerns when therapists attempt to distinguish fantasy from reality in the responses of the witness in the course of therapy. It is important that the therapist should be 'as open to the idea that the material presented as factual truth may be a distortion (even though real and meaningful to the witness), as they are to a fantasy being a representation of reality' (CPS, 2001b: para 10.1). The importance of keeping a careful record of therapy will be very clear in this situation.

The CPS guidance mentions recovered memories surfacing in therapy, some of which were clarified in a report published by the British Psychological Society (BPS), *Recovered Memories* (BPS, 1995). Recommendations for good practice were published with the approval of the Royal College of Psychiatrists in October 1997, 'Reported recovered memories of child sexual abuse – Recommendations for good practice and implications for training, continuing professional development and research' (Royal College of Psychiatrists, 1997). See also guidelines issued by the BPS in *The Psychologist* in May 2000 under the title 'Guidelines for Psychologists working with clients in contexts in which issues related to recovered memories may arise' (BPS, 2000). Since then, in cases of child sexual abuse further guidance on interviews of child witnesses in the context of child protection and in criminal cases has been issued (see Chapter 5).

4.11   Disclosures

The CPS guidance makes some clear requirements of therapists:

> Prosecutors must be informed that the witness has received therapy. Prosecutors must then obtain an assurance that the witness did not, in the therapy session(s), say anything inconsistent with the statements made by the witness to the police. Prosecutors may need to be made aware of the contents of the therapy sessions as well as other details specified in the paragraph above, when considering whether or not to prosecute and their duties of disclosure.

> (CPS, 2001b: para 11.15)

To comply with para 11.15, therapists will need to be informed when a client has or will become a witness in criminal proceedings. Therapists also have a responsibility under this guidance to tell the prosecution that therapy is taking (or has taken) place, and they are required to inform the prosecution of inconsistencies with earlier statements. Prosecutors also may need to know the content of therapy sessions. These disclosures, if unauthorised, would all normally constitute a breach of the therapist's duty of care and a breach of data protection legislation, which require a therapist to maintain client confidentiality. Disclosures may legally be made in accordance with explicit client consent, and/or a statutory duty, and/or a court order requiring disclosure. In the absence of client consent, the public interest may also afford some protection for a therapist's disclosure in these circumstances.

Further, in order to know what statements by the client may or may not be inconsistent, the therapist would need to have knowledge of the content of the client's earlier witness statements made in the case.

The last word ...

> It should be understood that those involved in the prosecution of an alleged offender have no authority to prevent an adult vulnerable or intimidated witness from receiving therapy.

> (CPS, 2001b: para 11.1)

5   Support and Protection for Child Witnesses

My client is 14, and she was raped. She wants to tell the police and knows that the abuser may be prosecuted. He and his mates all live locally. How can I help her? What does she need to know?

She was standing in the shop when her older brother's friend took those things, and now the police would like to interview her. He's really frightening and she is not sure about upsetting him or her brother. She is only young, she does not really remember everything clearly, and now she feels confused about what to do and what might happen.

He is eleven and he understands from his social worker that his step-father is likely to go to court for what he did. He needs help to understand what will happen next, and some psychological help to feel safe again.

5.1   Child protection law, practice and procedures

The law in England, Wales and Northern Ireland defines children as all those who are under the age of 18. The law affecting the rights of children includes the CA 1989, the United Nations Convention on the Rights of the Child (ratified by the UK in 1991) and the Human Rights Act 1998 (in force in the UK from 2 October 2000), which incorporates the ECHR and its Protocols into UK law. The Children and Families Act 2014 creates a new raft of reforms (particularly in relation to adoption, leaving care, residential care, family justice, school lunches, seat belts and smoking in cars, and provision for flexible working for parents) and these are gradually being implemented. For an outline of the changes, see www.gov.uk.

Under section 7(1) of the Human Rights Act 1998, a person who claims that a public authority has acted in a way that contravenes the ECHR may bring proceedings against that authority. Under section 22(4) of the Human Rights Act 1998, all proceedings brought by a public authority against a public authority are subject to the ECHR, even where the alleged breach of those rights occurred before the coming into force of the Human Rights Act 1998.

Child law includes statutes and subsidiary legislation (including those acts, orders and rules made by the UK Parliament that are applicable in England, Wales and Northern Ireland, and also additional legislation made by the government in Northern Ireland and by the Welsh Assembly). In addition, there is a body of case law (the common law) comprising the decisions of the courts as they interpret and apply the statutory legislation to issues in individual cases. Case law works on a hierarchical basis – the decisions of the higher courts bind those of the lower courts, which should in general obey the higher courts' rulings on specific legal issues.

In addition to law, there is a body of guidance, some of which is made under statutory powers and therefore carries a limited legal force. An example of this is *Working Together* (DfE, 2015a), made under section 7 of the Local Authority Act 1970, and which should be followed by schools and local authorities in England and Wales (with sanctions for non-compliance) unless they can justify with good reason why they did not do so. Relevant additional guidance documents issued for practitioners following the CA 1989 are listed in *Working Together*, Appendix C, and also in this book in Appendix 5.

The CA 1989 encourages families to stay together, imposing a duty on local authorities to provide services for children in need and their families and to reduce the necessity for children to be looked after away from home, as well as the need for child protection proceedings. Care or supervision orders can only be made where the criteria in the CA 1989 are met, and where an order is necessary for the welfare of the child. If there is concern about the welfare of a child, the family court may order a local authority to investigate the child's circumstances and if necessary the local authority may apply for a care order.

The CA 1989 introduced a new concept of parental responsibility, which unmarried fathers may gain in relation to their biological children. It also created ways in which other adults related to the child, such as grandparents or step-parents, may apply for parental responsibility through the courts. Individuals with parental responsibility may be able to apply to the court for a 'child arrangement order (contact)' or a 'child arrangement order (residence)'. The Act also created the concept of other orders governing aspects of a child's life, such as contact with others, residence, and the resolution of disputed aspects of childcare through prohibited steps (forbidding actions) and specific issues (permitting actions to take place).

The principles behind the CA 1989 and its guidance are that children are people whose rights are to be respected, not just 'objects of concern', and that children should wherever possible remain with their families, helped if necessary by provision of services, provided that their welfare is safeguarded. An atmosphere of negotiation and co-operation between professionals is encouraged. The welfare of the child is paramount, and, in the field of childcare and protection, professionals are expected to work together in a non-adversarial way for the benefit of the child.

Section 6 of the Human Rights Act 1998 makes it unlawful for public authorities to act in ways incompatible with ECHR rights. This includes courts, tribunals and local authorities, including both acts and omissions (section 6). Those affected may bring proceedings or rely on the ECHR (section 7) by way of an appeal, complaint or judicial review.

5.1.1 Legal definitions relevant to child protection

Authorised person:

(a)   In care and supervision proceedings, and in child assessment orders, this means the NSPCC or its officers, under sections 31(9) and 43(13) of the CA 1989. A person (other than a local authority) may be authorised by order of the Secretary of State to bring proceedings under section 31 for a care or supervision order, but no other organisation or body has been so authorised.

(b)   In emergency protection orders, proceedings may be brought by an 'authorised officer' of the local authority, an 'authorised person' (as defined in (a)), a 'designated' police officer or 'any other person'; see sections 31(9) and 44.

CAFCASS: The Children and Family Court Advisory and Support Service, which is responsible for family court social work services in England. In Wales, this service is provided by CAFCASS Cymru, and in Northern Ireland, by the Northern Ireland Guardian Ad Litem Agency (NIGALA). See Appendix 6 for contact details.

Care order: An order made under section 31(1)(a) of the CA 1989, placing a child in the care of a local authority. By section 31(11), this includes an interim care order made under section 38. By section 105, any reference to a child who is in the care of an authority is a reference to a child who is in their care by virtue of a care order.

Child: A person under the age of 18.

Child assessment order: An order under section 43 of the CA 1989 to produce the child and to comply with the court's directions relating to the assessment of the child. There are restrictions on keeping the child away from home under this section.

Child in need: Under section 17 of the CA 1989, 'a child is taken to be in need if: (a) he is unlikely to achieve or maintain, or to have the opportunity of achieving or maintaining, a reasonable standard of health or development without the provision for him of services by a local authority; (b) his health or development is likely to be significantly impaired or further impaired, without the provision for him of such services; or he is disabled'. See also Part 3 of the Children and Families Act 2014 relating to children with special needs or disabilities.

Child looked after: The term 'child looked after' is defined in section 22(1) of the CA 1989 and refers to a child who is subject to an interim care order made under section 38 or a full care order made under section 31(1)(a). It also includes a child who is accommodated by the local authority under section 20.

Child minder: Defined in section 71 of the Care Standards Act 2000 as a person who looks after one or more children under the age of 8, for reward, for a total period(s) exceeding 2 hours in any one day.

Child of the family: In relation to the parties to a marriage, under section 52 of the Matrimonial Causes Act 1973, this means: (a) a child of both of those parties; or (b) any other child, not being a child who is placed with those parties by a local authority or voluntary organisation, who has been treated by both of those parties as a child of their family.

Child protection: By the use of this term in this book, I intend to include all the legal measures that can be implemented to protect a child from the risk of serious harm, or to stop or prevent the continuation of any serious harm that has already occurred. This is a narrower meaning than the wider term 'safeguarding' (see below).

Children's guardian: A professional (usually a professionally qualified social worker who does not work for the local authority involved in the case) appointed by the court to represent the child's interests in court proceedings. Children's guardians are provided in England by CAFCASS, and in Wales by CAFCASS Cymru. In Northern Ireland they are referred to as 'Guardians ad Litem', and provided by the Northern Ireland Guardian Ad Litem Agency (NIGALA).

Children's home: Defined in section 1 of the Care Standards Act 2000 as a home that usually provides or is intended to provide care and accommodation wholly or mainly for children. Obviously, the section lists several exceptions, including the homes of parents, relatives or those with parental responsibility for the children in question.

Contact order: Defined in section 8(1) of the CA 1989 as 'an order requiring the person with whom a child lives, or is to live, to allow the child to visit or stay with the person named in the order, or for that person and the *child otherwise to have contact with each other*'.

Contact with a child in care: Section 34 of the CA 1989 creates a presumption that a child subject to a care order will have reasonable contact with his or her parents, and contains provisions for determination of contact issues by the court.

Development: Defined in section 31(9) of the CA 1989 as physical, intellectual, emotional, social or behavioural development.

Disabled: Defined in section 17(11) of the CA 1989 as:

> in relation to a child, means a child who is blind, deaf, or dumb or who suffers from mental disorder of any kind or who is substantially and permanently handicapped by illness, injury or congenital deformity or such other disability as may be prescribed.

Education supervision order: An order under section 36(1) of the CA 1989, putting the child with respect to whom the order is made under the supervision of a designated local education authority.

Emergency protection order: Under section 44 of the CA 1989, this order is a direction for a child to be produced and authorises the local authority either to remove the child to a safe place or to stop the child from being removed by others from a hospital or other safe place.

Family assistance order: An order made under section 16 of the CA 1989 appointing a probation officer or an officer of the local authority to advise, assist and (where appropriate) befriend any person named in the order for a period of 12 months or less. Named persons may include parents, guardians, those with whom the child lives, or the child himself.

Family court adviser: A social work practitioner directed by the court to assist it by providing dispute resolution services in section 8 applications and/or reports under section 7 of the CA 1989.

Guardian: Means a guardian appointed under section 5 of the CA 1989 for the child, but not for the child's estate. A guardian appointed under section 5 has parental responsibility for the child, following the death of one or both parents. (This role is not the same as that of the 'children's guardian', who is a person appointed by the court in child protection proceedings.)

Harm: Defined in section 31(9) of the CA 1989, meaning ill treatment or the impairment of health or development. Where the question of whether or not the harm is significant turns on the child's health and development, his or her health or development shall be compared with that which could be reasonably expected of a similar child, section 31(10).

Health: Under section 31 of the CA 1989, includes physical and mental health.

Hospital: Any health service hospital, and accommodation provided by the local authority and used as a hospital. It does not include special hospitals, which are those for people detained under the Mental Health Act 1983, providing secure hospital accommodation, section 105 of the CA 1989.

Ill treatment: Defined in section 31(9) of the CA 1989 and includes sexual abuse and forms of ill treatment that are not physical.

Kinship care: Care for a child by family members or friends of the family. Kinship care may be arranged privately, on a voluntary basis or as part of a care plan in the context of a care order.

Local authority:

(a)   Under section 52 of the CA 1989, a council of a county, a metropolitan district, a London borough or the Common Council of the City of London.

(b)   The local authority of a geographical area, including county councils, district councils, unitary authorities in England and Wales, Welsh county councils and Welsh county borough councils.

Local authority foster carer: Defined in section 22(C)(12) of the CA 1989 as a person with whom a child has been placed by a local authority under section 22. Local authority foster carers may include a family member, a relative of the child or any other suitable person.

Parent: The natural (birth) mother or father of a child, whether or not they are married to each other at the time of the birth or conception. When it says 'parent', the CA 1989 means the birth parents of a child, therefore including natural fathers without parental responsibility. Where it intends to mean 'a parent with parental responsibility', it says so specifically.

Parent with parental responsibility: All mothers have parental responsibility for children born to them. Fathers also have parental responsibility for their child if they married their child's mother before or after the child's birth. The biological father of a child who is not married to the mother is able to acquire parental responsibility in various ways under the CA 1989. This term therefore excludes the natural birth father of a child who has not acquired parental responsibility under the Act.

Parental responsibility: Defined in section 3 of the CA 1989 and includes all the rights, duties, powers, responsibilities and authority that a parent of a child has by law in relation to the child and his property. Parental responsibility can be acquired by unmarried fathers in respect of their child by registration of the birth with the mother after 1 December 2003, by court order or by a parental responsibility agreement under the CA 1989, and by others through residence or guardianship orders, or by a local authority under a care order. Parental responsibility can be shared with others. It ceases when the child reaches 18, on adoption, death, or cessation of the care order.

Parental responsibility agreement: Defined in section 4(1) of the CA 1989 as an agreement between the father and mother of a child providing for the father to have parental responsibility for the child (a father married to the mother of their child at the time of the birth will automatically have parental responsibility for that child, but a father not so married will not). Format for the agreement is set out in the Parental Responsibility Agreement Regulations 1991 (SI 1991/1478), as amended.

Private fostering: See section 66 of the CA 1989; to 'foster a child privately' means looking after a child under the age of 16 (or if disabled, 18), caring and providing accommodation for him or her; by someone who is not the child's parent, relative, or who has parental responsibility for the child.

Prohibited steps order: Defined in section 8(1) of the CA 1989. Means an order that no step that could be taken by a parent in meeting his parental responsibility for a child, and that is of a kind specified in the order, shall be taken by any person without the consent of the court.

Relative: In relation to a child, this means a grandparent, brother, sister, uncle or aunt (whether of the full blood or of the half blood or by affinity) or step-parent, see section 105 of the CA 1989.

Residence order: An order under section 8(1) of the CA 1989 settling the arrangements to be made as to the person with whom a child is to live. This confers parental responsibility on the person who holds the order.

Responsible person: Defined in Schedule 3, paragraph 1 to the CA 1989. In relation to a supervised child, it means: (a) any person who has parental responsibility for the child; and (b) any other person with whom the child is living.

Safeguarding: By the use of this term in this book, I intend a wider meaning for all those actions that will operate to enhance a child's health, development and welfare and prevent the risk of harm. This differs from the way in which some people use the term 'child protection', for which they intend the more specific meaning of legal actions to protect a child at risk of serious harm (see above).

Service: In relation to any provision made under Part III of the CA 1989 (local authority support for children and families), this means any facility.

Special educational needs: These arise when there is a learning difficulty that calls for special educational provision to be made. These terms are defined in section 318 of the Education Act 1996.

Special guardian: A special guardianship order confers parental responsibility on the holder of the order, which he may exercise alone, excluding the parent. The provisions are found in sections 14A–F of the CA 1989.

Specific issue order: An order under section 8(1) of the CA 1989 giving directions for the purpose of determining a specific issue that has arisen, or that may arise, in connection with any aspect of parental responsibility for a child.

Supervision order: An order under section 31(1)(b) of the CA 1989 and (except where express provision to the contrary is made) includes an interim supervision order made under section 38.

Supervised child/supervisor: In relation to a supervision order or an education supervision order, these mean, respectively, the child who is (or is to be) under supervision and the person under whose supervision he is (or is to be) by virtue of the order.

Upbringing: In relation to any child, this includes the care of the child but not his maintenance.

Voluntary organisation: Means a body (other than a public or local authority) whose activities are not carried on for profit.

5.1.2   Court process and legal orders in relation to children

The CA 1989 created a new unified court system consisting of three tiers, the High Court, the county court and the family proceedings court, each of which has concurrent jurisdiction and powers. Appeals from the family proceedings court go to the county court or High Court, and from the county court and High Court to the Court of Appeal and the Supreme Court. Cases may move up or down the tiers, transfers therefore being easier. The avoidance of delay is one of the underlying principles of the CA 1989. Another important principle in section 1(5) is non-intervention – that is, to make no order unless it is necessary in the interests of the child. This Act, along with its subsidiary rules, also created a new system of directions hearings to enable the courts to take firmer control of the timing of cases, admission of evidence and administrative matters.

There is insufficient space here to describe in detail the court orders listed in Table A, but please refer to the definitions in para 5.1.1.

The regularly updated looseleaf encyclopaedias, *Children Law and Practice* (Hershman and McFarlane) and *Clarke Hall and Morrison on Children* (White et al.), provide comprehensive details of current child protection practice. For briefer guidance, there are a number of resource books on child care practice, including one recently issued by the Law Society, *Good Practice in Child Care Cases* (2015). Details of all these publications can be found in Appendix 5.

Table A Court orders that may be made in relation to children

Order	*Section*	*Maximum duration**
Parental responsibility	4	Age 18
Guardianship	5	Age 18
CAO (Residence)	8	Age 18
CAO (Contact)	8	Age 16 (18 in exceptional circumstances)
Prohibited steps	8	Age 16 (18 in exceptional circumstances)
Specific issue	8	Age 16 (18 in exceptional circumstances)
Special guardianship order	14A	Age 18 (or earlier revocation)
Family assistance order	16	12 months
Care order	31	Age 18
Interim care order	38	First, not more than 8 weeks; remainder, maximum 4 weeks
Supervision order	31	Age 18, one year; may be extended to maximum total of 3 years
Contact with a child in care	34	For duration of care order
Education supervision order	36	One year; repeatedly extensible for 3 years; ceases at age 16
Child assessment	43	7 days
Emergency protection	44	8 days; extendable for further 3 days

* These orders may be brought to an end by court order, variation or discharge, and may be subject to additional provisions

Source: Mitchels, 2012.

5.1.3   Children in need of services

In England, Northern Ireland and Wales, the law imposes a duty to provide resources and services for children who are in need of support or services without which their health or welfare is likely to be impaired, and sets out the responsibilities and limitations of the provision of services by government and local authorities for 'children in need'.

There is not enough space here to explore in detail all the services available for children in need, but see *Children Law and Practice, Clarke Hall and Morrison on Children,* Mitchels (2012) and *Working Together* (DfE, 2015a) for further discussion regarding services for children in need in England and Wales; and see Chapter 8 of Long (2013) for provisions in Northern Ireland. CAFCASS, CAFCASS Cymru, and NIGALA may also be able to assist.

One of the services that may be provided for a child in need is counselling and psychotherapy, which may be deemed appropriate in any context, including school. If the child does not have the capacity to make his own decisions, then those with parental responsibility will have the right to make decisions for the child and also the right to see the child's social care records, as well as their therapy records (with certain exceptions allowing the service provider to maintain secrecy in order to safeguard the health or safety of the child or others, or to safeguard a police or other investigation in the context of child protection).

5.1.4   Children in need of care and protection

In England, Northern Ireland and Wales, the law imposes a duty of care on the state to safeguard and protect children living in its jurisdiction. The law operates in different ways in some of these jurisdictions but the basic principles on which child protection operates across jurisdictions are similar. Again, there is not enough space to explain these provisions in detail here, but see Mitchels (2012), *Children Law and Practice, Clarke Hall and Morrison on Children* and *Working Together* (DfE, 2015a); and see Chapter 8 of Long (2013) for provisions in Northern Ireland.

Working Together (DfE, 2015a) is the main guidance relevant to the jurisdiction of England and Wales, and it carries the force of law because it is issued under:

- section 7 of the Local Authority Social Services Act 1970, which requires local authorities in their social services functions to act under the general guidance of the Secretary of State;

- section 11(4) of the Children Act 2004, which requires each person or body to which the section 11 duty applies to have regard to any guidance given to them by the Secretary of State; and

- section 16 of the Children Act 2004, which states that local authorities and each of the statutory partners must, in exercising their functions relating to Local Safeguarding Children Boards (LSCBs), have regard to any guidance given to them by the Secretary of State.

Compliance with this guidance in England and Wales is not optional, and local authority chief executives and directors of children's services are required to follow this statutory guidance as they exercise their social services functions, unless exceptional reasons apply. It should also be read and followed by LSCB chairs, and senior managers within organisations who commission and provide services for children and families (including social workers and professionals from health services, adult services, the police, academy trusts, education and the voluntary and community sector) who have contact with children and families.

All relevant professionals should read this guidance and comply with it unless exceptional circumstances arise, so that they can respond to individual children's needs appropriately.

Good sources of information to keep updated on legal issues in relation to children are local authority lawyers, local authority child protection or safeguarding departments, the CAFCASS, CAFCASS Cymru in Wales and NIGALA, and also see the websites of the NSPCC, and other organisations listed in Appendix 6.

5.1.5   The rights of the child

The CA 1989 commences with a clear direction in section 1(1) that:

> When a court determines any question with respect to:
>
> (a) the upbringing of a child; or
>
> (b) the administration of a child's property or the application of any income arising from it,
>
> the child's welfare shall be the paramount consideration.

This means that after weighing all the factors, the court's decision will be made in accordance with the child's welfare.

The child's welfare is not always easy to determine, and so, in section 1(3), the CA 1989 sets out a list of criteria known as the 'welfare checklist', primarily intended as an aide-memoire, to which the court must have regard when considering an application to vary or discharge a special guardianship order or a contested section 8 order for contact, residence, specific issue or prohibited steps, and magistrates should always refer to the welfare checklist when considering their findings of fact and reasons for their decisions.

The welfare checklist is not compulsory in other circumstances, but it is always useful for practitioners to consider it. In relation to all orders, the court must not make the order or any of the orders unless it considers that doing so would be better for the child than making no order at all. If we refer to these criteria when making decisions or writing reports, we will ensure that we are complying with the principles of the Act.

5.1.6   The welfare checklist (cited from section 1(3) of the Children Act 1989)

(a)   The ascertainable wishes and feelings of the child concerned (considered in the light of his age and understanding).

(b)   His physical, emotional and educational needs.

(c)   The likely effect on him of any change in his circumstances.

(d)   His age, sex, background and any characteristics of his which the court considers relevant.

(e)   Any harm which he is suffering or which he is at risk of suffering.

(f)   How capable each of his parents, and any other person in relation to whom the court considers the question to be relevant, is of meeting his needs.

(g)   The range of powers available to the court under this Act in the proceedings in question.

5.2   Competence, consent and compellability in relation to child witnesses

5.2.1   Mental capacity and consent for adults

An adult with mental capacity may make his own decisions within the law, and may even make decisions that that could endanger his life or health or that others may consider unwise (such as the refusal of medical treatment), but those decisions may be legally valid. Adults are included in this chapter because sometimes adults may need to make decisions for the children for whom they hold parental responsibility (see para 5.2.4). Also the tests for mental capacity in relation to young people aged between 16 and 18 are very much the same as for adults (see para 5.2.2).

Mental capacity is a legal concept, according to which a person's ability to make rational, informed decisions is assessed. There is no single, definitive test for mental capacity to consent; however, the assessment of it is based on a set of principles in which it is situation-specific and depends upon the ability of the person to:

•   take in and understand information, including the risks and benefits of the decision to be made;

•   retain the information long enough to weigh up the factors make the decision; and

•   communicate his wishes.

For adults, law relating to mental capacity is now governed by the Mental Capacity Act 2005, the Mental Health Act 2007 and the Mental Capacity Act 2005 (Appropriate Body) (England) Regulations 2006 (SI 2006/2810). Relevant publications and websites are listed in Appendix 6.

5.2.2   Mental capacity for young people aged 16–18

The CA 1989 defines a 'child' as 'a person under the age of 18' (section 105). Children and young people under the age of 18 are also collectively referred to in many areas of law (including contract law) as 'minors'. People over the age of 18 are said to have reached the age of 'majority'. Section 1 of the Family Law Reform Act 1969 lowered the former age of majority of 21 to the current age of 18. A minor may make a valid contract for 'necessary' goods and services, including counselling and medical services.

The law on children's capacity to make decisions, and other people making decisions for children, is vitally important for all practitioners who work with children and young people. Whether children can agree the terms on which legal services or pre-trial therapy is offered may depend upon whether they have the legal capacity to make their own decisions. If they do not have capacity, then those with parental responsibility for the child can make the necessary decisions (see para 5.2.4).

For young people over the age of 16 years (and under the age of 18), the practical tests of mental capacity will be the same as for an adult (see para 5.2.1), although the law permits the High Court to step in and protect a young person under the age of 18 from decisions that may endanger their life or health.

Note: Mental capacity to make any particular decision is not only situation-specific, but may also be affected temporarily or permanently by illness, ability, substance use or abuse, medications, and psychological response to stressful or traumatic life events. Care should therefore be taken when assessing mental capacity in the presence of illness, trauma, or other circumstances where cognition may be affected, as someone with capacity one day may not have the same level of capacity the next (or vice versa).

Under section 8 of the Family Law Reform Act 1969, at the age of 16, a young person with mental capacity gains the right to give informed consent to medical or dental treatment, which includes psychological treatment and counselling. By implication, examinations or assessments must be included in this. The consent of the young person is as valid as that of an adult. A young person with mental illness, disability or psychiatric disturbance may also be subject to the Mental Health Act 1983.

If a young person consents to recommended medical or dental treatment (even if those with parental responsibility for the young person disagree for any reason), therefore, the medical or dental practitioner would be protected from a claim for damages for trespass to the person.

However, if the young person aged between 16 and 18 with mental capacity refuses recommended treatment, his views would be regarded in the same way as those of an adult, so his refusal and the reasons for it are important considerations for a court. If the young person suffers from an impairment of mental functioning or any other illness or condition that affects his mental capacity, and psychological and/or medical assessment is considered necessary, those with parental responsibility for the young person may in law be able to give valid consent, which will have the effect of protecting the medical or psychological practitioner from claims for damages for trespass to the person. In the event of a dispute between a young person and medical practitioners or those with parental responsibility, regarding consent for essential medical (or psychological) treatment, the issue may if necessary be taken before the High Court, which can provide the requisite authority (either under its inherent jurisdiction or under section 8 of the CA 1989) for a specific issue order.

However, please note that changes made to section 131 of the Mental Health Act 1983 by section 43 of the Mental Health Act 2007 mean that when a young person aged 16 or 17 has capacity (as defined in the Mental Capacity Act 2005) and does not consent to admission for treatment for a mental disorder (whether because the young person is overwhelmed, does not want to consent, or refuses to consent), that person cannot then be admitted informally on the basis of the consent of a person with parental responsibility (see Chapters 19 and 36 of the *Mental Health Act 1983: Code of Practice* (DoH, 2015) and section 131(4) of the Mental Health Act 1983).

Although in the past, there have been court decisions indicating that those with parental responsibility could technically give their consent for treatment despite the clear refusal of their child, since the inception of the Human Rights Act 1998, in the case of a child aged between 16 and 18 who has capacity, medical and other authorities are unlikely to rely on this, and court cases reflect the right of the child or young person with capacity to have his views respected. See the case of *R (on the application of Axon) v Secretary of State for Health and the Family Planning Association* [2006] EWHC 37 (Admin). In some circumstances, it will be possible for young people aged between 16 and 18 who lack capacity to be admitted to hospital and/or be treated on the basis of consent of those with parental responsibility for them (see DoH, 2015: 182–5, paras 19.53–19.70). However, the courts have made it clear that there are limits to the types of decisions that those with parental responsibility can make on behalf of their child, and the circumstances in which such decisions can be made.

If the decision is unsuitable for those with parental responsibility to make, then the matter may need to be referred to a court.

5.2.3 Mental capacity: children under 16 – competence in the context of the *Gillick* case

Children who are under the age of 16 may also be regarded as competent to make their own decisions (often referred to colloquially as 'Gillick competence'). This principle of law was settled by the House of Lords in the leading case of *Gillick v West Norfolk and Wisbech Area Health Authority and Another* [1986] 1 AC 112.

The rationale of the *Gillick* case was that a child's ability to make an informed decision may be assessed according to a number of factors, including:

- the nature and seriousness of the decision to be made;
- the child's age;
- the child's maturity;
- the child's understanding of the circumstances;
- the information given to the child to enable him to understand the potential benefits and risks of what is proposed and the consequences of consent or refusal.

It will be evident that the capacity of a child to make a decision is situation-specific and that, to have capacity, the child must have an informed understanding of the issues, including the risks and benefits involved and the consequences of refusal.

The ability to help a child make a decision will depend on the provision of age-appropriate information and explanations or answers to his questions. The more serious the decision, the greater the need for the child to possess sufficient maturity and understanding to evaluate his situation in its wider context. For this reason, the courts have steadfastly refused to set specific age limits for Gillick competence.

The steps for assessment of competence are set out in the *Mental Health Act 1983: Code of Practice* (DoH, 2015: 174, para 19.25):

> Practitioners should consider the following three questions which should be read in conjunction with the examples in the paragraphs below:
>
> 1. Has the child or young person been given the relevant information in an appropriate manner (such as age appropriate language)?
>
> 2. Have all practicable steps been taken to help the child or young person make the decision? The kind of support that might help the decision-making will vary, depending on the child or young person's circumstances.

Examples include:

- steps to help the child or young person feel at ease;
- ensuring that those with parental responsibility are available to support their child (if that is what the child or young person would like);
- giving the child or young person time to absorb information at their own pace; and
- considering whether the child or young person has any specific communication needs (and if so, adapting accordingly).

3. Can the child or young person decide whether to consent, or not to consent, to the proposed intervention?

A child may lack the competence to make the decision in question either because they have not as yet developed the necessary intelligence and understanding to make that particular decision; or for another reason, such as because their mental disorder adversely affects their ability to make the decision. In either case, the child will be considered to lack Gillick competence.

(DoH, 2015: 177, para 19.37)

Each case involving a child client must be decided on its own merits. If the child is under 16, it is the task of the therapist and any other professionals involved, with expert help if necessary, to talk through the situation with the child client. Together, they will need to explore and discuss the child's circumstances and the therapeutic or other options available (such as special measures), considering the possible outcome of each option open to the child, and then decide whether the child has the capacity to make the necessary decisions, including whether to enter into a therapeutic contract. In the context of a therapeutic relationship for pre-trial therapy, a child may need help to assess the necessary conditions to which the therapist may have to adhere in the context of the guidance, for example, in keeping records and making disclosures, or in the use of video or other recording equipment, making referrals, etc.

Consent for a therapeutic contract can be given for a young child under the age of 16 who is *not* 'Gillick competent' by:

- a person with parental responsibility for the child; or

- an order of the High Court.

If therapeutic treatment is considered necessary and the child or those with parental responsibility refuse, or if there is any issue about the competence of a child to make an informed decision, the matter can, if necessary, be referred for expert opinion and/or to the High Court. The High Court has the power to make an order in the best interests of the child and resolve disputes with a 'specific issue' order made under section 8 of the CA 1989. In the situation where a child is a witness in a criminal case, the welfare of the child is of primary importance for the police, the CPS and criminal court. The welfare of the child is paramount for the High Court, as it is for all levels of the family court in all child protection matters; see the welfare checklist at para 5.1.6.

In the case of emergency medical or psychiatric treatment, if urgent life-saving treatment is judged to be necessary and there is grave risk to the child if emergency treatment is not given, medical practitioners may rely on their own clinical judgement if those in a position to give consent are unavailable, just as they would for an adult.

Once a young person reaches the age of 18, even the High Court cannot overrule his wishes about medical examination, treatment or therapy, unless for any reason he lacks the mental capacity to make his own valid decisions, in which case adult rules apply.

5.2.4   Parental responsibility

People may assume that all parents have the power to make decisions for their children. This is not so. The ability of a parent, or anyone else, to make a decision for his child depends on the age of the child, and whether the child has capacity to make his own decisions, and also whether the adult concerned has 'parental responsibility', which is the legal basis for making decisions about a child, including giving valid consent for therapy.

Parental responsibility was a legal concept created by the CA 1989 and defined in section 3(1) as 'all the rights, duties, powers, responsibilities and authority which by law the parent of a child has in relation to a child and his property'. There may be new legislation that will further define the concept of parental responsibility.

More than one person can have parental responsibility for a child at the same time. Parental responsibility cannot be transferred or surrendered, but elements may be delegated; see section 2(9) of the CA 1989.

Who has parental responsibility?

See *Children Law and Practice* and *Clarke Hall and Morrison on Children* for more detail. Here is a brief summary.

Mothers and married fathers: Every mother (whether or not she is married) has parental responsibility for each child born to her; and every biological father who is married to the child's mother at the time of or subsequent to the conception of their child, automatically has parental responsibility for their child, which may be shared with others but will cease only on death or adoption.

Unmarried biological fathers: Unmarried fathers may acquire parental responsibility for their biological child in one of several ways, the first three of which can be removed only by order of the court:

- From 1 December 2003, in England and Wales (earlier in Northern Ireland) an unmarried father in most cases automatically acquires parental responsibility for his child if, with the mother's and his consent, he is named as the child's father on the register of births in the UK. This law does not operate retrospectively.

- By formal Parental Responsibility Agreement signed by the mother and father, witnessed by an officer at court, then registered. Copies may be obtained for a fee, in a similar way to obtaining a birth certificate (see Parental Responsibility Agreement Regulations 1991 (SI 1991/1478).

- The court can make an order under section 4(1)(a) of the CA 1989 awarding parental responsibility to the father, consistent with the interests of the child.

Parental responsibility can also be acquired by a child's biological father where:

- a residence order is made under section 8 of the CA 1989, directing the child to live with the father, and parental responsibility is awarded along with it;

- appointment as the child's guardian is made under section 5 of the CA 1989;

- the father marries the child's mother;

- certain placement or adoption orders are made under the Adoption and Children Act 2002.

Acquisition of parental responsibility by others: Parental responsibility may be acquired by others (including relatives, partners and guardians) in a variety of ways, for example by the appointment of a testamentary guardian, or by marriage to or civil partnership with a parent who has parental responsibility for the child, with the agreement of others who also hold parental responsibility. It may also be acquired by local authorities in care proceedings and by others by means of various court orders. Parental responsibility may then be shared with others who also hold it, and the exercise of parental responsibility may be limited by the court in certain cases.

What if there is no one with parental responsibility for a child? Some children (e.g. a child whose biological father is unknown and whose single mother dies without appointing a guardian) may have no one with legal parental responsibility for them. Relatives or others wishing to care for the child will then have to apply for parental responsibility under one of the applications listed above or, failing that, the local authority has a responsibility to assume the care of the child and can seek an appropriate order.

There is an additional provision in section 3(5) of the CA 1989 that those without parental responsibility may 'do what is reasonable in all the circumstances to safeguard and promote the welfare' of a child in their care. This provision is useful in day-to-day situations, for example allowing a babysitter, neighbour or relative who is temporarily looking after a child to take that child for medical help in an emergency. This provision is unlikely to apply to counselling, unless in an emergency.

5.2.5   Confidentiality

A client has the legal and ethical right to confidentiality, both in law and as part of the therapist's duty of care to the client, subject to certain legal limitations. The right to ask for confidentiality will depend on the mental capacity of the child client.

If the child does not have the capacity to make his own decisions, then those with parental responsibility will have the right to make decisions, and also the right to see the child's therapy records (with certain exceptions allowing the therapist and school to maintain secrecy in order to safeguard the health or safety of the child or others, or to safeguard a police or other investigation in the context of child protection).

In the context of pre-trial therapy, confidentiality for the therapy work is limited in accordance with the CPS guidance. The child (or those with parental responsibility for the child) will need to understand and agree the terms of the guidance (see para 5.3).

5.2.6   Competence to give evidence

Under section 53(1) of the YJCEA 1999, in principle, 'all persons are (whatever their age) competent to give evidence' provided that in accordance with section 53(2), that person can: (a) understand questions put to him as a witness; and (b) give answers to them which can be understood.

If the competence of a witness is questioned, the YJCEA 1999 requires the court to determine, on a balance of probabilities, whether or not the witness is competent; and it is the job of the party calling the witness to satisfy the court as to the witness's competence. See section 54(1) and (2) of the YJCEA 1999.

In determining the question of competence, the court shall treat the witness as having the benefit of any directions made under section 19 which the court has given or proposes to give regarding special measures, section 54(4) of the YJCEA 1999.

Note: Under section 54(6) of the YJCEA 1999, 'any questioning of the witness (where the court considers that necessary) shall be conducted by the court in the presence of the parties'. This means that if the witness is likely to be vulnerable or intimidated, those supporting the witness need to raise with the court the issue of any special measures to which the witness might be entitled under section 19 at the outset of the case, for the protection of the witness during any questioning regarding competence.

Expert evidence may be received to assist the court in making a decision as to competence, section 54(5) of the YJCEA 1999.

Competence is not dependant on the age of a child. See the case of *R v B* [2011] Crim LR 233, where the Court of Appeal held that:

> although the chronological age of the child will inevitably help to inform the judicial decision about competency, in the end the decision is a decision about the individual child and his or her competence to give evidence in the particular trial.

A competent witness is also compellable, i.e. the witness can be legally required to attend court and give evidence, or to give his evidence in another way under a court direction for the use of special measures. However, as *Achieving Best Evidence* points out:

> the fact that a witness is compellable does not mean that they can be legally required to give any kind of preliminary statement to the police – even the sort of statement that is made under this guidance.

(MoJ, 2011a: para 2.10)

5.2.7   Assessment of psychological risk and the welfare of the child witness

Child witnesses may live in an environment or social context which could pose a specific or generalised risk to the child or to others, and this may need to be taken into account; for example there may be proximity or involvement with gangs, criminal activities, living conditions in violent or highly oppressive situations, involvement in a culture of illegal dangerous substance abuse, etc. Child protection issues are discussed at para 5.1. Working with the psychological risk to a child or adult who is to be a witness in criminal proceedings is always a concern in the provision of pre-trial therapy. Therapists, police, CPS and the courts have to consider any area of potential risk to the health and welfare of the child to whom there is a duty of care in the context of both the legal proceedings and any therapeutic work.

For a helpful and practical resource relevant to the provision of therapy, see *Working with Risk in Counselling and Psychotherapy* (Reeves, 2015). Tim Bond also pays attention to the ethical issues of risk in his book *Standards and Ethics for Counselling in Action*, 4th edition (Bond, 2015: 77–79, 174 and 215–218).

Careful attention should be paid to risk assessment, which is vital in considering the needs of a child witness in the provision of pre-trial therapy. Some states of mind may carry with them an increased risk of suicidality or other forms of self-harm, and this may be exacerbated by the stress of giving evidence and legal proceedings.

The legal position is that the courts will expect the practitioner to take reasonable care of each child client, taking into account the circumstances of that particular child or young person and their specific situation. It is therefore advisable for the practitioner to seek guidance on the appropriate management of risk in relation to that specific client from the relevant professionals responsible for the client's health and welfare. For example, where appropriate, consultation with those responsible for the child's medical, social and physical care is advisable, within the bounds of client confidentiality and client consent.

Therapists have a duty to work within the limits of their professional competence. Appropriate training and experience is necessary when working with child witnesses. The therapist should be appropriately qualified, and familiar with court procedures and the requirements of the relevant guidance. The courts would regard it as an unacceptable risk to a child for a therapist to work with a child witness who presents material, issues, behaviours or any other circumstance (e.g. age, ethnicity, social circumstance, personal qualities, or a diagnosis of specific mental illness or disorder, etc.) which may challenge the therapist beyond the remit of his competence.

5.3   Interviews with child witnesses

Child witnesses are those under the age of 18 (section 16 of the YJCEA 2009, as amended by the Coroners and Justice Act 2009).

Interviews with child witnesses are covered in *Achieving Best Evidence*, paras 2.16–2.59 (MoJ, 2011a). Child protection issues, consent, medical examinations and psychiatric or psychological assessments should all inform the planning process for the evidence of child witnesses.

If a child is interviewed by video-recording, this can serve the purpose of gathering evidence in the investigation and in criminal proceedings, and also the child's evidence in chief. It can also be used to inform enquiries under section 47 of the CA 1989 regarding any significant harm and any actions needed to safeguard the child's welfare or that of other children, or in civil child care or disciplinary proceedings; see *Achieving Best Evidence* (MoJ, 2011a: paras 2.18–2.19). For more about video-recorded interviews, see para 3.5.

The interview with the child should be the responsibility of the police, but may be jointly shared with police and social care worker, with the one with the best rapport with the child taking the lead. The police should retain responsibility for planning and monitoring the interview. The local authority should retain its duty to make enquiries under section 47 of the CA 1989 by ensuring that the interview is properly planned and that the social care worker has an effective role in monitoring the interview (MoJ, 2011a: para 2.22). Regard should be had to the child's welfare, and the child should not be further traumatised by too many visits, or being asked to give his account of events too often. For this reason, joint interviews and joint investigations by police and social care can be helpful.

Consideration should be given to holding a discussion between the investigating officer and the CPS where necessary to discuss what special measures might be needed to assist the witness before and during the trial (see *Special Measures for vulnerable and intimidated witnesses: research exploring the decisions and actions taken by prosecutors in a sample of CPS file cases* (CPS, 2012), and MoJ, 2011a: para 2.28).

When assessing how a child's evidence should be obtained, interviewers should:

- consider each child as an individual;
- assess the child's individual needs whatever the offence;
- take account of the following characteristics of the child:
  - age,
  - gender,
  - culture,
  - religion,
  - physical and/or learning disability,
  - confidence and developmental level;
- consider the views of the child and their carer.

(MoJ, 2011a: para 2.29)

5.4   CPS guidance on the provision of psychological pre-trial therapy for child witnesses

The CPS issued guidance on 8 February 2001 on pre-trial therapy for children and young people, *Provision of Therapy for Child Witnesses Prior to a*

Criminal Trial: Practice Guidance (CPS, 2001a). There is a parallel version of this guidance in relation to pre-trial therapy for *Provision of Therapy for Vulnerable or Intimidated Adult Witnesses Prior to a Criminal Trial: Practice Guidance*, which, although dated 2001, came into force on 24 January 2002 (CPS, 2001b), available at www.cps.gov.uk; for discussion, see Chapter 4. These two documents remain in force as guidance to police, CPS and therapists, until they are revised or withdrawn. The CPS 2001 guidance in relation to pre-trial therapy for children is worded similarly to that for vulnerable adults. There is an argument for revision of these two guidance documents to take in new law and government guidance documents, and to bring them both into line with recent developments in psychological therapy modalities and practice. In relation to references to child protection procedures (CPS, 2001a), readers should now refer to *Working Together* (DfE, 2015a).

5.4.1   Key issues for pre-trial therapy with children

The CPS guidance has to balance the needs of the child witness and the interests of justice. The document is aimed at those who arrange or commission therapy, therapists and lawyers involved in making decisions in cases where pre-trial therapy is a consideration.

A key issue in a criminal trial, especially in relation to child witnesses, is that pre-trial discussions of any kind have a potential effect on the reliability, actual or perceived, of the evidence of the witness and the weight which will be given to that evidence in court. Pre-trial discussions may lead to allegations of coaching and, ultimately, the failure of the criminal case. It should also be borne in mind that the professionals concerned may themselves be called to court as witnesses in relation to any therapy undertaken prior to the criminal trial.

The overarching concept in the CPS guidance is the primary importance of the welfare of the child witness, even at the cost of the trial if necessary and the guidance is crystal clear on this (see CPS, 2001a: paras 4.3–4.6).

The CPS guidance states three issues relevant to pre-trial therapy:

- many child victims express the wish to see their abuser convicted and punished;
- there is a wider public interest in ensuring that abusers are brought to justice to prevent further abuse;
- all accused persons are entitled to a fair trial.

(CPS, 2001a: para 1.1)

5.4.2   Definitions

Therapy: In the CPS guidance, the term 'therapy' covers a range of psychological treatment approaches, but does not include physical therapy.

Psychotherapy – purpose:

> Psychotherapy includes interventions designed to decrease distress, psychological symptoms and maladaptive behaviour, or to improve adaptive and personal functioning through the use of interpersonal interaction, counselling or activities following a specific treatment plan. Treatment focuses on some facet of how clients feel (affect), think (cognition) and act (behaviour).

(Kazdin, 1990: 21–5, in CPS, 2001a: para 2.2)

Psychotherapy – modalities:

> Psychotherapies and counselling can be grouped in a number of ways; for example, psychodynamic, cognitive-behavioural, systemic, experiential. They are underpinned by different models of understanding and techniques, and vary in the context in which they are given (individual, family, group, etc.) and frequency of sessions.

(CPS, 2001a: para 2.3)

Psychotherapy may address a number of issues, including:

- treatment of emotional and behavioural disturbance, for example post-traumatic stress disorder;
- treatment of a child who has been highly traumatised and shows symptoms which give rise to concern for the child's mental health.

(CPS, 2001a: para 2.4.2)

Counselling: This will address a number of issues, including:

- the impact on the child of the abuse;
- improving the self-esteem and confidence of the child;
- providing the child with information with regard to, for example, abusive relationships. The aim of this is to enable the child to seek out assistance from a trusted adult if the child feels unsafe at some stage in the future.

(CPS, 2001a: para 2.4.1)

> Both counselling and psychotherapy may require long term involvement with the child, depending on the degree of trauma suffered and the child's cognitive ability.

(CPS, 2001a: para 2.4.2)

It will be seen from these definitions that counselling is seen generally as working on the impact of the event, developing self-esteem and confidence, information-giving with regard to dealing with and avoiding abusive situations, and helping the child to access appropriate support and protection. Psychotherapy is seen as more in-depth work with the witness on emotional, cognitive and behavioural issues.

The CPS guidance makes a distinction between 'formal preparation of a witness for giving evidence in court' and the provision of psychotherapy and counselling by qualified practitioners.

The preparation for court may be to:

- provide the child with information about the legal process;
- address any particular concerns or fears which the child may have in relation to giving evidence;
- reduce anxiety.

(CPS, 2001a: para 2.5)

> The timing of the preparation for court is important. If it is carried out too soon before evidence is given, the child's anxieties may be increased. On the other hand, if it is carried out at the last minute the child may feel rushed and be unable to assimilate the information given.

(CPS, 2001a: para 2.5)

Information should be available in a variety of forms to enable accessibility, for example, braille, British Sign Language, Maketon, etc. The CPS guidance refers to an earlier version, but *Achieving Best Evidence* (MoJ, 2011a) has information about preparation for court, see Chapter 3.

The CPS guidance suggests various materials, which are listed in the references section of the guidance. Those listed are now quite old, but are designed to assist with the preparation of the child witness for giving evidence in court. *The Young Witness Pack* (NSPCC and ChildLine, 1998), which is aimed at both children and young people, provides booklets for specific age groups. There is a video addition to the Pack entitled *Giving Evidence – What's It Really Like?* (NSPCC and ChildLine, 2000) which is suitable for older children.

5.4.3   Risks of pre-trial therapy

Discussions with a child witness before a trial which in any way touch on the proceedings or his evidence might potentially affect the quality and the reliability of the evidence of the child witness concerned. In particular, concerns arise about the possibility of a child witness being coached or led, causing him to give an inconsistent account of what happened, or perhaps contradicting his earlier statement to police or the content of an earlier video-recorded interview.

Another concern is that through discussions, a child witness could begin to imagine events differently, and perhaps come to recall them differently, so – intentionally or inadvertently – to fabricate evidence. This could happen to fill in gaps in information, or rationalisations to explain inconsistencies in the accounts of the witness and others. Fortified by discussions about the events, the child may become more convinced of his account, but nevertheless remain mistaken.

In therapy, therefore, it is vital that the work is undertaken with these risks in mind, to ensure that, as far as possible 'justice is seen to be done' and the actual or perceived risks are eliminated.

For this to happen, good record keeping in therapy is essential, see para 5.4.4.

5.4.4   Records, confidentiality and disclosures in pre-trial therapy

In pre-trial therapy, practitioners must pay particular attention to issues of confidentiality and record keeping, particularly with regard to information sharing. In relation to children, vulnerability, trauma, capacity and consent may be issues for undertaking psychological therapy and perhaps, too, in relation to the witness's competence to give evidence, assessment for special measures and arrangements for the trial hearing. Therapists will need to be aware of current law and their own professional body's guidance, in addition to the government guidance, and match all this as seamlessly as possible with their own policies and procedures. In the NHS, local authority and government-regulated practice, policies are set and will contractually bind therapists as part of their employment or contract for services to compliance with government guidance.

Child clients must know what to expect from their psychological therapy and where the boundaries of confidentiality lie. They need to be told, for example, that careful records of the therapy will be kept, and that disclosure of information concerning their pre-trial therapy is likely to be required by the court.

Therapy records should be accurate, up to date, and all material that may be relevant to the issues in the case must be preserved, and may have to be disclosed (CPS, 2001a: paras 3.7–3.8):

> Disclosure should not be viewed as a tool to enable the prosecution or defence to satisfy their curiosity. It is a principle designed to ensure that information that is of genuine relevance to a criminal case is available to the parties and the court.

(CPS, 2001a: para 3.10)

Requests for information to be obtained from third parties may be made at various stages in a criminal case by:

- the police;
- the prosecutor;

- the defence;
- the court.

(CPS, 2001a: para 3.12)

The requests should explain the issues in the case, so far as they are known, and be reasonably precise. Speculative inquiries are discouraged. The purpose should be to elicit a genuine and focused search for relevant documents or information. Careful maintenance of records of therapy will facilitate this focused approach. Where a therapist receives a request for information or documents, legal advice should be obtained before complying with the request. If, for example, the therapist is employed by a Social Services Department or NHS Hospital, the legal department of such a Department or Hospital will provide advice.

(CPS, 2001a: para 3.13)

Therapists have a duty of confidentiality to child clients, and the guidance recognises that it will usually only be appropriate to breach confidentiality in compliance with a court order. It emphasises that:

> Those aspects of the therapy that have no material relevance to criminal proceedings should not have to be disclosed. However, the issue of relevance may need to be reviewed at different stages of the criminal case, as more becomes known about the prosecution and defence cases.

(CPS, 2001a: para 3.15)

In addition to informal requests for information, if there are real grounds to believe that material which could affect the outcome of the prosecution is being withheld, an application may be made to the court for a witness summons to obtain the material. If, as will usually be the case, a therapist, having taken appropriate legal advice, believes that the material should not be disclosed, he or she may oppose the witness summons application. In that case the court may hold a hearing at which the therapist's employer may be legally represented. The court, having heard representations from the advocate representing the applicant for the witness summons and the advocate for the therapist's employer, will decide whether or not to issue a summons requiring the disclosure of the material.

(CPS, 2001a: para 3.14)

Note: This wording could benefit from clarification. It is assumed that a self-employed therapist may attend court in his own right.

The CPS guidance makes it very clear, in bold type '**Confidentiality cannot, therefore, be guaranteed in advance**'. (This means, in effect, that a therapist cannot promise a vulnerable child witness absolute confidentiality.) The guidance then goes on to state:

> Bearing this in mind, it is important that an understanding is reached with the child and carers at the outset of any therapy undertaken of the

circumstances under which material obtained during treatment may be required to be disclosed.

(CPS, 2001a: para 3.15)

5.4.5   Making decisions about pre-trial therapy

The CPS has a good deal of power in making decisions about prosecutions. Having considered the needs and the best interests of the child witnesses in consultation with the child, carers and other relevant professionals, the interests of justice must be weighed against any conflicting needs of the child, and the potential impact of any therapy on the child's evidence in the case. If the needs of the child (or any other vulnerable or intimidated adult witnesses) require therapy of a type that may adversely affect his evidence, then the case may have to be abandoned in the child or other vulnerable or intimidated witness's best interests:

> The Crown Prosecution Service (CPS) is responsible for reviewing and conducting the majority of criminal cases involving child victims and witnesses. Once a Crown Prosecutor considers that there is a realistic prospect of conviction, the public interest must be considered.

(CPS, 2001a: para 4.1)

This means that, in a criminal case, the CPS must decide in the public interest whether (or not) to bring a case against the accused. However, 'A primary consideration for Crown Prosecutors when taking decisions in these circumstances is the best interests of the child' (CPS, 2001a: para 4.1).

If the CPS decides to proceed with the case, then additional considerations will follow:

> The prosecution in these criminal cases must do what it can to:
>
> * identify cases in which the provision of therapy before the criminal trial might be thought to have some material impact on the evidence;
> * assess the likely consequences for the criminal trial in these cases;
> * ensure that these cases are dealt with as quickly as possible;
> * safeguard the confidentiality of therapy sessions wherever possible whilst ensuring that the defence and the court are aware of the existence of information which might undermine the prosecution case or assist the defence.

(CPS, 2001a: para 4.2)

> These questions are not unique to therapy which takes place before the criminal trial, but the ethical, medical, welfare and legal issues are of particular importance in these cases.

(CPS, 2001a: para 4.2)

Note, however, that the guidance is clear that the decision about whether or not a child should receive therapy is not a matter for the police or CPS to decide:

> Whether a child should receive therapy before the criminal trial is not a decision for the police or the Crown Prosecution Service. Such decisions can only be taken by all of the professionals from the agencies responsible for the welfare of the child, in consultation with the carers of the child and the child him or herself, if the child is of sufficient age and understanding.
>
> (CPS, 2001a: para 4.3)

> The best interests of the child are the paramount consideration in decisions about the provision of therapy before the criminal trial. In determining what is in the best interests of the child, due consideration should be given to ascertaining the wishes and feelings of the child in a manner appropriate to the child's age and understanding. When working with the child either for assessment or therapeutic purposes, account should be taken of the child's gender, race, religion, language, and (if appropriate), disability.
>
> (CPS, 2001a: para 4.4)

The provision of certain types of pre-trial psychological therapy, for example traumatic incident reduction, or other types of imaginal re-exposure therapies which might be used to alleviate the symptoms of PTSD, or any therapeutic modality requiring discussion of issues relevant to the case, might cause the evidence to become unreliable or unsafe, and the impact of therapy may go so far as to cause the police and the CPS to abandon the prosecution. As we saw earlier, the interests of justice have to be weighed against the needs of the witness, and sometimes there will be a compromise that will satisfy both needs. The CPS will advise on the impact of the therapy on the evidence, but the overriding principle that will apply in this situation, as stated in the CPS guidance (CPS, 2001a: paras 4.4–4.6) is the best interests and the wellbeing of the witness:

> If there is a demonstrable need for the provision of therapy and it is possible that the therapy will prejudice the criminal proceedings, consideration may need to be given to abandoning those proceedings in the interests of the child's wellbeing. In order that such consideration can be given, it is essential that information regarding therapy is communicated to the prosecutor.
>
> (CPS, 2001a: para 4.5)

There are some situations where therapy may be delayed until after the case is heard:

> Alternatively, there may be some children for whom it will be preferable to delay therapy until after the criminal case has been heard, to avoid the benefits of the therapy being undone.
>
> (CPS, 2001a: para 4.6)

This principle is repeated and expanded in the section in the CPS guidance on assessment:

> Some children are so severely traumatised that the short term provision of, for example, once or twice weekly therapeutic sessions may be either inadequate for their needs or positively disturbing for them, particularly if their home or alternative care situation has not been fully resolved. With certain children, therefore, it may be better to delay long-term therapeutic work until a placement is made within a containing environment and then commence more intensive therapeutic work.
>
> (CPS, 2001a: para 5.20)

> This may, in some cases, mean delaying therapy until the criminal proceedings are at an end (though in such cases prosecutors will wish to do all that they can to expedite the proceedings). This does not, however, preclude the important provision of general support for the child and family or briefer forms of more focused therapy.
>
> (CPS, 2001a: para 5.21)

> There is a possible psychological advantage for a highly traumatised child in a purposeful and carefully planned delay of intensive therapy until full physical and psychological safety has first been obtained for that child. Some forms of intensive trauma therapy may involve the child in some form of imaginal re-exposure to the traumatic events, carried out in a structured way in a physically and psychologically safe environment. If therapy for such a child were delayed for the duration of the legal proceedings, one might question whether the re-exposure to the traumatic events in the context of legal interviews and the stress of a cross-examination (even with special measures), without the support of therapy and a structured safe therapeutic environment, might cause further psychological damage to the child. If there is such a high degree of trauma, careful psychological assessment and safety for the child must be the first priority, followed by any necessary therapy, which should take precedence over the legal process if the best interests of the child require it.

A delay in providing therapy would greatly benefit the prosecution in that it removes a potential risk to the quality of the child's evidence. The substitution of 'general support' for the child and family instead of therapy should only happen if this is in the best interests of the child.

It is possible that further psychological research on the impact of post-traumatic stress in relation to the impact of a delay in therapy in these circumstances may shed some light on the validity of this provision from the perspective of the best interests of the child.

5.4.6   Guidelines on assessment for pre-trial therapy

> Assessment of the need for therapy of any child during the pre-trial period (when that child may become a witness in the subsequent trial) should only be undertaken following consultation with the relevant and other professionals

involved. This may be appropriate in the context of a strategy discussion or child protection conference convened under child protection procedures. If the child is not the subject of child protection processes, and it is judged desirable, a meeting of all relevant professionals might be convened for the purpose of discussing an assessment and treatment strategy.

(CPS, 2001a: para 5.9)

The professionals meeting should be to discuss the needs and best interests of the child, and may include discussion about the logistics of setting up a specialist assessment of the child, with agreement on who will undertake this assessment and which professional agencies will support the assessment, for example by bringing the child to appointments and working with the family (CPS, 2001a: para 5.10).

The point that priority must be given to the best interests of the child is again emphasised, and the impact of any therapy on the conduct of the criminal case should be fully discussed:

> The Crown Prosecution Service will advise, as requested on the likely effect of any particular type of therapy on the evidence of witnesses in individual cases and will need to be informed about any planned or ongoing therapy. Where a criminal case is at an advanced stage, it may be possible to consult the judge in chambers as to the potential consequences of a proposed course of action.

(CPS, 2001a: para 5.11)

More than one professional may be needed to carry out an assessment, and therapy may be carried out by a different person with appropriate qualifications and experience:

> It is vital that a trained professional person with a recognised competence in such assessments should see the child and any relevant family members. One or more careful assessment interviews should be conducted in order to determine whether and in what way the child is emotionally disturbed and also whether further treatment is needed. This could be as part of an assessment undertaken according to the Framework for the Assessment of Children in Need and their Families (Department of Health et al., 2000).

(CPS, 2001a: para 5.12)

The CPS guidance makes it clear that therapy is not considered as always being necessary. If it is advised, then the professionals will also discuss the best therapeutic approach for the child:

> It is important to note that not all children who are assessed in this way will need therapy. Final recommendations from the assessment will indicate the type of therapy or intervention, if any, required by the particular child. It will be important for such findings to be made available to other relevant agencies involved as soon as possible after the assessment is completed.

(CPS, 2001a: para 5.13)

Areas that should be addressed in an assessment may include the following:

- *Developmental factors*:

    > Children of the same age may have different levels of understanding. An assessment should therefore address the child's development in both emotional and cognitive terms, as well as any relevant physical illnesses or developmental problems which might affect a child's performance as a witness in court, and which could be worked with in the course of therapy provided prior to the criminal trial.

    (CPS, 2001a: para 5.15)

- *Specific needs*: A child with specific needs may, with the appropriate assistance, be a competent witness:

    > An assessment of children with specific needs, including physical and learning disabilities, hearing and speech impairments should be conducted in conjunction with specialist workers who are trained in these areas of work.

    (CPS, 2001a: para 5.16)

- *Suggestibility*: A child may be suggestible in an interview or during cross-examination in court:

    > It should be remembered that some children including young children, learning disabled children, very severely abused children who have been intimidated or physically beaten, or severely emotionally disturbed children are more likely to produce erroneous or ambiguous responses to leading questions from interviewers, than are less vulnerable or older children. Particular care, therefore, should be taken in the assessment of such vulnerable children to use short, plain, words, to ask open questions where possible and to avoid convoluted, hypothetical or other leading questions.

    (CPS, 2001a: para 5.17)

Achieving Best Evidence (MoJ, 2011a) provides clear guidance on interviews, questioning, evidence in the legal process and video-recorded evidence of children.

The CPS guidance provides advice on assessment skills and equipment:

> The assessor should use a limited range of selected assessment tools such as drawing materials and appropriate toys (for example, non-anatomical dolls) to supplement questioning within an assessment session. The use of anatomical dolls in assessment for therapy is unlikely to be necessary, since specific investigative work about alleged abuse (which may or may not involve anatomical dolls) will already have been undertaken in the joint investigative interview. The use of any materials which suggest or presume that abuse has taken place should be avoided.

(CPS, 2001a: para 5.18)

If deemed clinically appropriate, children should also have a separate psychological and/or developmental assessment to obtain baseline data on their cognitive and emotional functioning. Such a psychological assessment will indicate whether the child has specific needs which may require assistance in court, for example an intermediary or interpreter, as well as contributing to an understanding of the child's emotional needs.

(CPS, 2001a: para 5.19)

5.4.7 Guidelines on the use of pre-trial therapy

The CPS guidance makes a distinction in para 5.1 between 'formal preparation of a witness for giving evidence in court' and the 'use of psychotherapy and counselling by qualified practitioners'.

Therapists and those providing formal preparation for giving evidence in court need to be aware of the possible impact of their work on subsequent evidence. Some relevant training or experience would be necessary to create this awareness. The guidance states that 'some types of therapeutic work are more likely to be seen as prejudicial and therefore undermine the perception of the credibility and reliability of the witness, or to influence the memory of the witness in the account they give' (CPS, 2001a: para 5.2). When exploring the modalities that may be appropriate, the CPS guidance then becomes less clear in its wording, 'Preparation for court and carefully planned preventive work which does not focus on past abuse presents less of a problem than interpretive psychodynamic psychotherapy' (CPS, 2001a: para 5.2).

There are many therapeutic modalities, of which psychodynamic psychotherapy is just one, but to widen out the point being made, it would seem that the main two aspects causing concern for the CPS here are the use of interpretation, and also the possible discussion of past events relevant to the trial in the therapy.

However, as we have seen in the CPS guidance (CPS, 2001a: para 4.4), if intensive trauma therapy were considered absolutely necessary in the interests of the witness's mental health and welfare, then the trial may have to be abandoned if the therapy would adversely affect evidence which is vital to the case.

A clearly stated preferred modality is cognitive-behavioural therapy, to improve self-esteem and confidence, and/or including:

- the reduction of distress about the impending legal proceedings;
- the treatment of associated emotional and behavioural disturbance that does not require the rehearsal of abusive events.

(CPS, 2001a: para 5.3)

There should be careful recording of the therapeutic sessions (CPS, 2001a: para 5.4).

Last, to restate the most important principle, those involved in the prosecution of an alleged abuser have no authority to prevent a child from receiving therapy (CPS, 2001a: para 6.1).

5.4.8   Which therapist is appropriate to undertake pre-trial work?

Therapy may be provided through the NHS, voluntary sectors, or privately. The context may vary between Child and Adolescent Mental Health Services (CAMHS), NHS or private family therapy, or private or voluntary therapy in other settings. There is no specific universal register of which the author is aware of therapists appropriately qualified to work with child witnesses, perhaps partly because there are so many therapeutic modalities and training organisations. There are specialist professional organisations for the treatment of trauma, and others specialising in therapy with children and young people. Some of these are listed in Appendix 6. Some professional organisations for counsellors and psychotherapists, for example the British Association for Counselling and Psychotherapy (BACP) has specialist interest groups including working with children and young people.

Those who provide therapy for child witnesses should have appropriate training and supervision, and membership of an appropriate professional body or other recognised competence would be expected. The therapist should also have a good understanding of how the rules in criminal proceedings require the modification of techniques, see the CPS guidance (CPS, 2001a: para 5.7).

Paragraph 5.8 of the CPS guidance is now outdated, as it refers to:

> National Standards for Young Witness Preparation being issued as part of the current revision of the 1992 Memorandum of Good Practice on Video Recorded Interviews with Child Witnesses for Criminal Proceedings.

Achieving Best Evidence (MoJ, 2011a) provides detailed guidance on assessment, preparation and interviewing techniques for both adult and child witnesses. Other relevant guidance for further reading is listed in Appendix 5.

It will be seen that pre-trial therapy has to be undertaken by therapists who are confident in their ability to meet their client's needs in the context of preparing for court proceedings and at the same time to comply with the requirements of the judicial process. Specific training may be helpful for therapists who undertake pre-trial work. Section 7 of the CPS guidance (2001a) addresses the qualities expected of the therapists undertaking this work. Revisions of this guidance may reconsider both the therapeutic modalities considered appropriate and the recommended therapist qualities and training, recognising that these may vary according to the client needs and the nature of the case.

5.4.9 Potential problem areas in pre-trial therapy with children

The CPS guidance deals with problem areas at paras 5.22–5.25. It explains that there have been concerns when therapists attempt to distinguish fantasy from reality in the responses of the child in the course of therapy. It is important that the therapist should be 'as open to the idea that the material presented as factual truth may be a distortion, as they are to a fantasy being a representation of reality' (CPS, 2001a: para 5.22). The importance of keeping a careful record of therapy will be very clear in this situation.

The CPS guidance specifies modalities which are seen as clearly problematic, even if carefully conducted:

> There are therapeutic approaches that would very definitely present problems as far as evidential reliability is concerned. These would include hypnotherapy, psychodrama, regression techniques and unstructured groups.
>
> (CPS, 2001a: para 5.24)

> Prior to the criminal trial, group therapy where the specific recounting of abuse takes place is best avoided. The particular danger of this kind of group therapy is that the witness may adopt the experiences of others taking part in the therapy. Structured group therapy approaches which help in a neutral way to improve the child's self-esteem are less likely to cause difficulties. As a general principle, group therapy should not be offered to the child witness prior to the trial.
>
> (CPS, 2001a: para 6.10)

But:

> The professional background and training of the therapist, the provision of adequate supervision arrangements, the appropriateness and robustness of the policies of the agency providing therapy will all help to obviate problems.
>
> (CPS, 2001a: para 5.23)

The CPS guidance recommends training for therapists, the judiciary and the legal profession.

5.4.10 Conclusions: dos and don'ts in pre-trial therapy

> The police and the Crown Prosecution Service should be made aware that therapy is proposed, is being undertaken, or has been undertaken.
>
> (CPS, 2001a: para 6.2)

The nature of the therapy should be explained so that consideration can be given to whether or not the provision of such therapy is likely to impact on the criminal case. There should be a locally agreed mechanism for communicating this information and enabling it to be routed through the police to the Crown Prosecution Service using named contact points assigned to each individual child. Direct consultation between the professionals involved may be desirable in some circumstances and should be arranged in the same way.

(CPS, 2001a: para 6.3)

Those involved in the prosecution of an alleged abuser have no authority to prevent a child from receiving therapy.

(CPS, 2001a: para 6.1)

If the prosecutor advises that the proposed therapy may prejudice the criminal case, those responsible for the child's welfare should take this into account when deciding whether to agree to the therapy. It may still be in the best interests of the child to proceed with the therapy.

(CPS, 2001a: para 6.7)

However, the timing of the therapy could be important:

In newly arising allegations, therapy should not usually take place before a witness has provided a statement or, if appropriate, before a video-recorded interview has taken place. However, in existing cases where therapy is already under way, a decision about how to proceed may be best made after discussion at a multi-disciplinary meeting which includes the child's therapist. Clearly, when therapeutic work is in progress, disruption of therapy should be avoided even if new investigations must be conducted. If it is decided that leading questions or interpretations must be used to help a child in psychotherapy then the evidential implications of this should be understood and made clear.

(CPS, 2001a: para 6.6)

Records are of course important in this work. Professional therapists are expected to keep records, and to comply with data protection legislation and other relevant law. They should expect that their records will be required in court:

Records of therapy (which includes videos and tapes as well as notes) and other contacts with the witness must be maintained so that they can be produced if required by the court. They should include, in the case of therapy, details of those persons present and the content and length of the therapy sessions. It is not expected, for practical reasons, that verbatim written records will be kept.

(CPS, 2001a: para 6.4)

Children and their carers should understand the circumstances under which the material in the therapy may need to be disclosed. Disclosure of material may be requested by the police or CPS. By order of the court therapeutic records and material may be disclosed to the lawyers and also to the defendant.

The court is in charge of the evidence in the case and can make orders as to which material is relevant to the case and so to be disclosed, and if so, to whom:

> Maintaining a child's trust will remain important and it can be confirmed that those aspects of the therapy that have no material relevance to criminal proceedings will not have to be disclosed.

(CPS, 2001a: para 6.5)

The court may set limits on the extent of disclosure as appropriate to the case and the needs of the witness. The therapist may wish to be represented or to attend and be heard at a directions hearing on the matter of disclosure of the therapeutic material.

Therapists should be made aware of any impending criminal proceedings before commencing therapy. They should also 'be aware of the implications of using techniques which may result in the child's evidence being discredited' (CPS, 2001a: para 6.8). For example, in therapy, leading questions, exploring the substance of allegations, or discussing the evidence which the witness will give should be avoided (CPS, 2001a: para 6.9).

There are grey areas in the guidance in establishing which specific kinds of pre-trial therapy (apart from cognitive-behavioural therapy which is specifically mentioned) might be considered appropriate for witnesses, i.e. which modalities are less likely to prejudice the evidence.

If a child needs any form of therapy that will necessitate talking in detail about the events material to the case, for example specific trauma therapy involving intensive discussion or imaginal re-exposure to the traumatic events, then this is likely to be perceived as potentially damaging to the cogency of the witness's evidence, as the therapist may be thought to be going over the evidence and so 'rehearsing the witness' or 'coaching the witness' or in other ways affecting the witness's recall of the event. This may happen quite unintentionally on the part of the therapist, simply as a result of the recounting of events in the course of therapy.

> Children may derive therapeutic benefits from talking about their experiences, but any detailed recounting or re-enactment of the abuse may be perceived as coaching. Therapists should recognise that the criminal case is almost certain to fail as a consequence of this type of therapeutic work. This should be differentiated from the accepted practice of allowing witnesses, prior to giving evidence, to refresh their memory by reading the statement or viewing the video-recorded interview.

(CPS, 2001a: para 6.11)

However, as we have seen, if this sort of intensive trauma therapy were considered absolutely necessary in the interests of the child's mental health and welfare, then the child's welfare is of primary concern, and the trial may have to be abandoned if the therapy would adversely affect evidence which is vital to the case.

The CPS guidance warns:

> Professionals should avoid the use of jargon and take care to use language that will not be perceived, if repeated by a child witness, as evidence of the witness being instructed. The language content of the therapy and counselling sessions is guided by the child but equally it must be recognised that children do use different forms of language in differing situations and contexts.
>
> (CPS, 2001a: para 6.12)

> During therapy, witnesses should never be encouraged to extend their account of the abuse which they have suffered. However, it is acceptable to offer general reassurance and support to a child during this difficult process.
>
> (CPS, 2001a: para 6.13)

> Any disclosures of materially new allegations by the witness undergoing therapy, including possible disclosures of their own abusive behaviour, or any material departure from or inconsistency with the original allegations should be reported to the Social Services Department, Police and any other statutory agencies in accordance with the local area child protection committee (ACPC) procedures.
>
> (CPS, 2001a: para 6.14)

Note: In relation to CPS 2001a, readers will need now to refer to *Working Together* (DfE, 2015a) for up-to-date guidance on child protection procedures and terminology.

> Prosecutors *must* be informed that the witness has received therapy. Prosecutors *must* then obtain an assurance that the witness did not, in the therapy session(s), say anything inconsistent with the statements made by the witness to the police. Prosecutors may need to be made aware of the contents of the therapy sessions as well as other details specified in the paragraph above, when considering whether or not to prosecute and their duties of disclosure.
>
> (CPS, 2001a: para 6.15)

To comply with the CPS guidance above, therapists will need to be informed when a child client has or will become a witness in criminal proceedings. Therapists also have a responsibility under this guidance to tell the prosecution that therapy is taking (or has taken) place, and they are required to inform the prosecution of inconsistencies with earlier statements. Prosecutors also may need to know the content of therapy sessions. These disclosures, if unauthorised, would all normally constitute a breach of the therapist's duty of care and a breach of data protection legislation, which require a therapist to maintain client confidentiality. Disclosures may legally be made in accordance with explicit client consent, and/or a statutory duty, and/or a court order requiring disclosure. In the absence of client consent, the public interest may also afford some protection for a therapist's disclosure in these circumstances.

Further, in order to know what statements by the client may be inconsistent or not, the therapist would need to have knowledge of the content of the client's earlier witness' statements made in the case.

The last word. Just to reiterate:

> Those involved in the prosecution of an alleged abuser have no authority to prevent a child from receiving therapy.

> (CPS, 2001a: para 6.1)

> If the prosecutor advises that the proposed therapy may prejudice the criminal case, those responsible for the child's welfare should take this into account when deciding whether to agree to the therapy. It may still be in the best interests of the child to proceed with the therapy.

> (CPS, 2001a: para 6.7)

6   Victim Support

She was hit by the car and now the police are prosecuting the driver. She is only just out of hospital, she does not really remember the accident very clearly, and she feels confused about what will happen next. She would like some compensation for her injuries.

He is glad that the police took action against the man who attacked him, and he was glad the man went to prison. He is really frightened, and wants the parole board to know how he feels if they are thinking about early release. If they do let the offender out, he needs to be prepared for when the man comes out of prison.

The lad who mugged her is on probation. Is there anyone she can talk with about her concerns?

If the defendant pleads guilty, is there any way she can let the court know how she feels before he is sentenced?

6.1   *Code of Practice for Victims of Crime*

Issued in October 2013, under section 33 of the Domestic Violence, Crime and Victims Act 2004, the CA 1989 (MoJ, 2015), the *Victims' Code* was first issued by the Ministry of Justice in 2013 and then updated in October 2015. It was created in response to public concern and government strategy to support those who are victims of criminal conduct, and is available at www.cps.gov.uk. It implements relevant provisions of the EU Directive establishing minimum standards on the rights, support and protection of victims of crime (2012/29/EU); Directive 2011/92/EU combating the sexual abuse and sexual exploitation of children; and Directive 2011/36/EU preventing and combating the trafficking of human beings.

The *Victims' Code* applies to adults (MoJ, 2015: Chapter 2) and also to children and young people (MoJ, 2015; Chapter 3). It sets out who is entitled to services, who may provide services under the *Victims' Code* and what those services are.

The *Victims' Code* provides an excellent flowchart of the 'Victim's Journey through the Criminal Justice system' (MoJ, 2015: Introduction).

6.1.1   The 'service providers' (those who should provide services)

- The Criminal Cases Review Commission
- The Criminal Injuries Compensation Authority
- The Crown Prosecution Service (CPS)
- The First-tier Tribunal (Criminal Injuries Compensation)
- Her Majesty's Courts and Tribunals Service (HMCTS)
- Her Majesty's Prison Service
- National Offender Management Service (NOMS)
- The Parole Board
- Police and Crime Commissioners
- All police forces in England and Wales, the British Transport Police and the Ministry of Defence Police
- The National Probation Service
- The UK Supreme Court
- Witness Care Units
- Youth Offending Teams

(MoJ, 2015: para 8)

Other organisations may provide services but are not covered by the *Victims' Code* (MoJ, 2015: para 11).

6.1.2   Who is entitled to receive services?

Note: All those listed below are entitled to receive services under the *Victims' Code*, irrespective of whether any person has been charged or convicted of an offence relating to the criminal conduct, and regardless of whether or not the victim wishes to co-operate with the investigation (MoJ, 2015: para 29, and also see the entitlement to opt in or out of services in paras 37–38).

However, the *Victims' Code* also notes that if the victim is considering applying to the Criminal Injuries Compensation Authority (CICA), a CICA compensation award would be withheld unless the victim has co-operated as far as reasonably practicable in bringing the assailant to justice.

Entitlement does not depend on residence, and help will be given with language problems. Entitlement exists provided that the crime occurred in England and Wales (MoJ, 2015: para 21. Those entitled may refuse services or opt back in again whenever they wish if the case is still under active investigation by the police (MoJ, 2015: paras 37–38):

- Direct victims of crime, when an allegation has been made to the police (MoJ, 2015: para 20).

- Bereaved close relatives of a victim of crime (MoJ, 2015: para 23).

- Family spokesperson for families bereaved by crime (MoJ, 2015: paras 24–25).

- Family spokesperson for victims of crime who have a disability, or victims so badly injured by the crime that they cannot communicate (MoJ, 2015: para 26).

- A victim who is under 18 years of age and also his parent or guardian (MoJ, 2015: para 27).

- Businesses that are victims of crime (but not public sector bodies, their agencies or other subsidiary organisations) (MoJ, 2015: para 28).

Failure to provide services under the *Victims' Code* to a person who is entitled to receive them is not illegal, but it is possible that the *Code* might be used in evidence in the legal proceedings and taken into account in decision making.

6.1.3   Enhanced entitlements

Certain victims may receive 'enhanced entitlements':

- Victims of the most serious crime.
- Persistently targeted victims.
- Vulnerable or intimidated victims.

(MoJ, 2015: para 1.1)

Victims may belong to more than one of the above categories. Children and young people under the age of 18 will always be eligible for enhanced entitlements. Police are responsible for assessment for needs or support required (MoJ, 2015: para 1.4). Service providers must give opportunities for re-assessment if circumstances change (MoJ, 2015: para 1.5).

These victims will be entitled to special measures, which are listed in the *Victims' Code* (MoJ, 2015: paras 1.13–1.15). Please refer to Chapter 3 of this handbook for discussion of special measures and the services available for vulnerable and intimidated witnesses.

6.1.4   Definitions

Most serious crime: A 'victim of most serious crime' is defined as including:

> a close relative bereaved by criminal conduct, a victim of domestic violence, hate crime, terrorism, sexual offences, human trafficking, attempted murder, kidnap, false imprisonment, arson with intent to endanger life and wounding or causing grievous bodily harm with intent.

(MoJ, 2015: para 1.8)

Persistently targeted: 'Persistently targeted' means being 'targeted repeatedly as a direct victim of crime over a period of time, particularly if you have been deliberately targeted or you are a victim of a sustained campaign of harassment or stalking' (MoJ, 2015: para 1.9).

Vulnerable victim: A 'vulnerable victim' is defined in the *Victims' Code* (MoJ, 2015: para 1.10) to reflect the special measures provisions listed in section 16 of the YJCEA 1999.

You will be a vulnerable victim if:

    (a) you are under 18 years of age at the time of the offence, or

    (b) the quality of your evidence is likely to be affected because:

        i) you suffer from mental disorder within the meaning of the Mental Health Act 1983;

        ii) you otherwise have a significant impairment of intelligence and social functioning; or

        iii) you have a physical disability or are suffering from a physical disorder.

Intimidated victim: An 'intimidated victim' is defined as a person whose quality of evidence may be affected because of fear or distress about testifying in court (MoJ, 2015: para 1.11). Intimidation may result from the behaviour of others associated with the case, the nature and alleged circumstances of the offence, age, social and cultural background, religious beliefs or political opinions, ethnic origin, domestic and employment circumstances. Victims of human trafficking are automatically considered to be intimidated (MoJ, 2015: para 1.12).

6.1.5   Victims' entitlements pre-trial, during the hearing and sentencing

Under Chapter 2, Part A of the *Victims' Code*, adult victims are entitled to:

- receive a written acknowledgement that a crime has been reported, with basic details of the offence;
- an explanation of what to expect from the criminal justice process, by a leaflet or referral to a website, within 5 days of reporting the crime;
- a needs assessment to see if they are eligible for enhanced entitlement;
- have information about victims' services;
- have details automatically passed to victims' services within two days of reporting the crime to the police (victims can request this not to happen. Explicit consent for this referral is necessary for victims of sexual offences or domestic violence);
- an explanation within 5 days if there is a decision not to investigate the crime;
- be told if the investigation is concluded but nobody charged;
- be informed by the police, with reasons given, within 5 days (and in relation to the most serious crimes one working day) if a suspect is:

- arrested,
- interviewed under caution,
- released without charge,
- released on police bail, or if police bail conditions are changed or cancelled;

- agree timings for receipt of the information and services;
- be accompanied at police interview by a person of choice.

For those who are victims of most serious crime, persistently targeted or vulnerable or intimidated, there are additional entitlements (where appropriate):

- To have information on special measures explained.
- To be referred to a specialist organisation (where appropriate and available).
- To receive information on pre-trial therapy and counselling where appropriate.
- Where an investigation was concluded without charge, if the victim wishes, to be informed if an investigation is to be re-opened.
- To make a VPS. This is a statement which can be read out in court before sentencing, and allows the victim to have a say in the justice process. For more details about the VPS see the *Victims' Code* (MoJ, 2015: Chapter 1, paras 1.12–1.22).

Bereaved close relatives are entitled to the services of a Family Liaison Officer, assigned by the police.

Victims are entitled to a wide range of information about the criminal justice process and the progress of their specific case pre-trial and during the hearing, and to information about the disposal of the case, sentencing and any appeals. The duties are listed in relation to adults, in Chapter 1 of the *Victims' Code* in sections 2, 3 and 4 (paras 2.1–4.4), and in relation to children and young people, a similar list of duties is set out in Chapter 2 of the *Code*. Service providers should treat victims in a respectful, professional and sensitive manner, and without discrimination of any kind.

After the trial, the Witness Care Unit or the police will pay any expenses incurred in attending court to give evidence, provide information about the sentencing and use of the VPS.

6.1.6   Victims' entitlements post-trial and appeals

Where an appeal is lodged, a victim is entitled to information about its progress and outcome, the date and location of the hearing, and specified assistance at the court, together with information about victim support services where available. The victim is entitled to be made aware of any use made of the VPS in the appeal, see Chapter 1 of the *Victims' Code*, at section 5.

Following the trial, the Criminal Cases Review Commission undertakes reviews of convictions and sentences imposed as a result of the offender's criminal conduct. The Commission may refer a conviction or sentence for a fresh appeal if there is some new information or new argument which might mean the conviction is unsafe or the sentence too long.

When reviewing a case, the Commission will assess the potential impact on the victim and decide whether he should be notified. The Commission will record the reasons for its decisions as to the form of contact with the victim, and in appropriate cases will notify the police of those decisions. If the victim is to be notified, he will be informed of the review and the decision (see MoJ, 2015: paras 6.1–6.6).

Post-trial, the victim may receive support and advice about protection from unwanted contact (e.g. from social networking, mail, phone calls, etc.) from the offender through the victim's Victim Liaison Officer or the National Offender Management Service (tel: 0845 7585 112).

If the offender is on licence or is a young offender under the age of 18, the police, local probation service, Victim Liaison Officer or Youth Offending Team may be of help. The Probation Service Victim Contact Scheme (VCS) is offered to the victims of violent and sexual offences where the offender receives a sentence of 12 months or more, and information and support is available from a Victim Liaison Officer (for details see MoJ, 2015: paras 6.7–6.16). If the offender later commits a serious further offence, the victim is entitled to information about this in a Victim Summary Report (see MoJ, 2015: paras 6.17–6. 20).

Sex offenders are subject to 'notification requirements' (they must tell the police about some of their personal details) and these requirements may be reviewed. Victims of their offences may be entitled to make representations to be considered at a review (see MoJ, 2015: paras 6.21–6.23). Similarly, victims may be entitled to make representations to a Parole Board through the Probation Service Victim Contact Scheme and/or their VPS – this may be particularly important if the victim is worried, or has new evidence that the prisoner might currently pose a risk of danger to him (see MoJ, 2015: paras 6.24–6.31).

Victims of young offenders under the age of 18 may be contacted by the Youth Offending Team. In cases where a young offender is sentenced to less than 12 months in custody, 12 months or more for a non-sexual or non-violent offence or a community based order, the victim's views may be sought on sentencing or restorative justice initiatives (see MoJ, 2015: paras 6.32–6.33). Community resolutions are primarily aimed at first time offenders where genuine remorse has been expressed, and where the victim has agreed that he does not want the police to take formal action (MoJ, 2015: para 7.7).

6.1.7   Restorative justice

Section 7 of the *Victims' Code* (MoJ, 2015: paras 7.1–7.9) deals with restorative justice. This is the process of bringing together the victim and those responsible for the harm, to find a positive way forward. There is emphasis on the safety of the victim, and empowerment of the victim to have a say in agreeing activities for the offender to do as part of his taking responsibility for his actions in working to repair the harm that he has done. It can provide a means of closure for the victim, and sometimes for the offender, too, and it is a way to enable offenders to understand the impact of what they have done and to express their regret, and perhaps to develop greater empathy for those they have harmed.

6.1.8   Criminal injuries compensation

Compensation can be awarded by the CICA to the victims of crime, in specified circumstances, usually where the offender is unknown, or does not have the means to pay compensation. CICA contact details can be found in Appendix 4. For details of how to apply, and how to appeal a CICA decision to the First Tier Tribunal (Criminal Injuries Compensation) see section 8 of the *Victims' Code* (MoJ, 2015: paras 8.1–8.12).

CICA applications must be made within 2 years of the incident, and the time limit will only be extended in exceptional circumstances or where the application could not be made earlier.

The *Victims' Code* also notes that if the victim is considering applying to CICA, a CICA compensation award would be withheld unless the victim has co-operated as far as reasonably practicable in bringing the assailant to justice.

6.1.9   Complaints

Service providers should treat victims in a respectful, professional and sensitive manner, and without discrimination of any kind. Their duties are set out in detail in Chapter 2, Part B of the *Victims' Code*, and for a brief summary, see sections 6.1.5 and 6.1.6 (above). If they fail to act with professionalism, sensitivity and respect, or are discriminatory, or fail to provide the services to which a victim is entitled, a complaint may be made under the *Victims' Code* to the service provider, and this should be swiftly addressed. For complaints procedures, see section 9 of the *Victims' Code* (MoJ, 2015: paras 9.1–9.6).

If dissatisfied with the response received, further complaints about the service provider can be made to the Parliamentary Ombudsman and Health Service Ombudsman, both online at www.ombudsman.org.uk.

6.2   Entitlements for children and young people

Chapter 3, Part A, of the *Victims' Code* sets out the entitlements for children and young people aged under 18 who are the victims of crime. Parents and guardians are also entitled to help and support unless they are suspects in connection with the crime or such help for them is not in the best interests of the victim.

6.2.1   When reporting a crime

Briefly, when reporting a crime, a young witness is entitled to:

- receive written confirmation that he has reported a crime;

- a clear explanation of what happens next;

- a local or national leaflet or a website address with information for victims of crime within 5 days of reporting the crime;

- information about people the witness can talk to if he is upset and needs support, and how to get in touch with them;

- talk to the police to help work out a needs assessment to see whether the witness is eligible for enhanced entitlement;

- have details automatically passed to victims' services within 2 days of reporting the crime to the police. Note that victims can request this not to happen. (For adults, explicit consent for this referral is necessary for victims of sexual offences or domestic violence, but it is unclear whether this applies equally to young victims) (MoJ, 2015: Chapter 3, para 1.1).

6.2.2   When the police are investigating

When the police are investigating, a young witness is entitled to:

- be accompanied at police interview when making a witness statement by a person of the witness's choice, normally over the age of 18, and can be a parent, or family friend;

- ask for someone to help understand the questions being asked;

- make a video-recorded statement;

- be told about special measures available;

- make a Victim Personal Statement (VPS). This is a statement which can be read out in court before sentencing, and allows the victim to have a say in the justice process. For more details about the VPS, see the *Victims' Code* (MoJ, 2015: Chapter 1, paras 1.12–1.22);

• receive information from the police about the progress of the case and discuss how often the police will contact the victim;

• be told if no one is found to be a suspect, or if the case is closed, and to be told why, within one working day of the decision being made;

• be told if the suspect is arrested, interviewed or released by the police and have the reasons explained, within one working day of the event happening;

• be told if the suspect is let out on police bail or if police bail conditions change, within one working day of the event happening;

• speak with someone specially trained to listen and help to get over the crime (therapy or counselling). The guidance states that this is often provided by a specialist organisation (MoJ, 2015: Chapter 3, para 1.7).

6.2.3   When the trial is pending

When the trial is pending, a young witness is entitled to:

• be told if the suspect is charged or not, and if the police decide not to prosecute, and an explanation of the reasons, within one working day of the decision or event happening;

• be told how to ask for more information and/or a review of the CPS decision not to prosecute, if unhappy with the decision;

• the victim is entitled to have his or her views and those of his or her parent or guardian on an 'out of court disposal' to help police decide if this is appropriate;

• be told if the police decide to keep the suspect in custody;

• be told the outcome of a hearing;

• be told if the suspect is released on bail, and of any conditions imposed, and why;

• be told if bail is changed or cancelled and why;

• be informed why the CPS will:

  – not prosecute the case,

  – make big changes to the charges against the suspect,

  – stop the case;

• also, if it will benefit the victim, he may be offered a meeting with the CPS to explain the reasons for any of the three decisions above; or how to ask for a review of a CPS decision to stop the case or offer no evidence (MoJ, 2015: Chapter 3, paras 2.1–2.2).

6.2.4   When the trial is in preparation

When the trial is in preparation, a young witness is entitled to:

- be informed within one working day of a decision by the CPS to:

    - make big changes to the charges against the suspect,

    - stop the case,

    - not to prosecute the case (take it to court);

- be offered a meeting with CPS to explain the reasons for any of the decisions above; or how to ask for a review of a CPS decision to stop the case or not to prosecute;

- have information about the services of the Witness Care Unit (sometimes the police will fulfil this role if they are the main point of contact) (MoJ, 2015: Chapter 3, paras 2.7–2.9).

6.2.5   Witness Care Unit information

The Witness Care Unit should provide information for young witnesses about the following, see (MoJ 2015: Chapter 3, paras 2.4–2.10):

- Date, time and place of court hearings, court's decisions and what should happen next.

- Whether the suspect is in custody or released on bail.

- Whether the suspect is subject to an arrest warrant, and when this is implemented.

- If there is a not guilty plea, and what this will mean.

- To be informed within one day after CPS decision, if evidence has to be given by the victim.

- To see the written statement or video-recorded evidence to refresh memory before the trial.

- To have an explanation of information about the special measures which will available at the trial.

- To visit the court before the trial to see what it looks like, understand any special measures to be used, and practice using any special measures equipment, for example video links, and where possible, meet staff.

6.2.6   At the trial

At the trial, a young witness is entitled to the following:

- To meet the CPS prosecutor or representative and to be told what will happen in court, and how long the wait to give evidence may be.

- To use a different court entrance from the suspect and his family and friends.

- To wait in a separate area from the suspect and his family and friends.

- To be given a contact point at court where the victim can find out what is happening.

- To have any special measures arranged by the court staff when the court has ordered them.

- To give contact details to court staff in case the victim needs to leave the building for a short while.

- To watch the trial in a public gallery if the victim is not giving evidence.

- To have pre-recorded evidence played, and be cross-examined via a video-link (MoJ, 2015: Chapter 3, paras 3.1–3.2).

6.2.7   After the trial

After the trial, a young witness is entitled to the following:

- If the defendant is found guilty, to have the VPS read out or played in court before sentencing.

- To be paid any expenses for attendance at court within 10 working days after the correctly completed claim form is received by CPS.

- To be informed of the decision of the court and the sentence (MoJ, 2015: Chapter 3, paras 4.1–4.4).

Where an appeal is lodged, a victim is entitled to information about its progress and outcome, within one working day, to include:

- whether the appeal will go ahead;

- if the offender will be released on bail pending the appeal;

- dates, times and location of any further hearings;

- the outcome of the appeal and/or any changes to the sentence;

- information about victims' services;

- information about any use made of the VPS in the appeal, and the right to update the VPS to take in longer term effects of the crime on the victim;

- if the appeal is to the Court of Appeal, or to the UK Supreme Court, a copy of the judgment can be provided once it has been published. (See MoJ, 2015: Chapter 3, paras 5.1–5.3.)

6.2.8   After the sentence

The Victim Contact Scheme is for the victims of violent and sexual offences where the offender gets a custodial sentence of 12 months or more.

Where there was a violent and sexual offence for which the offender received a custodial sentence of 12 months or more, or is kept in a hospital for treatment because he is mentally unwell, the victim can have advice and help from a Victim Liaison Officer, who will keep the victim informed of the stages of the offender's sentence. In these cases, under the Victim Contact Scheme, a young witness is entitled to:

- ask for conditions to be put on the offender if they are released (e.g. not to make contact with the witness);
- be told when the offender is released from prison or hospital and any conditions put on them that relate to the witness;
- be told about any other important information that the Probation Trust think the victim should know;
- be told that the witness may choose to opt out of the Victim Contact Scheme, at any time

(MoJ, 2015: Chapter 3, paras 6.1–6.2)

Post-trial, young victims may receive support and advice about protection from unwanted contact (e.g. from social networking, mail, phone calls, etc.) from offenders through their Victim Liaison Officer or the National Offender Management Service (tel: 0300 060 6699). If the offender is on licence or is a young offender under the age of 18, the police, Victim Liaison Officer or Youth Offending Team may be of help (MoJ, 2015: Chapter 3, paras 6.7–6.8).

If the offender later escapes from prison, and the police think that the offender poses a risk of harm to the victim, they will inform the victim or his parent or guardian and let them know of any steps being taken to protect the child (MoJ, 2015: Chapter 3, para 6.9).

Similarly, victims may be entitled to make representations to a Parole Board through the Probation Service Victim Contact Scheme and/or provide their VPS – this may be particularly important if the victim is worried, or has new evidence that the prisoner might currently pose a risk of danger to him on release. A parent or guardian may apply to be present at part of the Parole Board hearing. The victim also may ask to read his VPS to the Parole Board via a live link or record it to be played at the hearing (MoJ, 2015: Chapter 3, paras 6.10–6.13).

Victims of young offenders under the age of 18 may be contacted by the Youth Offending Team, who will provide information on the progress of the offender's case, victims services and restorative justice (MoJ, 2015: Chapter 3, para 1.44).

6.2.9   Criminal injuries compensation

Compensation can be awarded by the CICA to adults and also to young victims of crime, in specified circumstances, usually where the offender is unknown, or does not have the means to pay compensation (see (MoJ, 2015: Chapter 3, paras 1.50–1.57). CICA contact details can be found in Appendix 6. For details of how to apply, and how to appeal a CICA decision to the First Tier Tribunal (Criminal Injuries Compensation) see MoJ, 2015 (section 8, paras 8.1–8.8).

If the applicant is under the age of 18, the *Victim's Code* advises that 'it is best if the CICA application is made by a responsible adult' on the applicant's behalf, within 2 years either of the date of the incident occurring or from the date when it was reported to the police (see MoJ, 2015: Chapter 3, para 8.3). If the incident occurred when the applicant was under 18 and it was reported to the police but no CICA claim was made, the time limit extends until the applicant reaches the age of 20. The time limit will only be extended in exceptional circumstances or where the application could not be made earlier.

6.2.10   Complaints

Service providers should treat children and young people who are victims in a respectful, professional and sensitive manner, and without discrimination of any kind. Their duties are set out in detail in Chapter 2, Part B of the *Victims' Code*, and for a brief summary, see paras 6.1.5 and 6.1.6. If they fail to act with professionalism, sensitivity and respect, or are discriminatory, or fail to provide the services to which a victim is entitled, a complaint may be made under the *Victims' Code* to the service provider, and this should be swiftly addressed. For complaints procedures, see MoJ, 2015 (Chapter 3, paras 9.1–9.4). If the child or young person is dissatisfied with the response received, further complaints about the service provider can be made to the Parliamentary Ombudsman and Health Service Ombudsman, both online at www.ombudsman.org.uk.

7 Supporting Child and Vulnerable Adult Witnesses after Legal Proceedings

> It is all very well – they have sent him to prison now – their job is done, but what about me? My life is never going to be the same again.

We have seen that there is support for children and vulnerable or intimidated adult witnesses in the course of legal proceedings, but after the case is concluded, often the levels of support may diminish, or no longer be available. It is after the trial that the witness may feel his stress more acutely – he may have been to some extent buoyed up by the adrenalin caused by the stress of the legal process, and once the trial is ended, there may be a psychological reaction, which may include a mixture of relief and also possibly a sense of low mood, or depression. There may, also, be anxieties remaining after the case, for which the witness may need both practical and psychological support and help. It is important for practitioners to see witnesses after the case is ended to discuss any concerns that may remain and be troubling, and to identify appropriate ways forward.

7.1 Counselling and psychotherapy after the case

7.1.1 Readiness for therapy

The codes of practice regarding pre-trial counselling and psychotherapy (therapy) for children and adult vulnerable or intimidated witnesses (CPS, 2001a, 2001b) apply pre-trial, and are very clear that if pre-trial therapy is necessary for the welfare of the witness, then the witness should receive the necessary therapy. Not all forms of therapy will adversely affect the evidence, and it may be that a form can be found that will be of sufficient help to the witness, at least as an interim measure, and which, if carried out by an experienced practitioner, will not adversely affect the witness's evidence or the case.

A witness may have needed more intensive therapy, of a modality involving discussion of the traumatic events, or revisiting the traumatic memories. These forms of therapy may be considered to be more likely to affect the quality or cogency of the evidence. Nevertheless, if that type of therapy was necessary for the health and wellbeing of the witnesses, then the required therapy should have gone ahead, even at the risk of the trial being abandoned by the CPS (see Chapters 4 and 5).

The same rationale applies to child witnesses:

> Those involved in the prosecution of an alleged abuser have no authority to prevent a child from receiving therapy.

> (CPS, 2001a: para 6.1)

> If the prosecutor advises that the proposed therapy may prejudice the criminal case, those responsible for the child's welfare should take this into account when deciding whether to agree to the therapy. It may still be in the best interests of the child to proceed with the therapy.

> (CPS, 2001a: para 6.7)

This rationale applies equally to vulnerable and intimidated adult witnesses:

> Whether a vulnerable or intimidated witness should receive therapy before the criminal trial is not a decision for the police or the Crown Prosecution Service. Such decisions can only be taken by the vulnerable or intimidated witness, in conjunction with the professionals from the agencies providing service to the witness.

> (CPS, 2001b: para 4.3)

> The best interests of the vulnerable or intimidated witness are the paramount consideration in decisions about the provision of therapy before the criminal trial. In determining what is in the best interests of the vulnerable or intimidated witness, it will be essential to consider the wishes and feelings of the witness and, where appropriate, of those who are emotionally significant to the witness. The witness will need to be given information on the nature of the therapy proposed in a form which is accessible. Account should be taken of issues associated with gender, race, culture, religion, language, disability and any communication difficulties both in initial discussions about the proposed therapy and in the provision of the therapy itself.

> (CPS, 2001b: para 4.4)

> If there is a demonstrable need for the provision of therapy and it is possible that the therapy will prejudice the criminal proceedings, consideration may need to be given to abandoning those proceedings in the interests of the wellbeing of the vulnerable or intimidated witness. In order that such

consideration can be given, it is essential that information regarding therapy is communicated to the prosecutor.

(CPS, 2001b: para 4.6)

The point is reiterated:

It should be understood that those involved in the prosecution of an alleged offender have no authority to prevent an adult vulnerable or intimidated witness from receiving therapy.

(CPS, 2001b: para 11.1)

However, the codes also refer to the possibility of delaying therapy until after the case. Certain forms of pre-trial support can be offered which are not counselling or psychotherapy, and if these were provided, they will have helped the witness develop confidence and self-esteem, preparing them for court without revisiting the events. The client may now be anxious to begin therapy and to address the issues which could not be discussed before or during the case.

There may be a wait after a trial while an appeal is pending. If the matter is appealed to the Court of Appeal or to the Supreme Court, there may be a longer waiting time during which the witness may remain anxious and uncertain of what will be the final outcome, and there may be anxiety or distress regarding uncertainty about the sentence and final disposal of the case. In some cases, therapy may have been delayed pending the hearing of the case, and if so, then the witness may not want to delay therapy further while waiting for an appeal to be heard. In these circumstances, the CPS can be asked to advise on legal procedural matters. Depending on the nature and grounds of the appeal, concerns about any further evidence from the witness may be unnecessary, unless for some reason there may need to be a re-hearing of the case. If there is no reason why therapy should be further delayed, and if it is in the best interests of the witness for therapy to go ahead, then is it arguable that it should do so.

7.1.2   NHS and private treatment options

Therapy may be available from the NHS or, for children and young people, from CAMHS. Referral is usually through a GP. An assessment and referral may have been carried out as part of the pre-trial witness assessment process. For witnesses who are not entitled to NHS services for any reason, or where the waiting period to access the NHS services offered is too long, there may be local private, and voluntary or charitable organisations providing therapy which may be able to assist. Many private therapists and organisations offer negotiable fees, or may work for donations, in order to assist those clients who are unable to afford full fees.

Websites for some national therapy professional organisations and helplines, such as the Samaritans, are listed in Appendix 4. If a witness is suffering from high levels of psychological stress (e.g. anxiety, panic attacks, post-traumatic stress, depression or thoughts of self-harm, etc.) and his day-to-day life is disturbed, or if he feels unable to carry on, or his normal level of functioning is clearly diminished, it is advisable for him to consult his doctor or GP, to consider whether medication and/or an NHS or private health referral for specialist psychological help may be appropriate.

Referrals to NHS services may be made via the GP.

Private therapy can be provided through self-referral, or through a referral by a private doctor, private psychologist or psychiatrist, or possibly through the GP. Sometimes a person may wish to obtain a private psychiatric or psychological report. This may be followed by private medical or psychological care, or the privately obtained report may be treated as a 'one off' report and if it recommends specified forms of psychological therapy and/or medication, where appropriate, those recommendations might then be taken over and implemented through the NHS system, via the patient's GP. The NHS system has the advantage that it is free to the patient (although medication may have to be paid for unless an exemption applies), and the NHS has a mental health crisis team which is available to the patient in the event of emergencies.

There is insufficient space here to give more than a brief outline and the web links to the NHS mental health care pathways available in England and Wales, as the options are complex, and may vary in each local area. The information below is derived from the NHS websites relevant for England and Wales. Further contacts and resources are listed in Appendix 6. Readers can find links to the NHS pathways for mental and physical illness at www.nhs.uk, and also to the pathways specific to mental health. The NHS 'Emotional Wellbeing' website at www.emotionalwellbeing.southcentral.nhs.uk provides links to the mental health care pathways, leading to explanations and resources.

Publicly funded mental health services in England and Wales form part of the physical and mental health services in the jurisdiction, and are governed by the National Health Service Act 2006, the Health and Social Care Act 2012, and other subsidiary legislation. These services should be provided free of charge, unless charging is specifically permitted in the legislation.

Mental health services in England are generally run in the following categories:

- adult services;

- Child and Adolescent mental Health Services (CAMHS);

- forensic services;

- learning disability services;

- older adults' services;

- substance misuse services.

How these services are organised in each local area may differ. This means some may not cover all mental health conditions, or only deal with people of a certain age. For example, some areas offer services for young people between the ages of 16 and 25 to help with transitions from children to adult services. Local GPs, or mental health care provider or relevant clinical commissioning group (CCG) should be able to provide information about services available in the area.

7.1.3   Choosing a therapist

The choice of a therapist is limited in the NHS system, which provides a structured approach to therapy, based on psychological assessments and levels of need. For a guide to good practice in the process of assessments and admissions for mental health treatment, see the *Mental Health Act 1983: Code of Practice* (DoH, 2015). This guidance is a significant help to understanding definitions and also an indication of what is expected in best practice. Only a small proportion of people with mental disorders are treated in hospital, or are subject to coercion under the provisions of the Mental Health Act 1983. The remainder are usually treated in primary care by their GP and/or others, and through other community-based services.

Therapists in private practice may also be employed by the NHS (e.g. under a part-time contract of service) or they may be commissioned to work on a self-employed basis (under a contract for services) as part of a NHS team for the holistic healthcare of a patient. The contract in either case will usually bind the therapist to work within the boundaries relevant to the NHS, and their actions will then be subject to the appropriate regulations and government guidance. The therapist will be expected to share information with the healthcare team on a need to know basis in accordance with the Caldicott guidelines (DoH, 2013).

Most therapists, whether employed or self-employed, will belong to one or more professional organisations, and therefore will be bound by a recognised code of ethics and conduct, and regulated by disciplinary procedures. In this way, these organisations provide a level of quality control and protection for clients using their services. Some organisations will also have internal levels of status in their membership which will indicate levels of members' qualification and experience, for example, therapy practitioners might be described as 'registered', 'accredited', 'senior accredited', etc. The website of each counselling and psychotherapy organisation will explain the structure, terminology and hierarchy of its membership. Professional organisations also usually make available to the public their code of ethics and practice, and complaints procedures, via websites and other forms of information. Some of these organisations are listed in Appendix 4. There are also a number of national advertising generic websites listing individual therapists which can then be searched by name, service required, or by geographical area. Some of these therapy advertising websites are also listed in Appendix 4. Note that these generic websites usually do not take responsibility for the therapists' work, but each therapist advertising on the website is individually responsible for his professional expertise and maintaining appropriate standards of care. To assist clients, each therapist should, ideally, set out his qualifications, experience, professional memberships and the types of therapy offered.

Usually, once a therapist or therapy organisation is approached, a client will be offered an assessment session to discuss his needs and what he would like to achieve through therapy, to get an idea about the types of therapy offered, and to discuss the terms of the therapy service (such as frequency, duration and cost of sessions, confidentiality, etc.), and then the client can consider whether or not he wishes to proceed. Often, such assessment sessions are offered free of charge or for a fixed fee, and treated as 'one off' sessions, to enable clients to understand how therapy works, and with no commitment for the client to return unless he decides to take up the therapy offered.

Organisations, agencies and employers may provide access to counselling and psychological services for their staff. The Human Resources or Occupational Health department of the organisation would usually maintain information about any available psychological or other health services for staff, and may manage a referral system.

7.2   Compensation and claims for damages

After a criminal trial, if the offender is found guilty or pleads guilty, an order may be made by the court for the payment of damages to the victim, as part of the sentence.

Victims may be entitled to take civil action for damages by way of compensation for injuries suffered and it is possible that civil proceedings may be appropriate.

Where there has been a criminal trial, but no finding of guilt or guilty plea; or where a criminal investigation was inconclusive; or in cases where a criminal trial was stopped, there may still be grounds for a civil action for damages by way of compensation for injuries suffered. In a criminal case the offence must be proved 'beyond reasonable doubt'. The burden of proof in a civil action is different, being on a 'balance of probabilities', and legal advice and support should be made available to the victim as soon as possible to assess damages and to advise on the best legal course of conduct.

A claim to the CICA may be made by both adults and young victims of crime, in specified circumstances, usually where the offender is unknown, or does not have the means to pay compensation. CICA contact details are listed in Appendix 4. For details of how to apply, and how to appeal a CICA decision to the First Tier Tribunal (Criminal Injuries Compensation), apply to CICA for information, and see MoJ, 2015 (section 8, paras 8.1–8.8).

If the applicant for compensation is under the age of 18, the *Victims' Code* advises that 'it is best if the CICA application is made by a responsible adult' on the applicant's behalf, within 2 years either of the date of the incident occurring or from the date when it was reported to the police (see MoJ, 2015: Chapter 3, para 1.51). If the incident occurred when the applicant was under 18 and it was reported to the police but no CICA claim was made, the time limit extends until the applicant reaches the age of 20. The time limit will only be extended in exceptional circumstances or where the application could not be made earlier.

7.3   Witness protection

After a case is ended, some witnesses may be afraid of reprisals from an offender, or those associated with the offender, or after an offender is released from prison. Information should be made available to the witness about the stages of the trial and sentence, including bail conditions and release dates (see Chapter 6, para 6.1.6). The police, CPS, Youth Offending Services and Probation Services may be of help where appropriate. Witness protection schemes are operated to assist those who are in fear of serious harm to themselves and/or their families. Information about these schemes should be made available to witnesses as part of their witness information pack, provided under the *Victims' Code* (MoJ, 2015) at the time of police investigation and preparation for the trial.

Appendix 1
Summary of Diagnostic Criteria for Post-traumatic Stress Disorder

The following is a summary. For the full diagnostic criteria for PTSD, please refer to the *Diagnostic and Statistical Manual of Mental Disorders*, 5th edition (DSM-5) (APA, 2013), pp 271–280 (as updated in the Supplement to 5th edition, August 2015). See www.dsm5.org.

A. Exposure to actual or threatened death, serious injury, or sexual violence in one (or more) of the following ways:

　　1.　Directly experiencing the traumatic event(s).
　　2.　Witnessing, in person, the event(s) as it occurred to others.
　　3.　Learning that the traumatic event(s) occurred to a close family member or close friend. In cases of actual or threatened death of a family member or friend, the event(s) must have been violent or accidental.
　　4.　Experiencing repeated or extreme exposure to aversive details of the traumatic event(s) (e.g. first responders collecting human remains; police officers repeatedly exposed to details of child abuse).
　　Note: Criterion A(4) does not apply to exposure through electronic media, television, movies, or pictures, unless this exposure is work related.

B. Presence of one (or more) of the following intrusion symptoms associated with the traumatic event(s), beginning after the traumatic events occurred:

　　1.　Recurrent and intrusive distressing memories of the traumatic event(s).
　　Note: In children older than 6 years, repetitive play may occur in which themes or aspects of the traumatic event(s) are expressed.
　　2.　Recurrent distressing dreams in which the content and/or the affect of the dream are related to the traumatic event(s).
　　Note: in children there may be frightening dreams without recognisable content.

3. Dissociative reactions (e.g. flashbacks) in which the individual feels or reacts as if the traumatic event(s) were recurring. (Such reactions may occur on a continuum, with the most extreme expression being a complete loss of awareness of present surroundings.)

Note: In children, re-enactment may occur in play.

4. Intense or prolonged psychological distress at exposure to internal or external cues that symbolise or resemble an aspect of the traumatic event(s)

5. Marked physiological reactions to internal or external cues that symbolise or resemble an aspect of the traumatic event(s).

C. Persistent avoidance of stimuli associated with the traumatic event(s), beginning after the traumatic event(s) occurred, as evidenced by one or both of the following:

1. Avoidance or efforts to avoid distressing memories, thoughts, or feelings about or closely associated with the traumatic event(s).

2. Avoidance or efforts to avoid external reminders (people, places, conversations, activities, objects, situations and situations) that arouse distressing memories, thoughts, or feelings about or closely associated with the traumatic event(s).

D. Negative alterations in cognitions or mood associated with the traumatic event(s), beginning or worsening after the traumatic event(s) occurred, as evidenced by two or more of the following:

1. Inability to remember an important aspect of the traumatic event(s) (typically due to dissociative amnesia and not to other factors such as head injury, alcohol, or drugs).

2. Persistent and exaggerated negative beliefs about oneself, others or the world (e.g. 'I am bad', 'No-one can be trusted', 'The world is completely dangerous', 'My whole nervous system is completely ruined').

3. Persistent distorted cognitions about the causes or consequences of the traumatic event(s) that lead the individual to blame himself/herself or others.

4. Persistent negative emotional state (e.g. fear, horror, anger, guilt or shame).

5. Markedly diminished interest or participation in significant activities.

6. Feeling of detachment or estrangement from others.

7. Persistent inability to experience positive emotions (e.g. inability to experience happiness, satisfaction, or loving feelings).

E. Marked alterations in arousal and reactivity associated with the traumatic event(s), beginning, or worsening after the traumatic event(s) occurred, as evidenced by two (or more) of the following:

1. Irritable behaviour and angry outbursts (with little or no provocation). Typically expressed as verbal or physical aggression towards people or objects.
2. Reckless or self-destructive behaviour.
3. Hypervigilance.
4. Exaggerated startle response.
5. Problems with concentration.
6. Sleep disturbance (e.g. difficulty falling or staying asleep or restless sleep).

F. The duration of the disturbance (criteria B, C, D and E) is more than 1 month.

G. The disturbance causes clinically significant distress or impairment in social, occupational or other important areas of functioning.

H. The disturbance is not attributable to the physiological effects of a substance (e.g. medication, alcohol) or another medical condition.

Specify whether:

With dissociative symptoms: The individual's symptoms meet the criteria for post-traumatic stress disorder, and in addition, in response to the stressor, the individual experiences persistent or recurrent symptoms of either of the following:

1. *Depersonalisation*: Persistent or recurrent experiences of feeling detached from, and as if one were the outside observer of, one's mental processes or body (e.g. as if one were in a dream; feeling a sense of unreality of self or body or of time moving slowly).
2. *Derealisation*: Persistent or recurrent experiences of unreality of surroundings (e.g. the world around the individual is experienced as unreal, dreamlike, distant or distorted).
    Note: to use this subtype, the dissociative symptoms must not be attributable to the effects of substance (e.g. blackouts, behaviour during alcohol intoxication) or another medical condition (e.g. complex partial seizures).

With delayed expression: If the full diagnostic criteria are not met until at least 6 months after the traumatic event(s) (although the onset and expression of some of the symptoms may be immediate).

Appendix 2
Stress Diagram and
Systemic Approach to
Stress Analysis

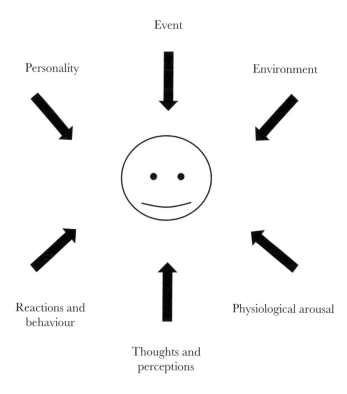

Event

Personality

Environment

Reactions and
behaviour

Physiological arousal

Thoughts and
perceptions

Questionnaire

A   Is there a specific problem causing me stress in my life?
B   Which situations cause me stress?
C   Are there times of day when I feel more stressed than at other times?
D   Are there places where I feel stressed?
E   Are there certain people around whom I experience stress?

A   Is there a specific problem causing stress in my life?

1.   Describe the problem.
2.   Which of my needs are not being met in this situation?
3.   Why or how are these needs not being met?
4.   Are my needs conflicting with those of others? If so, in what way?
5.   What needs to change?

B   Which situations cause me stress?

1.   Which situation(s) cause me stress?
2.   If there is more than one situation, do they have anything in common?
3.   What exactly is it about the situation(s) that cause me stress?
4.   Is it mainly people or circumstances here that are causing me the stress?
5.   Which of my needs are not being met in this situation?
6.   Why or how are these needs not being met?
7.   Are my needs conflicting with those of others? If so, in what way?
8.   What needs to change?

C   Are there times of day when I feel more stressed than at other times?

1.   What time of day do I feel most stressed?
2.   Where am I at that time?
3.   What is happening at that time?
4.   Who is around at that time?
5.   What is it about that time that is stressful?
6.   Which of my needs are not being met in this situation?
7.   Why or how are these needs not being met?
8.   Are my needs conflicting with those of others? If so, in what way?
9.   What needs to change?

D **Are there places where I feel stressed?**

1. In which places do I feel most stressed?
2. What is it about the place(s) that is stressful?
3. What is happening in these places?
4. Who is around in these places?
5. Which of my needs are not being met in these places?
6. Why or how are these needs not being met?
7. Are my needs conflicting with those of others? If so, in what way?
8. What needs to change?

E **Are there certain people around whom I experience stress?**

1. Are there specific individuals or a group of people who cause me stress?
2. Is it a type of person that I find stressful?
3. Do I feel stress when I am physically with them?
4. Do I feel stressed when I even think about them?
5. What is it about the way they are, or what they do, that troubles me?
6. Are they aware that they are causing me this stress?
7. What would happen if I talked about it with them? Is this possible?
8. If it is a type of person causing me stress (rather than a specific person), what could I change or manage better in myself to feel less troubled by this type of person? Can anything be done by others to help me to improve my situation?

Appendix 3
References and Further Reading

Note on Government publications:

- UK Government publications are available from The Stationery Office (TSO), PO Box 29, Norwich NR3 1GN, tel: 0870 600 5522, email: customer.services@tso.co.uk, www.tsoshop.co.uk.

- Northern Ireland Government publications are available from the Department of Health, Social Services and Public Safety, www.dhsspsni.gov.uk.

- For Welsh Government publications, see www.wales.gov.uk.

- The Department for Education (www.education.gov.uk), formerly Department for Children, Schools and Families, publishes policy regarding children's services in England.

- The Ministry of Justice (www.justice.gov.uk) publishes policy regarding the courts and tribunals in England and Wales.

American Psychiatric Association (APA) (2013) *Diagnostic and Statistical Manual of Mental Disorders*, 5th edition (DSM-5). Washington, DC: APA; updated in 2015, see http://psychiatryonline.org.

Andreasen, NJ (1984) *The Broken Brain*. New York, Harper and Row.

Association of Chief Police Officers (ACPO) (2010) *Advice on the Structure of Visually Recorded Interviews with Witnesses*. 1st edition. London: ACPO.

Association of Chief Police Officers (ACPO) (2013) *Advice on the Structure of Visually Recorded Interviews with Witnesses*. 2nd edition. London: ACPO.

Bartlett, P and Sandland, R (2013) *Mental Health Law: Policy and Practice*. 4th edition. Oxford: Oxford University Press.

Beckwith, S and Franklin, P (eds) (2011) *Oxford Handbook of Prescribing for Nurses and Allied Health Professionals*. Oxford: Oxford University Press.

Begley, S (2009) *The Plastic Mind*. London: Constable and Robinson.

Bond, T (2004) *Ethical Guidelines for Researching Counselling and Psychotherapy.* Rugby: British Association for Counselling and Psychotherapy.

Bond, T (2015) *Standards and Ethics for Counselling in Action.* 4th edition. London: Sage.

Bond, T and Mitchels, B (2014) *Confidentiality and Record Keeping in Counselling and Psychotherapy.* 2nd edition. London: Sage.

Bond, T and Sandhu, A (2005) *Therapists in Court: Providing Evidence and Supporting Witnesses.* London: Sage.

Bowlby, J (1969) *Attachment and Loss.* New York: Basic Books.

British Medical Association (BMA) (2000) *Consent, rights and choices in health care for children and young people.* London: BMA.

British Medical Association (BMA) *Mental Capacity Tool Kit.* Available from BMJ Bookshop, tel: 020 7383 6286, www.bma.org.uk.

British Psychological Society (BPS) (1995) *Recovered Memories – A report of a working party of the British Psychological Society,* January. Leicester: BPS

British Psychological Society (BPS) (2000) 'Guidelines for Psychologists working with clients in contexts in which issues related to recovered memories may arise', *The Psychologist,* 13 (5), May.

British Psychological Society (BPS) (2005) *Professional Practice Guidelines for Counselling Psychologists.* Leicester: BPS.

British Psychological Society (BPS) (2006) *Code of Ethics and Conduct.* Leicester: BPS.

Bracken, P (2002) *Trauma, Culture, Meaning and Philosophy.* London, Whurr.

Brazier, M (2003) *Medicine, Patients and the Law.* London: Penguin.

Breuer, J and Freud, S (1955) *Studies on Hysteria: Project for a scientific psychology.* London, Hogarth Press.

Brisch, K and Kronenberg, K (2002) *Treating Attachment Disorders: From Theory to Therapy.* Guildford: Guildford Press.

British Association for Counselling and Psychotherapy (BACP) (2015) *Ethical Framework for Good Practice in Counselling and Psychotherapy.* Lutterworth: BACP.

Chennu, C, et al. (2014) 'Spectral Signatures of Reorganised Brain Networks in Disorders of Consciousness', PLoS Comput Biol, 10 (10): e1003887. doi: 10.1371/journal.pcbi.1003887.

Cohen, K (1992) 'Some legal issues in counselling and psychotherapy', *British Journal of Guidance and Counselling,* 20 (1): 10–26.

College of Policing (2016) *Working with Victims and Witnesses*. Available at www.app.college.police.uk.

Crown Prosecution Service (England and Wales) (CPS) (2001a) (issued 8 February 2001) *Provision of Therapy for Child Witnesses Prior to a Criminal Trial: Practice Guidance*. London: CPS.

Crown Prosecution Service (England and Wales) (CPS) (2001b) (issued 24 January 2002) *Provision of Therapy for Vulnerable or Intimidated Adult Witnesses Prior to a Criminal Trial: Practice Guidance*. London: CPS. Also available at www.cps.gov.uk.

Crown Prosecution Service (England and Wales) (CPS) (2012) *Special Measures for vulnerable and intimidated witnesses: research exploring the decisions and actions taken by prosecutors in a sample of CPS file cases*. London: CPS.

Crown Prosecution Service (England and Wales) (CPS) (2014) *Guidelines on Prosecuting Cases of Child Sexual Abuse*. Now online, last updated 2014. London: CPS. Available at www.cps.gov.uk.

Crown Prosecution Service (England and Wales) (CPS) (2015) *Code for Crown Prosecutors*. Online legal guidance, available at www.cps.gov.uk.

Curle, A (2001) 'Social Healing of the Wounds of War'. *Committee for Conflict Transformation Support Newsletter*, 14, Autumn: 3–6.

Davis, M, et al. (1997) 'Amygdala and bed nucleus of the stria terminalis: differential roles in fear and anxiety measured with the acoustic startle reflex', *Philosophical Transactions of the Royal Society*, 352: 1675–1687.

Dent, H and Flin, R (1992) *Children as Witnesses*. Chichester: Wiley.

Department for Constitutional Affairs (DCA) (2003a) *Making Decisions: DCA Guide for Healthcare Professionals*. Available at www.dca.gov.uk.

Department for Constitutional Affairs (DCA) (2003b) *Making Decisions: DCA Guide for Social Care Professionals*. Available at www.dca.gov.uk.

Department for Constitutional Affairs (DCA) (2003c) *Making Decisions: DCA Guide for Legal Practitioners*. Available at www.dca.gov.uk.

Department for Constitutional Affairs (DCA) (2007) *Mental Capacity Act 2005: Code of Practice*. Available at www.publicguardian.gov.uk.

Department for Education (DfE) (2014) *Mental Health and Behaviour in Schools*. Last updated March 2016. Available at www.gov.uk.

Department for Education (DfE) (2015a) *Working Together to Safeguard Children: A Guide to Inter-Agency Working to Safeguard and Promote the*

Welfare of Children. Norwich: TSO. Issued March 2015. Available at www.education.gov.uk and from TSO.

Note that this new version of *Working Together* replaces earlier guidance on particular safeguarding issues, and in it, Appendix C lists the following helpful and fully downloadable supplementary guidance documents.

Department for Education guidance:

– Safeguarding children who may have been trafficked.

– Safeguarding children and young people who may have been affected by gang activity.

– Safeguarding children from female genital mutilation.

– Forced marriage.

– Safeguarding children from abuse linked to faith or belief.

– Radicalisation – prevent strategy.

– Radicalisation – channel guidance.

– Use of reasonable force in schools.

– Safeguarding children and young people from sexual exploitation.

– Safeguarding children in whom illness is fabricated or induced.

– Preventing and tackling bullying.

– Safeguarding children and safer recruitment in education.

– Information sharing: advice for practitioners.

– Keeping children safe in education.

– Safeguarding Disabled Children: Practice guidance.

– What to do if you're worried a child is being abused: advice for practitioners.

Department for Education:

– National Service Framework for Children, Young People and Maternity Services.

– What to do if you're worried a child is being abused.

Guidance issued by other government departments and agencies:

– Child Protection and the Dental Team: an Introduction to Safeguarding Children in Dental Practice.

- Department of Health: Responding to domestic abuse: A handbook for health professionals.

- Department of Health: Violence Against Women and Children.

- Department of Health: The Framework for the Assessment of Children in Need and their Families 2000: Practice guidance.

- Department of Health: Good Practice in Working with Parents with a Learning Difficulty.

- Department of Health: Recognised, Valued and Supported: Next Steps for the Carers Strategy.

- Department of Health: Mental Health Act 1983 Code of Practice: Guidance on the Visiting of Psychiatric Patients by Children.

- Foreign and Commonwealth Office/Home Office: Forced marriage.

- Home Office: Guidance on Teenage Relationship Abuse.

- Home Office Circular: 16/2005 Guidance on Offences Against Children.

- Home Office: Disclosure and Barring Services.

- Home Office: What is Domestic Violence?

- Ministry of Justice: Guidance on forced marriage.

- Ministry of Justice: Multi-Agency Public Protection Arrangements Guidance.

- Ministry of Justice: HM Prison Service Public Protection Manual.

- Ministry of Justice: Probation Service Guidance on Conducting Serious Further Offence Reviews Framework.

- Missing Children and Adults – a Cross Government Strategy.

- NHS National Treatment Agency: Guidance on development of Local Protocols between Drug and Alcohol Treatment Services and Local Safeguarding and Family Services.

- UK Border Agency: Arrangements to Safeguard and Promote Children's Welfare in UKBA.

- Youth Justice Board: Guidance on People who Present a Risk to Children.

Department for Education (DfE) (2015b) *Information sharing – advice for safeguarding practitioners*. Norwich: TSO. Available at www.gov.uk.

Department for Education (DfE) (2015c) *The Prevent Duty*. Available at www.gov.uk.

Department for Education (DfE) (2015d) *What to do if you are worried that a child is being abused*. Norwich: TSO. Available at www.gov.uk.

Department for Education and Skills (DfES) (2004a) *Every Child Matters: Change for Children Programme*. Ref: DfES/1081/2004. London: TSO.

Department of Health (DoH) (2000) *No Secrets – Guidance on developing and implementing multi-agency policies and procedures to protect vulnerable adults from abuse*. London: TSO.

Department of Health (DoH) (2003a) *Confidentiality: NHS Code of Practice*. London: Department of Health. Available at www.ecric.nhs.uk.

Department of Health (DoH) (2003b) *Department of Health: Mental Health Act; Code of Practice*. 2nd edition. Available at www.doh.gov.uk.

Department of Health (DoH) (2005) Mental Capacity Act 2005: *Deprivation of Liberty Safeguards – Code of Practice to supplement the main Mental Capacity Act 2005 Code of Practice*. Available at webarchive.nationalarchives.gov.uk.

Department of Health (DoH) (2009) *Reference Guide to Consent for Examination or Treatment*, 2nd edition. Available at www.gov.uk.

Department of Health (DoH) (2010) *Caldicott Guardian Manual, 2010*. Available at www.dh.gov.uk.

Department of Health (DoH) (2013) *Caldicott Review: information governance in the health care system*. www.gov.uk.

Department of Health (DoH) (2014a) *Care Act: Easy read Version*. Available at www.gov.uk.

Department of Health (DoH) (2014b) *Care and Support Statutory Guidance*. Available at www.gov.uk.

Department of Health (DoH) (2015) *Mental Health Act 1983: Code of Practice*. Available at www.gov.uk.

Department of Health, Home Office & Employment (DOEA) (2000a) *Assessing children in need and their families: practice guidance*. London: HMSO.

Department of Health, Home Office & Employment (DOEA) (2000b) *Framework for the assessment of children in need and their families*. London: HMSO.

Director of Public Prosecutions (DPP) (2014) *Policy for Prosecutors in respect of cases of Encouraging or Assisting Suicide*. Available at www.cps.gov.uk.

Dyregrov, A (1995) *Grief in Children: A handbook for adults.* London: Jessica Kingsley Publishers, Ltd.

Dyregrov, A (2010) *Supporting Traumatised Children and Teenagers.* London: Jessica Kingsley.

Dyregrov, A and Dyregrov, K (2008) *Effective Grief and Bereavement Support.* London: Jessica Kingsley.

Egendorf, A (1981) *Legacies of Vietnam.* Washington, DC: US Government Printing Office.

Feldman, D (2002) *Civil Liberties and Human Rights in England and Wales.* Oxford: Oxford University Press.

Freeth, R (2007) *Humanising Psychiatry and Mental Health Care: the challenge of the person centred approach.* London: Routledge.

Freud, S (1962) *The Aetiology of Hysteria.* London, Hogarth Press (first published 1896).

General Medical Council (GMC) (2004) *Confidentiality: Protecting and Providing Information.* www.gmc-uk.org.

General Medical Council (GMC) (2009) *Confidentiality.* www.gmc-uk.org.

General Medical Council (GMC) (2013) *Good Medical Practice.* London: GMC. Available at www.gmc-uk.org.

Golightly, M (2014) *Social Work and Mental Health.* London, Sage.

Grant, L and Kinman, G (2015) *Guide to Developing Emotional Resilience.* (download from Community Care Inform at www.ccinform.co.uk).

Griffin, J and Tyrrell, I (2001) *The shackled brain: how to release locked in patterns of trauma.* Chalvington: European Studies Institute.

Hale, B (2010) *Mental Health Law.* 5th edition. London: Sweet & Maxwell.

Harris Hendricks, J, Black, D and Kaplan, T (1993) *When Father Kills Mother: Guiding children through trauma and grief.* London: Routledge.

Herman, JL (1992) *Trauma and Recovery.* London: Harper Collins.

Hershman A and McFarlane, D, *Children Law and Practice* (Looseleaf). Bristol: Family Law.

Home Office and Department of Health (1992) *Memorandum of Good Practice on Video Recorded Interviews with Child Witnesses for Criminal Proceedings.* TSO: London.

Irish Association for Counselling and Psychotherapy (IACP) (2005) *Code or Ethics and Practice* (Information Sheet 7). Wicklow: IACP.

Information Commissioner's Office (ICO) (2005) *The impact assessment tools and handbook*. Available at www.ico.org.uk.

Information Commissioner's Office (ICO) (2010) *Privacy Notices Code of Practice*. Available at www.ico.org.uk.

Information Commissioner's Office (ICO) (2011a) *Data Sharing Code of Practice*. Available at www.ico.org.uk.

Information Commissioner's Office (ICO) (2011b) *Data Sharing Checklists*. Available at www.ico.org.uk.

Information Commissioner's Office (ICO) (2012) *Anonymisation: Managing Data Protection Risk Code of Practice*. Available at www.ico.org.uk.

Institute of Psychiatry and Rethink (2006) *Sharing Mental Health Information with Carers: Pointers to Good Practice for Service Providers* (Briefing Paper). London: Department of Health.

Jackson, E (2006) *Medical Law, Texts and Materials*. Oxford: Oxford University Press.

Janet, P (1889) *L' automatisme psychologique*. Paris: Alcan.

Jones, E (1964) *The Life and Work of Sigmund Freud*. Middlesex: Pelican.

Jones, R (2014) *Mental Capacity Act Manual*. 6th edition. London: Thompson Reuters.

Joseph, S (1998) 'Traumatic amnesia, repression and hippocampus injury due to emotional stress, corticosteroids and encephalins', *Child Psychiatry and Human Development*, 29 (2): 169–185.

Joseph, S (2012) *What Doesn't Kill Us: The new psychology of posttraumatic growth*. London: Pikatus Little Brown.

Kardiner, A (1941) *The Traumatic Neuroses of War*. New York: Hoeber.

Kazdin, AE (1990) 'Psychotherapy for children and adolescents', *Annual Review of Psychology*, 41: 21–54.

Kolb, LC (1987) 'Neurophysiological hypothesis explaining posttraumatic stress disorder', *American Journal of Psychiatry*, 144: 989–995.

LeDoux, JE (1987) 'Emotion'. In F Plum (ed), *Handbook of Physiology*. Bethseda: American Psychological Society, pp 416–459.

LeDoux, JE (1992) 'Emotion and the amygdala'. In JP Aggleton (ed), *The amygdala: neurobiological aspects of emotion, memory and mental dysfunction*. New York: Wiley-Liss.

Law Commission (1981) *Breach of Confidence* (Cmnd 8388). London: HMSO.

Law Society (2015) *Good Practice in Child Care Cases*. London: The Law Society.

Lord Laming (2003) *The Victoria Climbié Inquiry: Report of an Inquiry by Lord Laming*. Norwich: TSO.

Long, M (2013) *Child Care Law: A summary of the law in Northern Ireland*. London: British Association for Adoption and Fostering.

Mason, JK and Laurie, GT (2006) *Mason and McCall Smith's Law and Medical Ethics*. 7th edition. Oxford: Oxford University Press.

McGilchrist, I (2010) *The Master and His Emissary: The divided brain and the making of the Western world*. New Haven and London: Yale University Press.

Menowe, M and McCall Smith, A (eds) (1993) *The Duty to Rescue: Jurisprudence of AID*. Aldershot: Dartmouth.

Mental Health Tribunal (2013) *Annex E of Practice Direction. First-tier Tribunal, Health, Education and Social Care Chamber: statements and reports in mental health cases*. Tribunals Judiciary. Available at www.judiciary.gov.uk.

Ministry of Justice (MoJ) (2006) *Code of Practice for Victims of Crime*. London: TSO.

Ministry of Justice (MoJ) (2009) *Early Special Measures Discussions between the Police and the Crown Prosecution Service*. London: Office for Criminal Justice Reform.

Ministry of Justice (MoJ) (2011a) *Achieving Best Evidence in Criminal Proceedings: Guidance on interviewing victims and witnesses, and guidance on using special measures*. London: TSO.

Ministry of Justice (MoJ) (2011b) *Vulnerable and Intimidated Witnesses: A Police Service Guide*. London: TSO.

Ministry of Justice (MoJ) (2013a) *Code for Crown Prosecutors*. 7th edition. Available at www.cps.gov.uk.

Ministry of Justice (MoJ) (2013b) *Code of Practice for Victims of Crime*. London: TSO.

Ministry of Justice (MoJ) (2013c) *The Witness Charter: Standards of Care for Witnesses in the Criminal Justice System*. London: MoJ.

Ministry of Justice (MoJ) (2015) *Code of Practice for Victims of Crime*. London: TSO.

Mitchels, B (ed) (2012) *Child Care and Protection: Law and Practice*. 5th edition. London: Wildy, Simmonds & Hill.

Mitchels, B and Bond, T (2008) *Essential Law in Counselling and Psychotherapy*. London: British Association for Counselling and Psychotherapy and Sage.

Mitchels, B and Bond, T (2012) *Legal Issues Across Counselling and Psychotherapy Settings*. London: British Association for Counselling and Psychotherapy and Sage.

Myers, CS (1940) *Shell Shock in France* Cambridge: Cambridge University Press.

National Health Service (NHS), *The Information Governance Toolkit*. Version 13 (29 May 2015), available at www.igt.hscic.gov.uk.

National Society for the Prevention of Cruelty to Children (NSPCC) (1998) *Preparing Young Witnesses for Court – A Handbook for Child Witness Supporters*. London: NSPCC.

NSPCC and ChildLine (1998) *The Young Witness Pack*. London: NSPCC.

NSPCC and ChildLine (2000) *Giving Evidence – What's It Really Like?* London: NSPCC.

Office of the Children's Commissioner for England (OCCE) (2012) *'I thought I was the only one. The only one in the world' – The Office of the Children's Commissioner's Inquiry into Child Sexual Exploitation In Gangs and Groups – Interim Report* (S Berelowitz, C Firmin, G Edwards and S Gulyurtlu). London: OCCE. Also available at www.childrenscommissioner.gov.uk.

Office of the Children's Commissioner for England (OCCE (2015a) *Protecting children from harm – Looking into child sexual abuse in the family network* (version for young people). London: OCCE. Also available at www.childrenscommissioner.gov.uk.

Office of the Children's Commissioner for England (OCCE (2015b) *'If only someone had listened' – Office of the Children's Commissioner's Enquiry into Child Sexual Exploitation in Gangs and Groups* (children and young people's version). London: OCCE. Also available at www.childrenscommissioner.gov.uk.

Office of the Children's Commissioner for England (OCCE (2015c) *'Sex without consent, I suppose that is rape' – How young people understand consent to sex* (children and young people's version). London: OCCE. Also available at www.childrenscommissioner.gov.uk.

Office of the Children's Commissioner for England (OCCE (2015d) *'It's a lonely journey …' – A Rapid Evidence Assessment on child sexual abuse within the family environment* (children and young people's version). London: OCCE. Also available at www.childrenscommissioner.gov.uk.

Office of the Children's Commissioner for England (OCCE (2015e) *'Basically … porn is everywhere' – A Rapid Evidence Assessment of the Effect that Access and Exposure to Pornography has on Children and Young People* (children and young people's version). London: OCCE. Also available at www.childrenscommissioner.gov.uk.

Owen, A, Coleman, M, Boly, M, Davis, M, Laureys, S and Pickard, JD (2006) 'Detecting Awareness in the Vegetative State', *Science*, 313, 5792: 1402.

Pattenden, R (2003) *The Law of Professional–Client Confidentiality: Regulating the Disclosure of Confidential Personal Information.* Oxford: Oxford University Press.

Pattinson, SD (2006) *Medical Law and Ethics.* London: Sweet & Maxwell.

Pitman, RK, Shin, LM and Rauch, SL (2001) 'Investigating the pathogenesis of posttraumatic stress disorder with neuroimaging', *Journal of Clinical Psychiatry*, 62 (17): 47–55.

Prior, V and Glaser, D (2006) *Understanding Attachment and Attachment Disorders: Theory, Evidence, and Practice.* London: Jessica Kingsley.

Proctor, B (1986) 'Supervision: a co-operative exercise in accountability'. In M Marken and M Payne (eds), *Enabling and Ensuring: Supervision in Practice.* Leicester: National Youth Bureau.

Reder, P, et al. (1994) *Beyond Blame: Child Abuse Tragedies Revisited.* London and New York: Routledge.

Regel, S. and Joseph, S. (2010) *Post-traumatic stress.* Oxford: Oxford University Press.

Reeves, A (2010) *Working with Suicidal Clients.* London: Sage.

Reeves, A (2015) *Working with Risk in Counselling and Psychotherapy.* London: Sage.

Royal College of Psychiatrists (1997) 'Reported recovered memories of child sexual abuse – Recommendations for good practice and implications for training, continuing professional development and research', *Advances in Psychiatric Treatment*, 4: 343–344.

Ruck Keene, A, et al. (2014). *Court of Protection Handbook: A user's guide.* London: Legal Action Group.

Schatzberg, A, and Nemeroff, C (eds) (2009) *American Psychiatric Publishing Textbook of Psychopharmacology.* Washington: American Psychiatric Publishing.

Scottish Executive (2004a) *Protecting Children and Young People: The Charter.* Edinburgh: Scottish Executive. Available at www.gov.scot.

Scottish Executive (2004b) *Protecting Children and Young People: The Framework for Standards*. Edinburgh: Scottish Executive, www.scotland.gov.uk.

Scottish Executive (2006) *Getting it Right for Every Child*. Edinburgh: Scottish Executive.

Scottish Executive (2008a) *Interviewing Child Witnesses in Scotland*. Available at www.gov.scot.

Scottish Executive (2008b) *Code of Practice to Facilitate the Provision of Therapeutic Support to Child Witnesses in Court Proceedings*. Edinburgh: Scottish Executive.

Secretary of State for the Home Department and Secretary of State Northern Ireland (1998) *Legislation against Terrorism: A Consultation Paper*, Cmnd 4178. Norwich: TSO.

Seedall, R (2011) 'John Bowlby – from Psychoanalysis to Ethology: Unraveling the Roots of Attachment Theory', *Journal of Marital and Family Therapy*, 37, 4: 377–514.

Shepherd, B (2000) *A War of Nerves; Soldiers and Psychiatrists 1914–1994*. London: Jonathan Cape/Routledge.

Slade, A and Holmes, J (2014) *Attachment Theory*. London: Sage.

Spencer-Lane, T (2014) *Care Act Manual*. London: Sweet & Maxwell.

Taylor, D, Paton, C and Kapur, S (2015) *The Maudsley Prescribing Guidelines in Psychiatry*. 12th edition. London: Wiley-Blackwell.

Trumble, WR and Stevenson, A (eds) (2002) *The Shorter Oxford English Dictionary on Historical Principles*. Oxford: Oxford University Press.

van der Kolk, BA (1994) *The body keeps the score: memory and the evolving psychobiology of posttraumatic stress*. Boston, MA: General Hospital Trauma Clinic, Harvard Medical School, pp 253–265.

van der Kolk, BA (1997) 'The Psychobiology of Posttraumatic Stress Disorder', *Journal of Clinical Psychiatry*, 58 (9): 16–24.

van der Kolk, BA, McFarlane, AC and Weisaeth, L (1996) 'The body keeps the score – approaches to the psychobiology of Posttraumatic Stress Disorder'. In *Traumatic stress: the effects of overwhelming experience on mind, body and society*. New York: The Guildford Press.

van der Kolk, BA, et al. (1985) 'Inescapable shock, neurotransmitters, and addiction to trauma: toward a psychobiology of post traumatic stress', *Journal of Biological Psychiatry*, 20, 3: 314–325.

White, RAH, et al., Clarke Hall and Morrison on Children (Looseleaf). London: Lexis Nexis Butterworths.

Wilson, JP and Walker, AJ (1989) 'The psychobiology of trauma'. In JP Wilson, *Trauma, transformation and healing*. New York: Brunner/ Mazel, pp 21–37.

Winnicott, DW (1957) *The Child and the Family*. London: Tavistock.

World Health Organization (1992) *The ICD-10 Classification of Mental and Behavioural Disorders: Clinical descriptions and diagnostic guidelines* (10th revision). Geneva: World Health Organization.

Yealland, L, Lewis, R, Buzzard, E and Farquhar, E (1918) *Hysterical Disorders of Warfare*. London: Macmillan.

Yehuda, R, Southwick, SM, et al. (1990) 'Interactions of the hypothalamic-pituitary adrenal axis and the catecholaminergic system of the stress disorder'. In EL Giller, *Biological assessment and treatment of PTSD*. Washington, DC: American Psychiatric Press.

Yehuda, R, et al. (1990) 'Low urinary cortisol excretion in patients with PTSD', *Journal of Nervous and Mental Diseases*, 178: 366–369.

Appendix 4
Useful Organisations and Resources

Capacity

Enduring Power of Attorney (EPA), see www.guardianship.gov.uk.

Lasting Power of Attorney. From 1 October 2007, the EPA was replaced by the Lasting Power of Attorney made under the Mental Capacity Act 2005. For detailed information and all the relevant forms and guidance, see www.guardianship.gov.uk.

Courts

High Court of Justice: correspondence address – The Court Manager, Room E08, Royal Courts of Justice, The Strand, London, WC2A 2LL, tel: 020 7947 7309 (Customer Service Manager), fax: 020 7947 7339 (Customer Service Manager). In case of difficulty out of hours, contact the Royal Courts of Justice on 020 7947 6260. See also www.justice.gov.uk.

Other courts: addresses and contact numbers for other courts can be found at www.hmcourtsservice.gov.uk.

Northern Irish courts, publications, judicial decisions, tribunals and services: contact details can be found at www.courtsni.gov.uk.

Scottish courts: contact details can be found at www.scotcourts.gov.uk.

National Assembly for Wales: information on guidance in Wales can be found at www.wales.gov.uk.

Law

British and Irish Legal Information Institute (BAILII): publishes all High Court, Court of Appeal and Supreme Court judgments, www.bailii.org.

Care Council for Wales: publishes *Child Law for Social Workers in Wales* in English and Welsh, with regular updates, www.ccwales.org.uk.

Family Law: access to *Family Law Reports*, published by Jordan Publishing, www.familylaw.co.uk.

Family Law Directory, http://directory.familylaw.co.uk.

Family Law Week, www.familylawweek.co.uk.

Justis: online resource, www.justis.com.

UK statute law, www.legislation.gov.uk.

UK statutory instruments, www.opsi.gov.uk.

Organisations and agencies

Action for Children, www.actionforchildren.org.uk.

Action on Elder Abuse Astral House, 1268 London Road, London SW16 4ER, freephone helpline: 0880 8808 8042, www.elderabuse.org.uk.

Adoption UK 46 The Green, South Bar Street, Banbury, OX16 9AB tel: 01295 752240, fax: 01295 752241, helpline: 0844 848 7900 (10 am to 4 pm), www.adoptionuk.org.

Age Concern Astral House, 1268 London Road, London SW16 4ER, tel: 020 8765 7200, www.ageconcern.org.uk.

Alert, 27 Walpole Street, London SW3 4QS, tel: 020 7730 2800, www.donoharm.org.uk.

Alzheimer's Society Gordon House, 10 Green Coat Place, London SW1P 1PH, helpline: 0845 300 0336, www.alzheimers.org.uk.

A National Voice, www.anationalvoice.org.

An Roinn Slainte Republic of Ireland Department of Health, Hawkins House, Hawkins Street, Dublin 2, Ireland. The main switchboard for the Department is 01 6354000 if ringing from inside Ireland, and +353 1 6354000 if ringing from outside Ireland.

Association of Child Abuse Lawyers (ACAL), PO Box 974A, Surbiton, KT1 9XF, tel: 0208 390 4701, email info@childabuselawyers.com, www.childabuselawyers.com.

Association of Directors of Children's Services (ADCS) Ltd, Piccadilly House, 49 Piccadilly, Manchester, M1 2AP, tel: 0161 826 9484, email: info@adcs.org.uk, www.adcs.org.uk.

Association of Lawyers for Children (ALC), PO Box 283, East Molesey, Surrey KT8 OWH, tel: 0208 8224 7071, email: admin@alc.org.uk, www.alc.org.uk.

Barnardo's (children's charity), tel: 0800 008 7005, www.barnardos.org.uk.

British Association for Counselling and Psychotherapy, BACP House, 15 St John's Business Park, Lutterworth, Leicestershire LE17 4HB, tel: 01455 883300, fax: 01455 550243, email: bacp@bacp.co.uk, www.bacp.co.uk.

British Association of Play Therapists South Road, Weybridge, Surrey, KT13 9DZ, tel: 01932 828638, www.bapt.info.

British Medical Association (BMA), Tavistock Square, London WC1 9JP, tel: 020 7383 6286, www.bma.org.uk. The website has guidance on ethics, children, confidentiality, consent and capacity, health records and human rights.

British Association for Psychopharmacology (BAP), www.bap.org.uk.

British Psychological Society, St Andrews House, 48 Princess Road East, Leicester LE1 7DR, tel: 0116 254 9568, fax: 0116 227 1314, email: enquiry@bps.org.uk, www.bps.org.uk.

CAFCASS (Children and Family Court Advisory and Support Service), National Office, 3rd Floor, 21 Bloomsbury Street, London WC1B 3HF, tel: 0300 456 4000, fax: 0175 323 5249 (local offices are listed on the website or available from National Office), email: webenquiries@cafacss.gsi.gov.uk, www.cafcass.gov.uk.

CAFCASS Cymru National Office, Llys y Delyn, 107–111 Cowbridge Road East, Cardiff CF11 9AG, tel: 02920 647979, fax: 02920 398540, email: Cafcasscymru@Wales.gsi.gov.uk, http://cafcass.gov.wales; email for children and young people: MyVoiceCafcassCymru@Wales.gsi.gov.uk.

Care Quality Commission, www.cqc.org.uk.

Carers UK, Ruth Pitter House, 20–25 Glasshouse Yard, London EC1A 4JT, carers line, tel: 0808 808 7777, 020 7490 8824, www.carersonline.org.uk.

Childline NSPCC, Weston House, 42 Curtain Road, London EC2 3NH, tel: 0800 1111.

Child Maintenance Options, tel: 0800 988 0988 (Mon–Fri, 8 am–8 pm), www.cmoptions.org.uk.

Children's Commissioner, www.childrenscommissioner.gov.uk.

Children's Commissioner for Wales, www.childcom.org.uk.

Children's Society, www.childrenssociety.org.uk.

Children's Trust, www.thechildrenstrust.org.uk.

Citizens Advice Myddleton House, 115–123 Pentonville Road, London N1 9LZ, tel: 0207 940 7510.

Citizens Advice Witness Service, www.citizensadvice.org.uk.

Care Quality Commission, www.cqc.org.uk.

Community Care Inform Children, www.ccinform.co.uk.

Contact the Elderly, 15 Henrietta Street, Covent Garden, London WC2E 8QG, freephone: 0800 716543, www.contact-the-elderly.org.

Coram, www.coram.org.uk.

CoramBAAF Adoption and Fostering Academy, http://corambaaf.org.uk.

Coram Children's Legal Centre, www.childrenslegalcentre.com.

Coram Voice, www.coramvoice.org.uk.

Counselling Directory, www.counselling-directory.org.uk.

Court of Protection, see Public Guardianship Office below.

Courts and Tribunals Service, www.hmcourts-service.gov.uk.

Criminal Injuries Compensation Authority, Alexander Bain House, Atlantic Quay, 15 York Street, Glasgow G2 8JQ. Contact form available at www.gov.uk. Claim enquiries, tel: 0300 003 3601; from outside the UK: +44 (0)203 684 2517.

Crown Prosecution Service (England and Wales) has headquarters in London and York, and operates under a structure of 42 areas in England and Wales. London Office: 7th Floor, 50 Ludgate Hill, London, EC4M 7EX, tel: 020 7796 8000, fax: 020 7710 3447.

Dementia Care Trust, Kingsley House, Greenbank Road, Bristol BS5 6HE, tel: 0870 443 5325, 0117 952 5325, www.dct.org.uk.

Department of Health, www.dh.gov.uk.

Dignity in Dying (formerly the Voluntary Euthanasia Society), 181 Oxford Street, London W1D 2JT, tel: 0870 777 7868, email: exit@euthanasia.cc, www.dignityindying.org.uk.

Disclosure and Barring Service (DBS) England and Wales, DBS customer services, PO Box 110, Liverpool, L69 3JD, tel: 0870 90 90 811, minicom: 0870 90 90 344, Welsh language line: 0870 90 90 223, email: customerservices@dbs.gsi.gov.uk. Transgender applications: email: sensitive@dbs.gsi.gov.uk, www.gov.uk. Welsh language scheme: www.gov.uk. Northern Ireland: Information on the application process: www.nidirect.gov.uk. Information on the disclosure and barring programme in Northern Ireland: www.dojni.gov.uk.

Down's Syndrome Association, 155 Mitcham Road, London SW17 9PG, tel: 020 8682 4001, www.downs-syndrome.org.uk.

Family and Childcare Trust, The Bridge, 81 Southwark Bridge Road, London SE1 ONQ, tel: 0207 940 7510, email: info@familyandchildcaretrust.org, www.familyandchildcaretrust.org.

Family Justice Council, Office of the President of the Family Division, WG62, Royal Courts of Justice, Strand, London WC2A 2LL, tel: 020 7947 7333/7974, email: fjc@courtservice.gsi.gov.uk, www.judiciary.gov.uk.

Family Rights Group, www.frg.org.uk.

Fostering Network, www.fostering.net.

Foundation for People with Learning Disabilities, 7th Floor, 83 Victoria Street, London, SW1H 0HW, tel: 020 7802 0300, www.learningdisabilities.org.uk.

General Medical Council, 178 Great Portland Street, London W1W 5JE, general enquiries desk tel: 020 7580 7642, www.gmc-uk.org.

Headway (brain injury association), 4 King Edward Court, King Edward Street, Nottingham NG1 1EW, helpline: 0808 800 2244, 0115 924 0800 (Nottingham); 020 7841 0240 (London), www.headway.org.uk.

Help the Aged, St James' Walk, Clerkenwell Green, London EC1R 0BE, free welfare rights advice line: 0808 800 6565, www.helptheaged.org.uk.

Help the Hospices, Hospice House, 34–44 Britannia Street, London WC1X 9JG, helpline: 0879 903 3 903, www.hospiceinformation.info.

HM Chief Inspector of Education, Children's Services and Skills, www.gov.uk.

HM Revenue and Customs, www.hmrc.gov.uk.

Howard League for Penal Reform, www.howardleague.org.

Improving Access to Counselling and Psychotherapy (IAPT), www.iapt.nhs.uk. If you are an IAPT service provider, please check the NHS Choices website to ensure that your service is registered and the details are fully up to date. Alternatively, a range of helplines and other support resources can be found at the Helplines Partnership website:

– IAPT, good practice guidance on the use of self-help materials: www.iapt.nhs.uk.

– Helplines Partnership: www.helplines.org.

Information Commissioner's Office (ICO), Wycliffe House, Water Lane, Wilmslow, Cheshire, SK9 5AF, tel: 0303 123 1113, email: casework@ico.org.uk, www.ico.org.uk.

Judiciary, www.judiciary.gov.uk.

Lawyers in Local Government Child Care Lawyers Group, www.lawyersinlocalgovernment.org.uk.

Law Society of England and Wales, 113 Chancery Lane, London WC2A 1PL, tel: 020 7242 1222, www.lawsociety.org.uk.

Legal Aid Agency, Unit B8 Berkley Way, Viking Business Park, Jarrow, South Tyneside, NE31 1SF, email: contactcivil@legalaid.gsi.gov.uk.

Linacre Centre for Healthcare Ethics, 60 Grove End Road, London NW8 9NH, tel: 020 7806 4088, www.linacre.org.

Manic Depression Fellowship, Castle Works, 21 St George's Road, London, SE1 6ES, tel: 020 7793 2600, www.mdf.org.uk.

MedicAlert Foundation, 1 Bridge Wharf, 156 Caledonian Road, London, N1 9UU, tel: 0800 581 420, www.medicalert.org.uk.

MENCAP, 123 Golden Lane, London EC1Y 0RT, helpline: 0808 808 1111, tel: 020 7454 0454, www.mencap.org.uk.

Mental Health Care (link to South London and Maudsley NHS website with information about mental health, illnesses, professionals and mental health care), www.mentalhealthcare.org.uk.

Mental Health Tribunal, www.gov.uk.

Mental Health Practice Guidance Mental Health Practice, http://rcni.com.

Mental health care pathways, see NHS Choices. A Guide to Mental Health Services in England at www.nhs.uk.

Mind (National Association for Mental Health), 15–19 Broadway, Stratford, London E15 4BQ, tel: 020 8519 2122, Mind infoline: 08457 660 163, www.mind.org.uk and www.youngminds.org.uk.

Ministry of Justice, www.justice.gov.uk.

Motor Neurone Disease Association, PO Box 246, Northampton NN1 2P2, tel: 01604 250505, helpline: 08457 626262, www.mndassociation.org.uk.

NAGALRO (The Professional Association for Children's Guardians, Family Court Advisers and Independent Social Workers), PO Box 264, Esher, Surrey KT10 0WA, tel: 01372 818504, fax: 01372 818505, email: nagalro@globalnet.co.uk, www.nagalro.com.

National Assembly for Wales, information on guidance in Wales, www.wales.gov.uk.

National Association of Child Contact Centres (NACCC), 1 Heritage Mews, High Pavement, Nottingham NG1 1HN, tel: 0845 4500 280/0115 948 4557, email: contact@naccc.org.uk, www.naccc.org.uk.

National Autistic Society, helpline: 0808 800 1050, www.autism.org.uk.

National Offender Management Service, victim helpline: 0845 7585 112.

National Society for the Prevention of Cruelty to Children, Weston House, 42 Curtain Road, London EC2A 3NH, www.nspcc.org.uk.

- help for adults concerned about a child, tel: 0808 800 5000.

- help for children and young people – ChildLine, tel: 0800 1111.

National Youth Offender Service, www.nyas.net.

NICE, www.nice.org.uk; www.nice.org.uk. Common mental health problems, see www.nice.org.uk. Clinical guidelines, see www.rcpsych.ac.uk.

Northern Ireland Guardian Ad Litem Agency, email: admin@nigala.hscni.net.

Office of the High Commissioner for Human Rights, www.ohchr.org.

Official Solicitor and Public Trustee Victory House, 30–34 Kingsway, London WC2B 6EX, tel: 020 7911 7127, email: enquiries@offsol.gsi.gov.uk, www.gov.uk.

Office of Public Sector Information (OPSI) (sets standards and provides a practical framework for opening up and encouraging the re-use of public sector information), www.legislation.gov.uk, www.opsi.gov.uk.

Ombudsman for Children's Office, Millennium House, 52–56 Great Strand Street, Dublin 1, Ireland. Complaints freephone: 1800 20 20 40. Tel: 01 865 6800, fax: 01 874 7333, email: oco@oco.ie, www.oco.ie.

Patient's Association, PO Box 935, Harrow, Middlesex HA1 3YJ, tel: 020 8423 9119, helpline: 0845 608 4455.

Patient Concern, PO Box 23732, London SW5 9FY, tel: 020 7373 0794, www.patientconcern.org.uk.

Patient Information Advisory Group (PIAG). Provides the minutes of PIAG meetings and guidance on the use of powers provided under section 60 of the Health and Social Care Act 2001 which allow confidentiality requirements to be set aside in limited circumstances for purposes such as research and public health work. PIAG also provides guidance on issues of major significance that are brought to its attention.

Prevention of Professional Abuse Network POPAN, 1 Wyvil Court, Wyvil Road, London SW8 2TG, tel: 020 7622 6334, support line: 0845 4 500 300, www.popan.org.uk.

Play Therapy UK (PTUK), www.playtherapy.org.uk.

Play Therapy Register, www.playtherapyregister.org.uk (set up by the Department of Health).

PTSD UK, www.ptsduk.org.

Public Guardianship Office, Archway Tower, 2 Junction Road, London N19 5SZ, customer service helpline: 0845 330 2900, enquiry line: 0845 330 2900, www.guardianship.gov.uk.

Rape Crisis, helpline 0808 802 9999 (12–14.30 daily and 19.00–21.30 daily), www.rasasc.org.uk.

Refugee Council, www.refugeecouncil.org.uk.

RESCARE (Society for children and adults with learning disabilities and their families), Stephen Jackson House, 31 Buxton Road, Heavily, Stockport, SK2 6LS, helpline: 0161 477 1640, www.rescare.org.uk.

Resolution, PO Box 302, Orpington, Kent BR6 8QX, tel: 020 3195 2469/020 3195 0190, email: info@resolution.org.uk, www.resolution.org.uk.

Respond, Third Floor, 24–32 Stephenson Way, London NW1 2HD, helpline: 0808 808 0700, www.respond.org.uk.

Rethink (formerly National Schizophrenia Fellowship), 17 Oxford Street, Southampton, SO14 3DJ, general enquiries: 0845 456 0455, advice line: 020 8974 6814, www.rethink.org.

Royal College of Psychiatrists Publications, www.rcpsych.ac.uk.

Samaritans, Freepost RSRB-KKBY-CYJK, PO Box 9090, Stirling, FK8 2SA, tel: 116 123 (UK), email: jo@samaritans.org, www.samaritans.org. Use any of these contact details to find a local branch.

SANE, 1st Floor, Cityside House, 40 Alder Street, London E1 1EE, helpline: 0845 767 8000, www.sane.org.uk.

Save the Children UK (children's charity, with a wide range of assistance), 1 St John's Lane, London EC1M 4AR, helpline: 020 7012 6400, www.savethechildren.org.uk.

Scottish Voluntary Euthanasia Society, www.euthanasia.cc.

Scope (major disability charity with a focus on cerebral palsy), 6 Market Road, London N7 9PW, tel: 020 7619 7257, cerebral palsy helpline: 0808 800 3333, www.scope.org.uk.

Solicitors Regulation Authority, The Cube, 199 Wharfside Road, Birmingham, B1 1RN, tel: 0370 606 2577, www.sra.org.uk.

Speakability, 1 Royal Street, London SE1 7LL, tel: 020 7261 9572, helpline: 080 8808 9572, www.speakability.org.uk.

Solicitors for the Elderly, PO Box 9, Peterborough PE4 7NN, tel: 01733 326769, www.solicitorsfortheelderly.com.

Stroke Association Stroke House, 240 City Road, London, EC1V 2PR, tel: 020 7566 0300, helpline: 0845 30 33 100, www.stroke.org.uk.

Supporting Justice, 68 King William Street, London EC4N 7DZ, tel: 020 7959 2465, direct dial: 020 7959 2462, mobile: 07525 855284.

Survivors Trust, Eastlands Court Business Centre, St Peter's Road, Rugby, CV21 3QP, tel: 01788 550554, www.thesurvivorstrust.org.

UK Council for Psychotherapy (UKCP), 2 Wakley Street, London, EC1V 7LT, tel: 020 7014 9955, www.ukcp.org.uk.

Victim Support Service, www.victimsupport.org.uk.

Voice UK, National Family Carer Network, email: voice@voiceuk.org.uk, www.familycarers.org.uk.

Who Cares Trust, www.thewhocarestrust.org.uk.

Index

The index entries for 'children and young people', 'intimidated witnesses', 'victims of crime' and 'vulnerable witnesses' are selective; more detail can be found via the entries for narrower topics. The letter B after a page number indicates a box; where there are two or more boxes on the page, both or all are referred to unless otherwise indicated.